The concept of predistribution is increasingly setting the agenda in progressive politics. But what does it mean? The predistributive agenda is concerned with how states can alter the underlying distribution of market outcomes so they no longer rely solely on *post hoc* redistribution to achieve economic efficiency and social justice. It therefore offers an effective means of tackling economic and social inequality alongside traditional welfare policies, emphasising employability, human capital, and skills, as well as structuring markets to promote greater equity.

At the same time, experts have warned that any shift away from a welfare state underpinned by traditional programmes of redistribution is potentially misguided: redistribution and predistribution should be complementary rather than alternative strategies. This book explores how far key concerns of the predistribution agenda relate to social democratic politics in Western European societies, in particular how to secure the support of middle-income voters, women, families, and younger generational cohorts in an era of austerity.

This book examines the key debates surrounding the emergence and development of predistributive thought with contributions from leading international scholars and policy-makers.

In the series:

After the Third Way: The Future of Social Democracy in Europe
Edited by Olaf Cramme and Patrick Diamond
ISBN: 978 1 84885 992 0 (HB); 978 1 84885 993 7 (PB)

Europe's Immigration Challenge: Reconciling Work, Welfare and Mobility
Edited by Elena Jurado and Grete Brochmann
ISBN: 978 1 78076 225 8 (HB); 978 1 78076 226 5 (PB)

Left Without a Future? Social Justice in Anxious Times
Anthony Painter
ISBN: 978 1 78076 660 7 (HB); 978 1 78076 661 4 (PB)

Progressive Politics after the Crash: Governing from the Left
Edited by Olaf Cramme, Patrick Diamond and Michael McTernan
ISBN: 978 1 78076 763 5 (HB); 978 1 78076 764 2 (PB)

Governing Britain: Power, Politics and the Prime Minister
Patrick Diamond
ISBN: 978 1 78076 581 5 (HB); 978 1 78076 582 2 (PB)

The Europe Dilemma: Britain and the Drama of EU Integration
Roger Liddle
ISBN: 978 1 78076 222 7 (HB); 978 1 78076 223 4 (PB)

The Predistribution Agenda: Tackling Inequality and Supporting Sustainable Growth
Edited by Claudia Chwalisz and Patrick Diamond
ISBN: 978 1 78453 440 0 (HB); 978 1 78453 441 7 (PB)

Edited by Claudia Chwalisz and Patrick Diamond

the predistribution agenda

Tackling Inequality and Supporting Sustainable Growth

I.B. TAURIS

LONDON · NEW YORK

Published in 2015 by
I.B.Tauris & Co. Ltd
London • New York
www.ibtauris.com

Copyright © 2015 Policy Network

The right of Claudia Chwalisz and Patrick Diamond
to be identified as the editors of this work has been asserted by them in
accordance with the Copyright, Designs and Patents Act 1988.

ISBN: 978 1 78453 440 0 (HB)
ISBN: 978 1 78453 441 7 (PB)
eISBN: 978 0 85772 910 1

A full CIP record for this book is available from the British Library
A full CIP record is available from the Library of Congress

Library of Congress Catalog Card Number: available

Typeset by Riverside Publishing Solutions, Salisbury SP4 6NQ
Printed and bound in Great Britain by T.J. International, Padstow, Cornwall

About Policy Network

Policy Network is a leading thinktank and international political network based in London. It promotes strategic thinking on progressive solutions to the challenges of the twenty-first century and the future of social democracy, impacting upon policy debates in the UK, the rest of Europe and the wider world.

Through a distinctly collaborative and cross-national approach to research, events and publications, the thinktank has acquired a reputation as a highly valued platform for perceptive and challenging political analysis, debate and exchange. Building from our origins in the late 1990s, the network has become an unrivalled international point-of-contact between political thinkers and opinion formers, serving as a bridge between the worlds of politics, academia, public policy-making, business, civil society and the media.

www.policy-network.net

'The market economy as it is organised today is leading to ever-greater polarisation of people's economic fortunes, and straining the postwar welfare state to breaking point. This important and wide-ranging collection of essays addresses how to change the framework within which markets operate in order to bring about a less unequal and therefore more sustainable economy.'

—Diane Coyle,
Professor of Economics, University of Manchester and Founder,
Enlightenment Economics

'A comprehensive rebuttal of the argument that European social democracy lacks the ingenuity to challenge post-crash inequality, this book contains numerous ideas which could underpin the political project we need to revive our electoral fortunes'

—**Tristram Hunt**

Contents

Acknowledgements

This volume originates in the collaboration between Policy Network and the Foundation for European Progressive Studies (FEPS) in a research programme on predistribution and changing welfare states. As international progressive thinktanks in London and Brussels, we have drawn together our respective political networks to engage centre-left academics, policy experts and thinkers from Europe and the USA on key debates surrounding how states can alter the underlying distribution of market outcomes so as not to rely on tax and spend redistribution to tackle inequality and support sustainable and inclusive growth.

We would like to convey our thanks to St Catherine's College, University of Oxford and the Renner Institute for the partnership that facilitated and informed a two day conference in Oxford in July 2014. It provided the starting point for this volume, and we are extremely grateful and indebted to the presenters and delegates at that transatlantic gathering. It offered a rigorous analysis of the social policy landscape and critical exploration of how predistributive policies can ensure long-term growth, fairer social and economic outcomes, and sustainable social models throughout Europe. *The Predistribution Agenda* draws on the policy ideas and political frameworks presented and debated in this volume. In addition to the book's contributors, we would like to thank Julia Lynch, Bruno Palier, David Soskice, Julian Le Grand, Andy Green, Laurence Weerts, Nicholas Costello, Andreas Schieder, Nick Pearce, Dan Corry, and Fran Bennett for enriching the debate and discussions at St Catherine's College.

We are extremely grateful to Michael McTernan for his intellectual contribution to shaping the conference, as well as to Emma Kinloch and Katherine Roberts in the Policy Network team for their vital support in its organisation. Roger Liddle, Policy Network's chair, provided inspiration and constant guidance to the project. Finally, we would like to thank Ania Skrzypek and Ernst Stetter of FEPS for the rewarding partnership.

Contributors

Karen M. Anderson is Associate Professor of Social Policy at the University of Southampton. Her research falls within the field of comparative politics, with a focus on the politics of welfare state change, the relationship between welfare states and labour markets, and trade unions as political actors.

Lucy Barnes is Lecturer in Quantitative Politics at the University of Kent and an External Research Associate at the Centre for Competitive Advantage in the Global Economy at the University of Warwick. Her research focuses on the comparative political economy of advanced industrial democracies, with particular attention on the politics of taxation, inequality and redistribution. Her recent publications include pieces in the *Socioeconomic Review*, *Political Studies*, and major university presses.

Rémi Bazillier is Assistant Professor of Economics at the University of Orléans. His research is specialised in development economics, labour economics, corporate social responsibility and migration. He is a Research Group Member of the Foundation for European Progressive Studies (FEPS).

Marius R. Busemeyer is Professor of Political Science at the University of Konstanz. His research focuses on comparative political economy, welfare states, public spending, social democratic parties and theories of institutional change. His most recent books are *The Political Economy of Collective Skill Systems* (co-edited, 2012) and *Skills and Inequality: Partisan Politics and the Political Economy of Education Reforms in Western Welfare States* (2014).

Claudia Chwalisz is Senior Policy Researcher at Policy Network. Her research focuses on resolving the tensions between representative and responsible government fueling support for populist anti-establishment parties, as well as welfare state revision and renewal in post-crisis Europe. She edits Policy Network's Populism Observatory and is the author of *The Populist Signal: Why Politics and Democracy Need to Change* (2015). She is also a Crook Public Service Fellow at the Sir Bernard Crick Centre for the Public Understanding of Politics, University of Sheffield.

Paul de Beer is Co-Director of the Amsterdam Institute for Advanced Labour Studies and Henri Polak Chair for Industrial Relations at the University of Amsterdam. He is also the Scientific Director of the Scientific Bureau of the Dutch Trade Union Movement, De Burcht.

Patrick Diamond is Vice Chair of Policy Network and Lecturer in Public Policy at Queen Mary, University of London. He is the former Head of Policy Planning in 10 Downing Street and Senior Policy Adviser to the Prime Minister. His recent publications include *After the Third Way* (co-edited, 2012), *Governing Britain: Power, Politics and the Prime Minister* (2013), *Progressive Politics after the Crash: Governing from the Left* (co-edited, 2013).

Ingrid Esser is Assistant Professor of Sociology at the Swedish Institute for Social Research at Stockholm University. Her research focuses on the sociology of work, work values, job preferences, job quality, matching in the labour market, well-being and health, as well as stress around the work–family life interface. Her most recent publication is *The State and the Future of the Swedish Model* (co-authored, 2014) for the NordMod2030 project.

Andrew Gamble is Professorial Fellow at the Sheffield Political Economy Research Institute. He is also Professor Emeritus of Politics and Fellow Emeritus of Queen's College at the University of Cambridge. He is a fellow of the British Academy and the UK Academy of Social Sciences. His main research interests lie in political economy, political theory and political history. In 2005, he received the Isaiah Berlin Prize from the Political Studies Association for lifetime contribution to political studies. His most recent book is *Crisis Without End? The Unravelling of Western Prosperity* (2014).

Paul Gregg is Professor of Economic and Social Policy, and Director of the Centre for Analysis and Social Policy at the University of Bath. He is also a programme director at the Centre for Market and Public Organisation covering Families, Children and Welfare. His research focuses on youth unemployment, workless households, child poverty, intergenerational mobility and the drivers of social disadvantage. His most recent book is *The Labour Market in Winter: The State of Working Britain* (with Jonathan Wadsworth, 2011).

Alfred Gusenbauer is Chair of the Foundation for European Progressive Studies (FEPS) 'Next Left' research programme. He is the former federal chancellor of Austria and the former leader of the SPÖ (Social Democratic Party of Austria). He is also the first Leitner Global Fellow at the Columbia University School of International and Public Affairs and is a guest lecturer at the IGLP of Harvard Law School. He is also Senator of the European Academy of Science and chair of the Renner Institut.

Jacob S. Hacker is Stanley B. Resor Professor of Political Science and Director of the Institute for Social and Policy Studies at Yale University. He is also Vice President of the National Academy of Social Insurance, and a former Junior Fellow of the Harvard Society of Fellows. He writes primarily on the politics of US health and social policy, and is the author of *Winner-Take-All Politics: How Washington Made the Rich Richer—And Turned Its Back on the Middle Class* (with Paul Pierson, 2010) and *American Amnesia: The Forgotten Roots of American Prosperity* (with Paul Pierson, forthcoming).

Peter A. Hall is Krupp Foundation Professor of European Studies at Harvard University and Co-Director of the Program on Successful Societies for the Canadian Institute for Advanced Research. His most recent books are *Social Resilience in the Neoliberal Era* (co-edited, 2013) and *The Politics of Representation in the Global Age: Identification, Mobilization and Adjudication* (co-edited, 2014).

Anke Hassel is Professor of Public Policy at the Hertie School of Governance and Adjunct Professor of the Graduate School of Social Sciences at Bremen University. Her key areas of research interest and expertise are comparative political economy, varieties of capitalism, the role of labour, trade unions and labour markets.

Evelyne Huber is Morehead Alumni Professor of Political Science and Chair of the Department of Political Science at the University of North Carolina, Chapel Hill. Her most recent books include *Democracy and the Left: Social Policy and Inequality in Latin America* (with John D. Stephens, 2012) and *The Oxford Handbook of Transformations of the State* (co-edited, 2014).

Alan Manning is Professor of Economics in the Department of Economics at the London School of Economics and Director of the Community

Programme at the LSE's Centre for Economic Performance. His research is on labour markets in general, imperfect competition (monopsony), minimum wages, job polarisation, immigration, and gender in particular.

Sophie Moullin is in the joint doctoral program in Sociology and Social Policy at Princeton University, as the Elliotte Robinson Little '25 Fellow in Sociology. She is a member of Princeton's Office of Population Research (OPR) in the Woodrow Wilson School and a former Senior Policy Adviser in the UK Prime Minister's Strategy Unit. Her research focuses on demography, economic sociology, family, and stratification, investigating the relationship between socio-emotional health and socio-economic inequality. Her publications include *Just Care* (2008) and *Why Progressives Should be Pro-Family* (2012).

Geoff Mulgan is Chief Executive of Nesta and is a Visiting Professor at LSE, UCL, Melbourne University and a regular lecturer at the China Executive Leadership Academy. He is also the current Chair of the Studio Schools Trust and the Social Innovation Exchange. He is a former Director of the Government's Strategy Unit, Head of Policy in the Prime Minister's office, and Chief Adviser to Gordon Brown MP. His latest book is *The Locust and the Bee: Predators and Creators in Capitalism's Future* (2013).

Ania Skrzypek is Senior Research Fellow at the Foundation for European Progressive Studies (FEPS). She co-ordinates the 'Next Left' programme and specialises in the political history of the European Union, with a focus on the development of pan-European party political systems. She previously worked as a researcher in the Institute of Political Sciences at the University of Warsaw.

John D. Stephens is Gerhard E. Lenski, Jr. Professor of Political Science and Sociology and Director of the Center for European Studies at the University of North Carolina, Chapel Hill. His current research focuses on the study of social investment policy in Europe and Latin America.

Ernst Stetter has been Secretary General of the Foundation for European Progressive Studies (FEPS) since its creation in 2008. He is an economist and political scientist who comments regularly on EU affairs. He formerly worked for the Friedrich Ebert Stiftung (FEST) holding various positions, including Head of the Central Europe Unit, Head of Africa Department, Director of the Paris office and Director of the EU office in Brussels.

Dimitris Tsarouhas is Assistant Professor of International Relations at Bilkent University. He is also a Research Associate of the Hellenic Foundation for European and Foreign Policy (ELIAMEP) and the Center for European Studies (CES), and a Research Group Member of the Foundation for European Progressive Studies (FEPS). His research interests include Europeanisation, social democracy and labour politics.

Pieter Vanhuysse is Professor of Comparative Welfare State Research at the University of Southern Denmark. His research focuses on the comparative politics and political sociology of welfare states, public policies, intergenerational policy conflict, and population ageing. His books include *Divide and Pacify: Strategic Social Policies and Political Protests in Post-Communist Democracies* (2006) and *Ageing Populations in Post-Industrial Democracies* (co-edited, 2012), which was nominated for the American Sociological Association's Best Book Award for Political Sociology.

Anne Wren is a Research Associate at the Institute for International Integration Studies at Trinity College, Dublin, where she directed a Marie Curie Excellence Team research project on 'Political Responses to Economic Change: De-Industrialization, Globalization and Service Sector Development'. Her current research focus is on the institutional underpinnings of growth and employment creation in traded knowledge-intensive sectors, the distributional and political implications of service expansion, and the political economy of the 'great recession'. Her most recent book is *The Political Economy of the Service Transition* (edited, 2013).

Preface

Ernst Stetter

P olitics used to be a mission. Those embarking on it would be driven by a sense of duty to serve others, while engaging in a battle of ideas aimed at winning the hearts and minds of a majority. Running to win parliamentary mandates or defend them, politicians used to be courageous and ready to take risks in expressing opinions, which might, at first, have seemed impossible to hold. There is conscious application of the disenchanting term 'used to'. Today, it seems that such a world of politics is alive only in books and in blurred memories.

Today, mainstream politics is framed by a trifold, disempowering set of convictions. The first is the belief that these are the days of globalisation, which in itself is an unstoppable force. The second is the idea that the new industrial revolution (with technological developments such as digitisation) and the societal trends (such as ageing demographics and individualisation) are self-governing changes. And the third is the legacy of the 2008 crisis, over the course of which neoliberal thinking was not exposed as erosive, but to the contrary prevailed – dictating the criteria of evaluation for all possible exit scenarios. Together, these three appear as vastly impersonalised, powerful forces to which the established world of politics appears only able to respond, react or readjust.

This depiction of the present situation is a long way from the inspiration, hope and security for which people long. There is no reason to assume that the present generation and the so-called future generations – namely the youth of today – will aspire to less than their predecessors and be ready to settle for less, simply because the analysis claims that 'they will be the first group to have it worse than their parents'.

Such anticipation is precisely the reason why nowadays there is so little trust in the state, its institutions and the established parties. To make matters worse, the fact that politicians generally tend to give in to the idea that their survival depends on balancing their programmes and presenting themselves as a 'risk-free' option for voters enhances the disconnect between politics and citizens. It is these very citizens who battle with diverse dangers and anxieties resulting from the dominant capitalist order on a daily basis. Since they feel unable to count on anyone else to stand up and seek new ways of empowering them, they tend to search for comfort in those who at least brutally articulate their concerns (even if they do it in irresponsibly radical or populist ways).

Although these trends are more visible on the national level, they also exist more widely across Europe. The last European elections in 2014 saw a stabilisation in voter turnout, but at the cost of heightened power for the extremist and protest forces. The current European Parliament is not only more fragmented, but also has become a stage on which the European project is fundamentally questioned and contempt for the views of others is more frequently expressed. This is a reason for great concern, as it would indicate that the core values that used to underpin the integration processes are under pressure. They are no longer a shield for the EU, which to so many appears to have neither social ambition nor means to fulfil any greater dream of a better future for all.

In this gloomy context, a search for a progressive alternative is a matter of considerable responsibility for the future course of affairs. There is a great need to formulate a new, plausible alternative that would hold credentials of economic accountability, social ambition and political answerability. It must be feasible in the light of – though not wholly dictated by – the debate regarding scarcity of resources and the limitations that this puts on implementation. It must show belief in the potential of people, emphasising the principles of commonly enabled emancipation as opposed to being confined by deliberations regarding growing individualism.

This spirit was the principal inspiration for choosing the theme 'Pre-distributive Social Policy: Changing Welfare States in a Knowledge-Driven Economy' as a leading thread of the deliberations that took place in Oxford, in July 2014. This was the second debate organised by FEPS, Policy Network and the Renner Institut at St Catherine's College Oxford. It served to link the transatlantic dialogue on predistribution on one hand and the European search for a new path, in the context of the FEPS Next Left research programme and its specific devotion to the 'future of welfare societies', on the other. The programme of the seminar itself subsequently featured three content components: a focus on the evolution of the labour market, challenges in the field of education and skills, and finally the ambition for a new social model.

It is therefore a great privilege and pleasure to present this book – a result of the debates at and around the seminar. Thanks to an extraordinary number of outstanding scholars involved, the content is undoubtedly rich, remarkable and noteworthy. The articles included provide not only food for thought, but they can also serve as a set of policy proposals. As such, they are a contribution to a further politically strategic conversation on the aspirations, challenges and choices that the centre-left in Europe must face in order for it to become the democratic force for change in the years to come. In this context, I would like to congratulate all of the authors and participants, and especially express my gratitude to Alfred Gusenbauer, Roger Liddle, Patrick Diamond, Ania Skrzypek, Michael McTernan and Claudia Chwalisz for making this project such an accomplishment.

Foreword
The Promise of Predistribution

Jacob S. Hacker

I magine for a moment that you are a highway engineer. Your job is to balance speed and safety – to ensure that people can get where they need to go without putting their lives on the line. Now imagine your supervisor tells you that the only thing you are allowed to do is redirect cars from the most congested roads to the least congested. No redesign of roads, no safety requirements for automobiles, no regulation of entry and exit to the highways, no speed limits, no congestion pricing, nothing. Just reallocation of cars on the existing roadways.

You know that redirecting traffic will reduce problems for some. You also know that it will create new hassles for others, people who may have figured out faster routes or paid to live away from the gridlock and now feel they are being held back to achieve some greater cause that has little do with them. And who knows whether any of this will make people safer overall? You have the tools for getting the balance right, but you are not allowed to use them. You are trapped in a box.

When it comes to pursuing growth and justice, progressives today are not unlike that unfortunate highway engineer: caught in a box that was built for past political battles. They have accepted a narrowing of the tools they are supposed to use to manage the economic challenges that post-industrial societies face. Their highways are the structures of contemporary capitalism; the traffic they need to master is the increasingly unequal patterns of growth that pulse through these structures. And the strictures that they face – and that, indeed, they too rarely even recognise as constraints – concern the proper role of the state in a modern knowledge economy.

When I first spoke of 'predistribution' in 2011, I thought what I was saying would be uncontroversial, if not all that catchy.[1] I was doubly wrong: it was controversial *and* catchy. The attacks from the right were to be expected; more surprising was the resistance on the left to the idea that after-the-fact redistribution – letting the market rip and then cleaning up afterward – was no longer a viable governing approach. Even more surprising was the attraction of the awkward neologism itself, so much so that many started using it as a catch-all label for progressive strategies that accommodated fiscal austerity, a meaning exactly the opposite of my original intent.

So I am gratified and humbled to introduce this collection of informed and wise chapters on the promise of a predistribution agenda. The chapters to come differ on many details, but they agree on the value of broadening the toolkit of progressive governance and going back to the basics of economic design. In introducing them, I want to pull out what I see as their major implications for our present political and economic challenges – and what I am convinced is their hopeful message for our ability to meet those challenges.

The Forgotten Roots of Modern Prosperity

Predistribution is not a strategy for doing more with less. It is a strategy for doing more with more – more policy options for creating healthy societies and more public investment for ensuring broad-based growth. The current backdrop of public austerity precipitated by private market failures is only the surface manifestation of a deeper problem: an institutionalised conception of the state that progressives helped construct during the unstable bubbles of the 1990s and 2000s.

In that crabbed conception, government's primary function is to redistribute the rewards of decentralised economic growth to ensure that no one is left too far behind. When it comes to economic policy, the state should 'steer, not row', as David Osborne and Ted Gaebler put it in the book that became the bible of America's New Democrats, *Reinventing Government*.[2] Government does not generate prosperity – it does not row. Its goal is to make sure the drivers of prosperity are heading in the right direction. Sometimes you need to redirect traffic, but in doing so you are inevitably interfering with the underlying dynamism of the system.

President Clinton's Treasury Secretary, Lawrence Summers, put this view best in a 2001 interview:

> There is something about this epoch in history that really puts a premium on incentives, on decentralisation, on allowing small economic energy to bubble up rather than a more top-down, more directed approach.[3]

Summers was speaking, of course, about the ongoing revolution in information technology that occurred during his tenure (ironically, just after the dot.com crash and rescue of the giant hedge fund Long-Term Capital Management, which presaged the devastating financial crisis to come).

In the minds of many policy elites, the high-tech boom was linked with changes in the financial sector that Clinton and Summers also supported: public deficit reduction alongside private financial speculation. Summers even compared the increasingly complex technologies of finance to high-speed aeroplanes.[4] Like jets, we could not do without these multiplying financial products – we just had to figure out how to make them a little safer.

This managerial, ameliorative view of the state crumbles in the face of two basic realities. First, since the dawn of the modern age, government has been at the heart of innovation and growth, broadly understood. Those breakthroughs that Summers extolled and breathless commentators ascribed to the genius of Steve Jobs or Bill Gates – virtually all of them emerged out of public research and funding. As the economist Mariana Mazzucato has shown, every component of Jobs's iconic iPhone – even the software behind that pleasant voice that asks you to repeat your questions – emerged from basic R&D done by publicly-funded scientists in Europe and the USA.[5]

Or consider the 100 innovations lauded each year by *R&D Magazine*: innovations that have included HDTV, the nicoderm smoking cessation patch, the anti-cancer drug Taxol, the ATM, and LCD. In recent years, according to research conducted at UC Davis, over two thirds of the winners have come from partnerships involving business and government. In 2006, the last year of the study, nearly 90 per cent of the organisations that produced award-winning innovations in the USA benefited from federal funding. By contrast, that year just two award-winning innovations were developed by Fortune 500 companies.[6]

Even more importantly, most of the public health and medical breakthroughs that have revolutionised our lives (and which even cautious estimates suggest are worth much more than the increases in income we have enjoyed) can be credited to the regulatory and investment power of the state. The MRI, for example, emerged from of a series of US National Science Foundation grants starting in the mid-1950s. The laser, also vital to medical practice as well as consumer electronics and much else, grew out of military-funded research. In drug development, a 1995 investigation by researchers at MIT found that government research led to 11 of the 14 most medically significant drugs over the prior quarter century. Another study showed that public funding of research was instrumental in the development of more than 70 per cent of the drugs, with the greatest therapeutic value introduced between 1965 and 1992 (most of the rest received public funding and research during clinical trials). The same is true of virtually all the biggest medical breakthroughs of recent decades.

According to a 1997 study of important scientific papers cited in medical industry patents, nearly three quarters of those funded by US sources were financed by the federal government.[7]

Though the USA is falling behind other rich nations in measures of population health, including longevity and infant mortality, the gains that have occurred owe overwhelmingly to federal action. Just two prominent policies – the efforts to stem smoking and the improvement in air quality created by the Clean Air Act – account for the majority of gains in Americans' life expectancy since the 1970s.[8]

Government rows, and it rows hard. And if it stops rowing – and the cutbacks in R&D, infrastructure, medical innovation, and education all augur badly – we will be much poorer and sicker in the future than we would be otherwise.

Second, and even more important, the translation of growth into shared prosperity is hardly an automatic process. It requires active democratic governance. Take the current US situation of 'profits without prosperity', in which overall growth has rebounded but little of it is going into long-term investment or workers' paychecks. As much as Democrats derided the trickle-down philosophy of supply-side tax cuts, financial deregulation and the hands-off approach to corporate governance were premised on a similar assumption: that the generation of higher valuations on Wall Street was an inevitable precursor of higher incomes on Main Street.

In fact, the growing share of the economy that goes into finance – or into overpriced health services or environmentally destructive energy practices – is a double negative. It pulls money and talent from more productive sectors while imposing enormous costs and risks on everyone but favoured insiders. What economists call 'rent-seeking' – the generation of excess returns for privileged players through the exercise of market power, political influence, or both – does not just occur when special interests wheedle special deals from the government. Far more common, it reflects the government's passivity in the face of major market distortions that benefit a favoured few at the expense of almost everyone else. Nowhere has this been truer than in the financial sector, which has come to capture more than a third of all corporate profits in the USA, even as the cost of financial intermediation has risen, employment in the sector has barely budged, and the rest of the economy has suffered the devastating consequences of financial instability.[9]

The negative effects on corporate behaviour are not just limited to the financial sector itself. With greater pressure for immediate shareholder returns, US managers outside the financial sector have focused more and more on paying dividends and keeping stock prices up, rather than growing companies over the long term. Indeed, over 90 per cent of the profits earned by companies that were in the S&P 500 from 2003–12 went to stock buybacks (54 per cent) and dividends (37 per cent).[10] Put another way, less than one in 10 dollars of profit was invested in future growth or distributed to workers as higher pay. No wonder big US corporations are not innovating much.

While all of us ultimately pay the price, the costs and risks imposed by rent-seeking sectors like finance are greatest for those who are most vulnerable to economic swings and most dependent on wage income – to the outsiders in the insider economy. And here we arrive at the greatest promise of predistribution: restoring the foundations of middle-class democracy.

The Investment Imperative

The foundation of inclusive markets is public investment: in projects that make society richer and in the skills and capacities of citizens, especially the young and those who are least likely to experience employment and achievement without such investment. The public foundations of twentieth-century prosperity included electrification, modern transportation and communication networks, and the municipal infrastructure that made possible running water, indoor plumbing, and so much else that enabled cities to become healthy hubs for innovation and advancement.

For the twenty-first century, the list must expand so as to include the infrastructure for advanced digital communication, newer and more efficient forms of mass transit, and platforms for a green-energy economy, such as smart electric grids. These projects are genuine investments in the future, they are extraordinarily attractive today given low interest rates and a backlog of needs, and they should be treated separately from ordinary public transfers in government accounts. But they will not occur with public dollars and public action to facilitate private investment.

Public investment is not about 'picking winners' once and for all. Technologies and projects should be chosen through competitive processes of resource allocation, as has been true in R&D and science funding for decades. Just as in private investment, some bets will not pay off, and nimble policies will be needed to ensure that projects can be carried through without excess litigation or delay. But investment in public goods will not happen without governments taking the lead. No one within America's military–industrial–academic complex (President Eisenhower's original formulation of the famous phrase) could be certain that they were creating the jobs of tomorrow.

But when they laid the groundwork for the internet and modern computing, they acted with a faith that government had a vital – indeed, essential – role to play in fostering human development. We need that faith again.

We also need to rekindle our faith in public investment in education and training, from early childhood development to the continuing skills improvement that a knowledge-based economy demands. To be sure, public resources should be used prudently, and reducing the unit cost of human capital investments is one way to boost net benefits. (A second way is to focus resources where the returns are greatest – which means that even universal programmes should ensure that special resources are devoted to the least advantaged.) But we should never forget just how large the benefits are. As the University of Chicago's James Heckman has persuasively argued, even conservative estimates of the returns of early childhood interventions – from increased productivity to improved life outcomes (including health outcomes) to reduced costs for public assistance – make them among the best investments that governments can make, helping children grow up to be productive adults while improving the parenting abilities of their caretakers.[11] Indeed, increasing evidence suggests that even public help that looks like consumption, such as food aid or medical assistance, has a significant investment component, improving life outcomes for affected children (including children *in utero*) decades later.[12]

Another high-returns investment is ensuring that young adults finish college without enormous debt (and that any debt takes the form of income-contingent payments, to reduce the risk of default and burden on young people as they build careers or businesses). During the 2012 presidential campaign, the eventual GOP nominee Mitt Romney told a young questioner who asked how he could pay the ever-rising cost of college: 'It would be popular for me to stand up and say I'm going to give you government money to pay for your college, but I'm not going to promise that ... And don't expect the government to forgive the debt that you take on.'[13]

This is a terribly blinkered view: Why shouldn't public money be used to invest in the higher productivity and better social outcomes that advanced education provides? As scholars have delved deeper and deeper into the returns of education, they have found more and more evidence that the social returns are extraordinarily large – perhaps larger than the private returns, which are widely acknowledged to be substantial.[14] Just as some nominally private activities produce negative costs for societies, others (like high-quality, post-secondary education) produce positive benefits. What unites these two kinds of externalities is that neither are fully taken into account by those engaged in the activities themselves. We should be discouraging actions that harm the rest of us, shifting the costs to society back onto those who are imposing them. And we should be encouraging actions that help the rest of us – not out of the goodness of our heart, but for our own long-term good.

The Pillars of Predistribution

Investment takes time to pay off, and we will be paying the price for past under-investment for a long time to come. How can we create jobs and expand productivity *now*, and no less importantly, ensure that those taking these jobs receive a decent share of the productivity gains that their work helps make possible? The chapters to come provide many answers to this vital question. But a few of their common prescriptions stand out.

To begin with, the central pillar of successful societies is fulfilling and socially valuable work for as many citizens as possible. That means macroeconomic policies that ensure tight labour markets – in the present environment, substantial public investment – and rules and levies that reduce the risks of financial instability. The most promising financial constraints are also the simplest: a financial transaction tax that reduces speculative activity, strict limits on leverage, and public requirements for open, transparent exchanges.

Ensuring high levels of labour force participation also requires moving to support work in myriad ways: with regulations and subsidies that bring up wages, with benefits that are portable from job to job, and with support for families that allows parents to balance work and child care and children to balance work and elderly care.

The Beveridge/FDR model of the welfare state was built on the assumption of a male breadwinner, his bargaining power augmented by expanding labour unions, who was able to earn enough through his wages to support a family. No one can make this assumption today. We live in a post-labour economic world, with the rewards of growth going mostly to those who hold or are paid in the form of capital. No longer can we comfort ourselves with the belief that wage increases will naturally track productivity gains, nor can we be content with wealth so radically maldistributed that the richest 16,000 American families have more aggregate wealth than everyone in the bottom two thirds of the US wealth distribution.[15]

Instead, there must be a renewed emphasis on minimum wage requirements, high labour standards in public contracting, and the promotion of alternatives to unions, such as work councils, that can provide workers with a chance to share concerns and ideas that improve both fairness and efficiency. At the same time, we should not neglect the role of corporate governance in restoring the link between profits and prosperity: boards should include worker representation, manipulation of stock prices through buybacks and similar financial ploys should be prohibited, and there should be a heavy emphasis on transparent executive pay packages geared to long-term corporate performance relative to industry peers, rather than short-term shifts in share prices. And to the extent possible, workers should be part of this deal, receiving a share of company profits as well as a wage or salary.

Far more happily, we also live in a world of vastly greater gender and racial equality, though much progress still needs to be made. We often conceive of efforts to end discrimination and promote equality of opportunity as all about social justice. But they are also measures to better utilise the dispersed talent of diverse societies. Recently, Chicago and Stanford economists have shown just how much these efforts matter: they find that between 1960 and 2008, as much as a fifth of overall US growth was simply due to women and people of colour entering and using their skills in traditionally closed-off professional occupations.[16] A society that fails to promote the skills and opportunities of all its members is leaving money on the table.

Speaking of money on the table: the threat to our social and economic well-being – and ultimately our planet – posed by climate change provides the opportunity for a new understanding of our common wealth. Carbon emissions put a tax on all of us, destroying what we share without compensation. Any solution to the problem must involve putting a price on this destruction. These payments – a carbon tax or tradeable emission rights – should be transformed into wealth for all of society. Some of the proceeds should be put into green energy infrastructure, but the rest should be placed in a trust, invested in the real economy, that provides some form of an individual property claim for all citizens.

Predistribution: A Policy Toolkit for Progressives

Too often, the strains faced by post-industrial societies prompt fatalism. Together with the ameliorative view of the state just criticised, this fatalism strikes at the heart of the case for active governance that sustains the progressive spirit. The fact is that advanced industrial societies have tackled great challenges before. We can only rebuild public trust in the ability of governing institutions to address our present challenges step-by-step, over many years, through the hard work of gaining and using democratic authority. But we can, and we must begin now.

For those who understand that innovation and progress depends on a state that can row as well as steer, on creating the public foundations of prosperity as well as restricting private activities that threaten it, nothing could be more important than articulating a realistic, robust approach to high-wage full employment in the twenty-first century. A predistribution agenda does not make all the hard choices easy. But like the engineer who is allowed to open his toolkit, we are at least able to recognise what the real choices are.

Notes

1. Jacob S. Hacker, 'The foundations of middle class democracy', in *Priorities for a New Political Economy: Memos to the Left* (London: Policy Network, 2011), pp. 33–8. My thinking about the role of the state in fostering prosperity has been deeply influenced by my more than a decade-long collaboration with Paul Pierson. This chapter draws ideas from our most recent collaboration, *Winner-Take-All Politics: How Washington Made the Rich Richer—And Turned Its Back on the Middle Class* (New York: Simon & Schuster, 2010), as well as the book we are now completing, *American Amnesia: The Forgotten Roots of American Prosperity* (New York: Simon & Schuster, forthcoming).

2. David Osborne and Ted Gaebler, *Reinventing Government: How the Entrepreneurial Spirit is Transforming the Public Sector* (New York: Basic Books, 1992).

3. Interview with Lawrence Summers for 'The Commanding Heights', WGBH Public Radio, conducted 24 April 2001. Available at http://www.pbs.org/wgbh/commandingheights/shared/minitext/int_lawrencesummers (accessed 29 November 2012).

4. Lawrence H. Summers, 'International financial crises: causes, prevention, and cures', *American Economic Review* (2000), pp. 1–16.

5. Mariana Mazzucato, *The Entrepreneurial State: Debunking Public vs. Private Sector Myths* (London: Anthem Press, 2013). The voice-powered assistant on iPhones, named 'Siri,' was developed by the Stanford Research Institute (later, just SRI) in collaboration with the Defense Department.

6. Fred Block and Matthew R. Keller, 'Where do innovations come from? Changes in the US economy, 1970–2006', *Socio-Economic Review* 7/3 (2000), pp. 459–83.

7. Gar Alperovitz and Lew Daly, *Unjust Deserts: How the Rich Are Taking Our Common Inheritance and Why We Should Take It Back* (New York: The New Press, 2008), pp. 83–4; 'The Benefits of Medical Research and the Role of the NIH', Joint Economic Committee, US Senate, May 2000. Available at http://www.faseb.org/portals/2/pdfs/opa/2008/nih_research_benefits.pdf (accessed 3 December 2014); Francis Narin, Kimberly S. Hamilton, and

Dominic Olivastro, 'The increasing linkage between US technology and public science', *Research Policy* 26/3 (1997), pp. 317–30.

8. John Zaracostas, 'US Clean Air Act Cited as Big First Step in Emissions Control', McClatchy DC, 23 September 2014. Available at http://www.mcclatchydc. com/2014/09/23/240800_us-clean-air-act-cited-as-big (accessed 1 December 2012); Steven A. Schroeder and Howard K. Koh, 'Tobacco control 50 years after the 1964 Surgeon General's report', *JAMA* 311 (2014), pp. 141–3.

9. Thomas Philippon, 'Has the US finance industry become less efficient? On the theory and measurement of financial intermediation', National Bureau of Economic Research Working Paper Series, No. 18077 (2012).

10. William Lazonick, 'Profits without prosperity', *Harvard Business Review* (September 2014 issue). Available at https://hbr.org/2014/09/profits-without-prosperity (accessed 1 December 2014).

11. James J. Heckman, *Giving Kids a Fair Chance* (Cambridge: MIT Press, 2013).

12. See, for example, Hilary W. Hoynes, Diane Whitmore Schanzenbach, and Douglas Almond, 'Long run impacts of childhood access to the safety net', National Bureau of Economic Research Working Paper Series, No. 18535 (2012).

13. David Firestone, 'Romney in Ohio: Want college? Can't afford it? Too bad', *New York Times*, 5 March 2012. Available at http://takingnote.blogs.nytimes. com//2012/03/05/romney-in-ohio-want-college-cant-afford-it-too-bad (accessed 1 December 2014).

14. Michael Hout, 'Social and economic returns to college education in the United States', *Annual Review of Sociology* 38 (2012), pp. 379–400.

15. Emmanuel Saez and Gabriel Zucman, 'Wealth inequality in the United States since 1913: Evidence from capitalized income tax data', National Bureau of Economic Research Working Paper Series, No. 20625 (2014).

16. Chang-Tai Hsieh, Erik Hurst, Charles I. Johnes, and Peter Klenow, 'The allocation of talent and US economic growth', National Bureau of Economic Research Working Paper Series, No. 18963 (2013).

Predistribution: A New Governing Prospectus for the Centre-left

Claudia Chwalisz and Patrick Diamond

'Predistribution' is a new label for an idea with a long pedigree in the radical political tradition, bridging the eighteenth century political philosopher Thomas Paine with the influential twentieth century economist James Meade: the objective of radically reforming markets and property relations to systematically empower the wage-earning classes, 'treating the root causes of inequality rather than attending only to the symptoms'.[1] A predistributive strategy is prepared to explicitly challenge unequal concentrations of capital, wealth and power promoting the goal of a 'property-owning democracy' where every individual has a stake in the capitalist system by virtue of being a citizen. Three centuries after Paine published *The Rights of Man*, advanced Western economies are still characterised by deep and enduring inequalities that reappear across generations. As such, Paine's words still carry enormous resonance:

> For all men being originally equals, no one by birth could have the right to set up his own family in perpetual preference to all others forever, and tho' himself might deserve some decent degree of honours of his contemporaries, yet his descendants might be far too unworthy to inherit them.[2]

This chapter provides a synoptic introduction to the burgeoning public policy literature on predistribution and the politics that animate the idea.

'Social Democratic Strategy': 'Beveridge-Plus-Keynes'

Predistribution is focused above all on an age-old social democratic concern: how to reconcile productive efficiency with social justice in a market capitalist economy. The pursuit of social justice constituted the central thread running through European social democracy since Eduard Bernstein famously articulated the case for 'reformist socialism' at the end of the nineteenth century, breaking with Marxist orthodoxy. What followed was decades of continuous centre-left reinvention and reform across western Europe, culminating in the 'golden age' of postwar social democracy summarised by Gøsta Esping-Andersen (1995) as the era of 'Beveridge-Plus-Keynes'. Since then, the world in which social democratic politics operates has continued to change profoundly. Not only has the West experienced one of the most serious and destabilising financial crises of the modern era: capitalism itself is undergoing major structural transformation. The fiscal pressures unleashed by the crisis are placing unprecedented strain on the postwar welfare state. Meanwhile, the international context is being redefined by the growing power of emerging market economies, and the relative decline of the West. This is the time, more than ever, to construct a new strategy and governing prospectus for the centre-left in Europe.

The pivotal issue for social democracy is that while the world has been transformed, its political agenda has too often remained trapped in the doctrines and narratives of the post-1945 era. Centralising 'statist' social democracy remains ingrained in the ideological 'DNA' of most European parties. The assumption since World War II has been that a well-resourced Keynesian welfare state would achieve greater social equality, with government intervention 'humanising' capitalist markets. Between the 1940s and the 1970s, the corporatist social democratic model was largely successful in significantly improving life chances: narrowing the gap between rich and poor; undertaking transfers from the wealthy to the needy; insuring people against social 'risks' such as sickness, unemployment, and old age; and providing guaranteed access to high-quality public services, smoothing out inequalities across the life cycle.

The strategy in recent decades has, nonetheless, increasingly been found wanting: in most advanced economies, globalised markets have produced rising levels of inequality which the population finds intolerable, both economically and morally. Growing reliance on redistribution especially in countries with a high level of inequality in the primary income distribution has led to a severe backlash against the tax state, feeding resentment towards the poor, while appearing to justify the neoliberal critique of the role of government. States have sought to pursue a variety of distributive objectives, but they often spend more than they can conceivably raise in taxes given heightened 'taxpayer resistance', adding to the problem of rising public debt.[3] Government interventions such as 'Quantitative Easing' (QE) after the 2008 crisis have, in turn, further accentuated inequality, boosting relative asset values and the owners of capital as real household incomes have stagnated.[4]

It is clear there are growing limits to the redistributive capacities of the state given the likelihood of stagnant growth and severe fiscal constraint in the decade ahead.[5] We have to find new routes to social justice and a more equal society for the 'new hard times' through which we are living.[6] This is the context in which the debate about 'predistribution' has recently emerged, especially in the USA and the UK, as Yale professor Jacob Hacker coined the phrase, and renowned American economist Joseph Stiglitz has been using the term to describe his latest report, *Rewriting the Rules of the American Economy: An Agenda for Growth and Shared Prosperity.*[7] Increasingly, the debate has spread to continental Europe, where the French Prime Minister Manuel Valls has embraced "prédistribution". It is a concept which recommends that the state should seek to prevent inequalities from occurring at the outset, rather than relying on traditional mechanisms of 'tax-and-spend' redistribution to tackle inequalities after they have occurred.[8] This is a pressing issue, as the last 30 years have witnessed a dramatic rise in income inequality across the advanced capitalist democracies.[9]

The aim of predistributive policy is to promote market reforms that encourage a more equal distribution of economic power, assets and rewards even before government 'collects taxes or pays out benefits'.[10] Predistribution seeks to restructure the market economy, ensuring fairer outcomes for all can be secured without sacrificing long-term growth and productivity. This is a strategy where, as Matzner and Streek attest, 'equality, rather than being wrought from the economy at the expense of efficiency, is built into the organisation of the production process itself'.[11] Rather than wholly relying on the distributive sphere of social policy, the aim of predistribution is to address the structural context of contemporary capitalism: the quality of work and the satisfaction it generates; the allocation of 'good' and 'lousy' jobs; the prevailing framework of employment rights and market flexibilities; and the extent to which markets work in the public interest by treating all consumers, including the most vulnerable, equitably. The aim of predistributive market design is to eliminate biases that benefit privileged groups, promoting public interest objectives that reduce the need for *post hoc* government intervention. This chapter argues that in addition to 'non-monetary' interventions, strategies of social investment complement and reinforce predistribution, in turn upgrading the productive potential of the workforce and the economy.

Of course, predistribution is a governing prospectus, not an election-winning slogan. It carries important insights about social democratic policy in the post-crisis era. Today, the traditional redistributive model of the state is facing an unprecedented crisis. The equilibrium between markets and social justice that characterised the postwar age is breaking down. The West is experiencing 'a crisis without end': a slow, protracted recovery, interest rates at extraordinarily low levels, a major risk of deflation, and an ongoing process of fiscal adjustment and austerity.[12] Moreover, the increasing internationalisation of economic life implies that social inequalities are no longer reversible within any single nation state. The question is whether a model of predistribution can plausibly fill the strategic void opened up by the decay of the 'Beveridge-Plus-Keynes' formula. A new social and economic framework focused on predistribution addresses three overriding concerns: the promotion of economic efficiency; the realisation of social justice; and the search for a new growth model after the crisis.

First, economic efficiency: predistribution provides a cogent rationale for an active state in an era where public spending is severely constrained, where many governments are implementing tough fiscal consolidation programmes, and where austerity in the light of low growth and secular stagnation is likely to remain for the foreseeable future.

The predistribution agenda acknowledges that the welfare state's redistributive capacity was receding prior to the crisis. In part, this reflects structural changes since the 1970s and 1980s, alongside neoliberal policy regimes that have weakened the egalitarian impact of welfare systems. Demographic change with increasing old-age dependency ratios has put increased pressure on health and social care spending, reducing the resources available for policies to boost opportunity through pre-school investment, education, training and re-skilling. Unsurprisingly, many European societies have witnessed declining rates of relative economic mobility since the 1960s and 1970s, with negative consequences for long-term productivity and economic growth.

Predistributive policies aim to raise the underlying growth rate of the economy, as well as advancing equality, integral to a new social contract for the knowledge economy.[13] The effort to widen social justice is not achieved at the expense of economic efficiency, but ought to be treated as complementary to it. Improving long-run economic performance in western Europe will be enhanced by greater equality of opportunities and outcomes. For example, constraining low-wage adjustment strategies should help to improve productivity and strengthen efficiency in labour and product markets.[14] The objective should be to break out of the low-wage, low productivity trajectory which has been especially prevalent in the 'Anglo-liberal' economies, improving skill-levels, productivity and living standards.

The second pillar of this framework is social justice: a predistributive policy agenda seeks to achieve more equal social and economic outcomes by reshaping markets, not only compensating the 'losers'. Past decades have witnessed a dramatic rise in income and asset inequalities in advanced capitalist democracies, alongside stagnation in median incomes, growing job polarisation, as well as increasing levels of long-term unemployment. Markets are producing more inequalities than ever, as the share of growth absorbed by capital at the expense of labour has markedly increased. Moreover, as profitability in the corporate sector has declined, real wages have been severely squeezed.[15] Not only is the capacity of traditional welfare systems to ameliorate capitalism's unequal character declining, social and economic inequalities are increasing in their intensity.

Third, predistribution addresses the need for a new growth model: a predistributive agenda strives for long-term, sustainable, inclusive growth. Rates of Western economic growth have recovered from the depths of the post-2008 recession, but growth remains anaemic and intermittent. There is no emerging 'growth paradigm' that appears capable of reviving Western prosperity; the impact of 'digitisation' in key sectors has so far been uneven; at the same time, lack of effective co-ordination and governance of the financial system hinders any sustained recovery in the world economy.[16] Some commentators have questioned whether a new concept of growth is required that better takes account of income inequality, environmental sustainability, and human well-being.[17] Moreover, low levels of income inequality are correlated with faster and more durable growth.[18]

In today's economy, austerity programmes and the financial crisis are hitting those most in need hardest, together with the burden of rising youth unemployment and long-term joblessness in Europe. The emphasis on reducing inequalities by reforming systems of capitalist production rather than relying on *post hoc* intervention through the welfare state are ever more necessary. The overall aim is to redraw the framework in which capitalist markets operate, strengthening both equity *and* efficiency, rather than compensating the 'losers' for the adverse outcomes markets produce. Some key examples of predistributive policy reforms are given below:

Financial System Reform

- Tougher financial market regulation to mitigate 'moral hazard' ensuring that taxpayers are not required to bail out failing banks and financial institutions;
- Limiting executive pay awards by giving shareholders and employees the right to veto excessive pay claims and bonuses.

Corporate Governance Reform

- Busting monopolies and cartels across product and capital markets supporting start-ups and small- and medium-sized business (SME) formation;

- A corporate governance system for large companies that gives workers a genuine 'voice' in the management of the firm alongside the promotion of profit-sharing schemes.

Labour Market Reform

- Measures to boost the National Minimum Wage (NMW) and 'living wage' to help the lowest paid strengthening the relative position of labour market 'outsiders' and encouraging unionisation in traditionally casualised sectors;
- Labour market reforms that improve flexibility for workers as well as firms: the purpose is not to outlaw dismissal exacerbating 'insider/ outsider' cleavages, but to ensure marginalised groups such as single parents and disabled people can have sustained contact with the labour market by offering greater employment flexibility;
- Redesigning procurement rules to ensure fair employment throughout the public and private sectors that are delivering public goods and services;
- Defining social norms and rules of the game that combat the culture of low pay in the corporate sector reinforcing legal regulations and rules.

Market Redesign

- Regulatory interventions in markets that protect the rights of vulnerable consumers, especially in sectors such as energy, transport and food;
- Another market reform would entail improving the accessibility of information about price and quality available to consumers, while removing privileges that reduce economic efficiency. Preferential taxation of 'buy-to-let' investments in the UK, for example, raises demand for housing assets, forcing up rents leading to higher housing benefit payments. The removal of tax breaks would reduce the need for retrospective intervention through the benefits system.

A Property-Owning Democracy

- The overall aim ought to be forging a 'property-owning democracy' giving the majority a fair share in the wealth and capital of the nation while tackling inherited concentrations of wealth among the privileged.[19] This should include a proportion of wages being paid in shares or other forms of capital so that wage-earners can increase their independence, autonomy and 'effective freedom'.

This is not to claim that social democrats ought to abandon the traditional welfare state, and its attendant mechanisms of egalitarian redistribution. On the contrary, markets produce inherently imperfect outcomes: there are citizens who are unable to participate in markets and who rely on state-funded 'solidaristic' provision to ensure opportunity and security throughout their lives. Moreover, greater equality of economic outcomes in the advanced industrialised democracies is necessary to ensure a more stable and cohesive society. The lesson of recent decades is surely that *both* predistributive and redistributive strategies are necessary to build a fairer, more equal society. As such, redistribution and predistribution ought to be viewed as two sides of the same coin. However, a greater focus on strategic predistributive interventions ought to mean that *less* redistribution is necessary later on.

Alongside measures to ensure that capitalist markets produce fairer outcomes in the distribution of primary incomes, predistribution should focus on how to improve equality of life chances through targeted early intervention: a complementary strategy of 'social investment'. Over the last fifteen years, many western European countries have sought to shift the focus of the welfare state, correcting inequalities a priori and investing in the earliest years of citizens' lives. Nonetheless, more needs to be done to advance and embed a social investment state. There is a risk that in the light of the crisis and the imperative of fiscal consolidation, states focus on protecting traditional welfare transfers rather than underwriting 'equality-boosting' programmes: pre-school education, parenting and family support, high-quality childcare from nought to adolescence, extra tutorial provision for those from low income households, and asset policies (such as British Labour's Child Trust Fund) that give the poorest children a capital stake for the future.

The Nature of Economic and Social Inequality

In the debate about what determines inequality in contemporary capitalist economies, various factors are invariably cited in a vast and growing literature.[20] Rising levels of immigration are one driver, combined with declining rates of unionisation. Both were believed to have weakened the bargaining power of low-skilled workers, accompanied by a fall in the relative value of the minimum wage. Another factor is the growth of international trade and the globalisation of labour, product and capital markets since the 1980s and 1990s. As the balance of economic advantage shifts to the east, industrial manufacturing and low-cost service sector jobs in Western economies become increasingly uncompetitive or even obsolete.[21] Each of these explanations has received considerable attention from politicians and policy-makers. There is evidence that such factors have each contributed to rising inequality of primary incomes in the USA and the UK, as well as countries as diverse as Germany, Japan, Spain and Portugal.

Nonetheless, one of the most significant drivers of income inequality in the advanced economies remains 'skill-biased' technological change,[22] as Figure 1 below makes clear. Although the table dates from 1997, the same findings are confirmed in the 2015 presidential report.[23] Technology increases the proportion of relatively skilled jobs at the higher end of the labour market, while skewing the wage distribution towards those with the most 'high-value' human capital. There is considerable debate within the economics profession about the impact of technological change, but it appears to be a powerful driver of inequality mediated by the level of education and skills.

FIGURE 1   The Drivers of Economic Inequality.

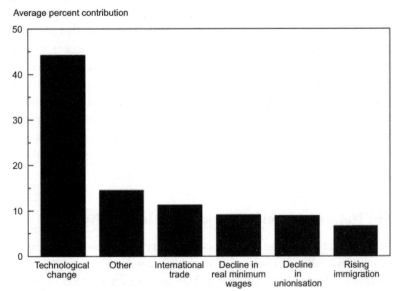

Source: Federal Reserve Bank of New York, as cited in the Economic Report of the President (1997).[24]

The Organisation for Economic Co-operation and Development (OECD) has recently predicted that jobs requiring 'highly-educated' workers will rise by 20 per cent in the next decade; on the other hand, low-skilled jobs are likely to fall by more than 10 per cent in the advanced economies.[25]

Moreover, low-skilled workers are increasingly vulnerable to the threat of redundancy and unemployment in a period of intense economic restructuring. In the EU28 countries, 84 per cent of working-age adults with 'higher' (tertiary level) skills are currently working, compared to less than half of those with low level skills. Moreover, downward pressure on wages and fear of unemployment is leading to heightened economic insecurity for those on median incomes. Across the OECD, 'middle income' households have experienced a far sharper decline in incomes than was the case during the last economic crisis in the 1970s.

Nonetheless, the recent focus on *income* inequality and rising Gini co-efficients in the aftermath of the financial crisis and 'great recession' may have distracted attention from the central importance of equality of opportunity, in particular how far children and young people from low income households and disadvantaged neighbourhoods have opportunities to realise their potential. This question is ably addressed in Jeremy Fishkin's recent book *Bottlenecks*,[26] which analyses how economic and educational structures often act surreptitiously to reduce the availability of opportunities for all. Fishkin insists that public policy should focus not on narrow goals such as pursuing a particular definition of academic excellence, but on how government interventions can maximise the ability of every individual to pursue a fulfilling and independent life where they can fully exercise their various capabilities. This insight is at the core of the predistributive agenda.

This Book

The contributors to this volume consider the predistribution agenda from a variety of comparative perspectives ranging across disciplines and countries. The focus throughout is on fashioning credible policy solutions, addressing the *politics* of predistribution. Forging a strategic 'market-shaping' state for the post-crisis era requires a model of progressive leadership that confronts 'insider' sectional interests, shifting resources across the income distribution, across generations, across localities, and across the life cycle. A concerted strategy of predistribution entails a new way of practicing social democratic politics – no longer promising fiscal rewards for every voter 'interest group' – but recognising that only a commitment to societal fairness predicated on 'shared sacrifice' will ensure our societies make the transition from the current crisis to a stable social and economic settlement beyond.

Navigating between politics and markets makes it necessary to identify the historical agents and institutions that will promote support for radical predistributive policies, forging new coalitions of mutual interest. Historically, welfare states have been the product of particular patterns of class affiliation, mediated by the property relations of modern capitalism.[27] Among the most significant challenges for social democratic parties since the 1960s and 1970s has been the secular decline of the manual working-class, combined with rising scepticism about what states can accomplish imposing fiscal limits alongside declining trust in the role of government.[28] This had led some to enthusiastically predict the *end* of egalitarian social democracy.[29]

Nonetheless, the centre-left should not be too pessimistic about its prospects. There are, of course, serious obstacles and constraints to the realisation of social justice and a more equal society, but there are still fresh strategic opportunities to be seized in fashioning new coalitions of political support. Anne Wren points to the growing importance of the service economy which provides significant opportunities for increasing women's participation in the labour market: women have a comparative advantage in high-value services compared to sectors such as agriculture and industry.[30] Paid employment for women is increasingly necessary both because 'dual earner' households have a lower poverty risk, and to ensure the fiscal sustainability of the welfare state given rapid population ageing. Facilitating women's inclusion in the labour market entails public subsidisation of care for children and older adults, as well as employment flexibility including the right to work part-time. As Wren attests: 'In political terms, parties of the centre-left are well positioned to pursue this agenda: the demand for these types of policies amongst women in particular is well recognised, and is closely linked with their higher levels of support for the left.'[31]

The remainder of this chapter addresses the framework of predistribution and its link to the development of the social investment state as envisaged by Wren. It is important to maintain a conceptual distinction between 'predistribution' and 'social investment': predistributive policies focus on regulatory interventions designed to transform the rules of the game in which markets operate; social investment is predominantly concerned with the optimal allocation of public spending in order to maximise equity and efficiency.[32] Nonetheless, both approaches focus on equipping individuals for change in dynamic, globalising market economies, rather than 'repairing' adverse outcomes that have already been inflicted. Predistribution and social investment are complementary strategies: predistribution relies on raising the underlying rate of productivity in the economy, changing the context in which markets operate in order to improve real wages and relative living standards. At the same time, improving productivity entails strategic 'social investment' throughout the life cycle, focused in particular on low-income households. Social investment policies, in turn, require faster growth and stronger government tax revenues through enhanced productivity and market efficiency.

Predistribution and the Social Investment State

A core theme of this volume is that rising inequality and lower earnings mobility in capitalist democracies are unlikely to be addressed without more effective strategic intervention by governments that improves the relative position of individuals from low-income households. In the burgeoning predistribution literature, government action is envisaged less as a mechanism for compensating individuals for disadvantage that has already occurred, but as a means of reducing the damage inflicted by markets, using instruments of anticipatory intervention that promote more equal opportunities. Predistribution, as its originator Jacob Hacker from Yale University attests, requires: 'A focus on market outcomes that encourage a more equal distribution of economic power and rewards even before government collects taxes or pays out benefits'.[33]

As such, predistribution is not limited merely to reducing poverty and social disadvantage. The test for predistribution policies is whether they can help to reverse what the economist, Miles Corak, refers to as 'The Great Gatsby curve':[34] the tendency in industrialised societies for a child's life chances to be increasingly determined by their parents' material circumstances. Since the crisis, the incidence of poverty and unemployment has been distributed even more unevenly among social groups: children are at highest risk of poverty, especially those with a low-skilled parent in a 'single earner' household. This has given rise across Europe to a process of 'dualisation' where societies are increasingly divided between knowledge-rich 'winners' and knowledge-poor 'losers'.[35] More unequal societies, according to Corak, are less likely to be characterised by higher rates of inter-generational mobility. Shifting the state's role from 'remedial' compensatory approaches to a 'pre-emptive' strategy of investing in the human and social capital of disadvantaged groups is intended to get opportunity and economic mobility flowing again. That requires a fundamental shift, combining income redistribution with pro-active investment throughout the life cycle.

This approach further underlines the central importance of education policy, in particular measures that are designed to shift the balance of human capital acquisition towards children from disadvantaged households. Surprisingly perhaps, education policy appears to have slipped down the agenda in recent years in many countries. In Britain, the education reforms undertaken by the Blair and Brown governments were politically controversial as they gave a major role to private and third sector providers. This attenuated ideological divisions within the Labour Party. Moreover, the claim that education policy was the most effective instrument to offset the inequalities generated by globalisation, a hallmark of 'third way' ideas, was exposed as problematic. Rising public investment in education and skills had not stemmed the tide of social and economic inequality in the industrialised countries. As Busemeyer highlights in a subsequent chapter of this book, the quality of the vocational education and training system at the post-secondary education stage is strongly related to overall levels of socio-economic inequality.

Of course, securing political legitimacy for pro-active social investment in education, pre-school provision, family support, and adult skills is seldom straightforward. Increasingly, voters in developed state economies are less likely to have children given falling birth-rates, and might resent extra support being given to families in an era of belt-tightening and austerity. In the New Labour years, low-income adults in UK households without children fared poorly in relation to poverty alleviation. Furthermore, in public attitude surveys, education, early intervention and childcare do not generally register as major issues of concern for voters.[36] Comparative data indicates that in many European countries, voters are more concerned about 'old' social risks, notably unemployment, pension adequacy, and fear of losing their home. Most welfare systems are characterised by a growing 'elderly bias', explicable given the ageing population. However, there is a constant danger of unbalanced welfare coverage further disadvantaging younger families with children. The risk is that governments will continue to support older citizens while neglecting the imperative of investing in the young.

Educational Performance

The economist Stephen Nickell argues that despite growing scepticism about the efficacy of education policy, human capital effects are vastly underestimated in the reproduction of inequality.[37] The recent OECD report comparing educational performance between countries has provided a 'wake-up call' for policy-makers. According to the OECD, 'England is the only country in the world where the generation approaching retirement is more literate and numerate than the youngest'.[38] Out of 24 industrialised countries, English 16–24 year olds rank 22nd in literacy and 21st in numeracy. More worryingly, young people in England have among the lowest levels of proficiency in Information and Communications Technology (ICT). As a consequence, 'the talent pool of highly skilled adults in England and Northern Ireland is likely to shrink relative to other countries'.[39]

It is striking that the OECD report has largely been ignored by the major political parties. The Conservatives sought to blame the previous Labour government for the UK's comparative weakness in educational achievement. Nonetheless, the post-2010 UK coalition government appeared to have no credible agenda for addressing the central drivers of low performance – in particular, that too many pupils from low income households are only able to access 'low-performing' schools.[40] Moreover, Labour has been reticent about the OECD's findings, presumably because the report emphasises the need for bold but contentious reforms of the English school system.

Policy-makers have historically focused on the role that formal educational institutions, most prominently schools, play in addressing the educational challenge underlined by the OECD report. The debate about how schools are organised so as to maximise the potential for continuous educational improvement remains crucially important. However, it ought to be remembered that most learning occurs outside the school day, particularly during the influential early years, developing the cognitive framework for subsequent human capital acquisition. Research by Dearden et al. shows that by the age of three years, a 23 per cent gap in cognitive outcomes has opened up between children from the richest and poorest households.[41] According to Anne West, a leading educational researcher, 'there is an achievement gap between children from poor family backgrounds and others. This is not unique to the UK, but found in all countries of the OECD'.[42] A combination of 'monetary' and 'non-monetary' variables – the quality of the home-learning environment, family background, parental education, resources within the household – are all crucial factors in explaining such cognitive differences. This poses a key challenge for policy-makers who want to make the initial distribution of endowments more equitable in accordance with the social investment and predistribution paradigms.

Capability and Character

Indeed, research consistently underlines that parental 'confidence' and 'peer effects' have a crucial impact on children's life chances alongside formal schooling. Traditionally, policy has tended to emphasise the importance of institutions, understating the role played by informal networks, including family, friends and peers, on children's outcomes. Predistribution is not only concerned with market reforms alongside sustained investment in the education and skills system, but with reinforcing the capabilities, resilience, and well-being of individuals, especially the most disadvantaged, giving them more power in relation to markets.[43] It is essential to focus support on the most deprived households, as the impact of child poverty is mediated by the reduced availability of parental resources.[44]

The perpetuation of low aspirations are a further critical factor in structural disadvantage: there is evidence that parents in low income households have lower levels of 'self-efficacy' – less self-confidence and belief in their own capabilities. Recent research in the social sciences has focused on the importance of 'character' in shaping cognitive outcomes and its inculcation in children through their parents: 'character' alludes to the individual's ability to exhibit drive, agency and determination, all of which are attributes of later success in life.[45]

Social Investment: Policy Implications

As such, this chapter makes the argument that an effective predistribution strategy needs to challenge and reshape markets, while at the same time boosting productivity and growth by investing in the education, skills and human capital of the entire population, particularly the most disadvantaged, through a social investment state. The key insight for policy-makers is to focus on what occurs outside formal institutions through the home environment, with parents, and among peers. Their influence is, in many ways, as significant as what takes place in schools and learning institutions, although the two are often self-reinforcing. In addition to the 'non-monetary' regulatory interventions outlined in a previous section of this chapter, the following social investment policy measures ought to be prioritised by future governments.

Refocus Early Intervention Strategies

Additional interventions in the early years have been a priority for policy-makers across the political spectrum, especially in the Nordic countries in the postwar era. Although the previous UK Labour administration invested heavily in nursery provision, the early years have never received the concerted attention given to schools and the National Health Service (NHS). As a result, childcare is now more expensive in the UK than in most comparable economies. There are growing concerns about the adequacy of coverage, the emergence of 'postcode lotteries', and lower levels of quality in childcare settings. As a consequence, the UK has a relatively low rate of female employment and a large gender pay gap, ranking 15th in the OECD league table. There are three vital dimensions of policy that should be addressed. First, ensure that resources and infrastructure are weighted towards the most disadvantaged groups within a universal childcare system. Second, give priority to parental involvement, not only in childcare settings themselves, but in the management and governance of 'Sure Start' children's centres. This dimension of parental empowerment has recently been neglected, and ought to be strengthened. Finally, additional measures are necessary to promote female employment, including increased availability of family leave shared between mothers and fathers.

Boost Parenting Support

In an increasingly disruptive, insecure economic environment characterised by a number of pervasive social stress factors, parents need more effective support. Mentoring has proven beneficial effects, where more experienced parents support those facing difficulties. Formal parenting programmes can also be productive, but often more informal support built around Sure Start, early years' provision, and schools and youth centres is necessary. Initiatives such as 'Nurse-Family Partnerships' originally pioneered in the USA where nurses support parents in disadvantaged households from the pre-natal stage through to early childhood are also vital.

Improve the Quality of Parenting

There is an extensive and wide-ranging public policy literature on the potential of behavioural change strategies to significantly improve parenting outcomes. How parents interact with their children can have a crucial impact on later achievement. For example, parents who regularly read to their children significantly improve cognitive outcomes; responding appropriately to misbehaviour can also help to prevent later conduct disorders and cognitive impairments.[46] It is important to remember that parenting is not always provided by biological parents, but a range of care-givers, including grandparents and family friends.

Parental Responsibilities

Parents have the right to support and to be able to access state-funded services, but parents have reciprocal duties and obligations too, including ensuring their children's school attendance and good behaviour. Where responsibilities are not met, mechanisms such as 'home-school contracts' and parenting orders are necessary to ensure that the underlying causes of negative behaviour are adequately addressed.

Extend the 'Pupil Premium' and Reform the System of School Choice

The pupil premium in England has provided schools who admit pupils from disadvantaged households with an additional £900 per child in 2013–14. Nonetheless, the evidence is that children from low-income households continue to access those schools that are consistently poor performers.[47] This needs to be addressed by boosting the premium available for pupils from disadvantaged backgrounds, while opening up the school selection process to avoid residential segregation. At the same time, highly performing schools need additional incentives to expand provision.

Reform teacher credentials and standardised student qualifications to make teaching a prestigious profession

Improving teacher quality by making teaching a prestigious profession can help balance inequalities between poorly and highly performing schools. Ensuring all teachers are required to attain a competitive teaching master's degree with an emphasis on pedagogy would level the playing field. If only the best students are able to become teachers in the first place, the disparity between 'good' and 'bad' schools narrows as only the brightest and most creative minds are teaching at all schools. Countries like Finland, which is consistently at the top of the OECD's Programme for International Student Assessment (PISA), demonstrate how this does not need to be achieved through financial incentives, as Finnish teachers are paid roughly the same amount as teachers in the UK. Rather, what attracts individuals to the position is the freedom afforded to them when it comes to developing the curriculum and teaching it in innovative ways. The lack of standardised exams and rigorous testing permit this flexibility. While this proposal would be difficult to implement politically, the leading countries in educational attainment show the potential of such policies to mitigate inequality.

Promote Multi-Agency Working Across Public Services

Improving the situation that faces the most disadvantaged children and young people requires not only input from schools and Sure Start centres, but public services locally and nationally. The impact of health inequalities on human capital acquisition and relative social mobility, for example, is now well-documented. In New York, a 'children's zone' model has been established to provide intensive support to disadvantaged families in low-income neighbourhoods. Moreover, expanding social investment to focus on pupils from low-income households will reap long-term benefits. For example, the Institute for Public Policy Research (IPPR) has estimated that provision of universal affordable childcare across the UK will significantly boost the female employment rate and government tax revenues: an initial, up-front investment achieves average returns of £20,050 over four years. In the long term, predistributive policies have the potential to pay for themselves: engaging women in the labour market more effectively through maternity benefits and childcare provision has been among the most successful social policy interventions of the last 30 years.[48]

Future governments will, nevertheless, have to demonstrate how this is to be funded. Various thinktanks have proposed to rationalise tax credits and childcare subsidies into increased supply-side funding for early years' provision. Alternative options include withdrawing benefits for relatively well-off pensioners such as free travel and the Winter Fuel Allowance, as well as taxing capital, property, wealth and inheritance more efficiently. For example, a lifetime gifts tax could raise £1 billion; abolishing higher-rate tax relief on pensions would generate a further £7 billion; a property-based tax could raise a further £3 billion for the UK Exchequer; a further crackdown on tax avoidance could raise substantial sums: in the UK, approximately £35 billion a year is lost due to tax evasion.[49] Raising the burden of taxation is never popular. This challenges the claim that predistribution does not necessitate hard choices, making it attractive to 'preference-accommodating' politicians. It is more necessary than ever to explicitly challenge unjustified concentrations of capital ownership and wealth inequality.

According to the political scientist Lucy Barnes, support for progressive taxation has risen markedly since the crisis, but while many voters do not believe that the rich pay enough tax, there is little appetite for a return to 'big' government.[50] Two principles ought to be enunciated in the public debate about social investment and taxation. Firstly, additional wealth taxes ought to be 'hypothecated': pooled into a specific investment fund designed to offset adverse 'social inheritance', boosting opportunities for those from disadvantaged backgrounds. Secondly, the 'better-off' older generations must acknowledge that younger people and families increasingly need support: modest tax rises and benefit rationalisation is necessary to ensure inter-generational reciprocity. The American political scientist Harold Lasswell famously argued that politics is about 'who gets what, when and how'; it is vital to bridge the inter-generational gap.

Conclusion

However well-targeted and resourced, early intervention programmes, family support, and education are not the solution to every social and economic problem. Nonetheless, it is difficult to envisage that rising inequality and lower earnings mobility can be addressed without more effective intervention that boosts the relative position of children and young people from low income households, alongside sustained predistributive reforms of capitalist markets. This chapter has argued that strategies of social investment and predistribution are inherently interconnected and mutually reinforcing. There is little purpose in improving the relative position of the most disadvantaged groups early in the life cycle if they then confront highly inegalitarian labour, capital and product markets which foster permanent reliance on the traditional welfare state.

Moreover, preventing the inter-generational transmission of disadvantage is an urgent moral and political imperative. As support for the welfare state has declined among high-skilled workers in service-orientated knowledge economies,[51] a predistribution agenda provides a fresh rationale for public investment which also benefits higher income groups through universal childcare, education, family support, and so on. The expansion of service employment among highly skilled women is a major political opportunity for the centre-left, forging a progressive alliance for a 'new welfare state', providing further opportunities to bridge the 'winners' and the 'losers' of economic and social change.

Until recently, the political dimension of how actors and institutions influence policy formation and resource allocation has been underplayed in much of the literature on predistribution. The chapters in this collection aim to remedy that gap. They make clear that the strategic aim of predistribution should be to ensure a decent minimum income for all, to provide access to social investment and services, alongside a fair distribution of assets, capital and wealth as Thomas Paine envisaged, identifying new means to provide collective security – the *sine qua non* of social democracy. As such, it is vital to integrate predistribution with social investment, developing future strategies that can achieve economic efficiency, social justice and sustainable growth in the 'new hard times' that are reshaping our world.

Notes

1. Martin O'Neill and Thad Williamson, 'The Promise of Predistribution' (London: Policy Network, 2012). Available at http://www.policy-network.net/ pno_detail.aspx?ID=4262&title=The-promise-of-predistribution (accessed 21 March 2015).
2. Thomas Paine, *Common Sense* (Philadelphia, 1776). Available at http://www. gutenberg.org (accessed 18 May 2015).
3. Wolfgang Streek, 'How will capitalism end?', *New Left Review* 87 (2014), pp. 35–64; Tony Atkinson, *Public Economics in an Age of Austerity* (New York: Routledge, 2014).
4. Andrew Gamble, *Crisis Without End* (Basingstoke: Palgrave Macmillan, 2014).
5. Andrew Gamble, *The Spectre at the Feast: Capitalist Crisis and the Politics of Recession* (Basingstoke: Palgrave Macmillian, 2009).
6. Miles Kahler and David A. Lake, *Politics in the New Hard Times* (New York: Cornell University Press, 2013).
7. Stiglitz, Joseph. 2015. *Rewriting the Rules of the American Economy: An Agenda for Growth and Shared Prosperity.* New York: Roosevelt Institute.
8. Jacob Hacker, 'The institutional foundations of middle class democracy' (London: Policy Network, 2011). Available at http://www.policy-network.net/ pno_detail.aspx?ID=3998&title=The+institutional+foundations+of+middle-class+democracy (accessed 21 March 2015).
9. OECD. 2011. *Divided We Stand: Why Inequality Keeps Rising.* OECD Publishing. http://dx.doi.org/10.1787/9789264119536-en.
10. *Ibid.*
11. Egon Matzner and Wolfgang Streek, *Beyond Keynesianism: The Socio-economics of Production and Full Employment* (Brookfield: Elgar, 1991), p. 16.
12. Gamble, *Crisis Without End.*
13. See concluding chapter in this volume.
14. Matzner and Streek, *Beyond Keynesianism.*

15. Wendy Carlin, 'A Progressive Economic Strategy' (London: Policy Network, 2012). Available at http://www.policy-network.net/publications_detail.aspx?ID=4269 (accessed 21 March 2015).
16. Gamble, *Crisis Without End*.
17. See Andrew Gamble's contribution in this volume.
18. Jonathan Ostry, Andrew Berg and Charalambos Tsangarides, 'Redistribution, Inequality, and Growth', IMF Staff Discussion Note (2014), pp. 2–3. Available at http://www.imf.org/external/pubs/ft/sdn/2014/sdn1402.pdf (accessed 21 March 2015).
19. O'Neill and Williamson, 'The Promise of Predistribution'.
20. OECD. 2011. *Divided We Stand: Why Inequality Keeps Rising*. OECD Publishing. http://dx.doi.org/10.1787/9789264119536-en.
21. Anne Wren, *The Political Economy of the Service Transition* (Oxford: Oxford University Press, 2014).
22. David Autor, Lawrence Katz and Alan Krueger, 'Computing inequality: Have computers changed the labor market?' *Quarterly Journal of Economics* 113/4 (1998), pp. 1169–1212. Autor et al.'s analysis is based on data from the 1990s, but the broad picture of the key drivers of inequality in the advanced economies still holds true.
23. Economic Report of the President (Washington: United States Government Printing Office, 2015), pp. 146, 309. Available at https://www.whitehouse.gov/sites/default/files/docs/cea_2015_erp.pdf (accessed 18 May 2015).
24. OECD Centre for Educational Research and Innovation, 'Education at a Glance' (Paris: OECD, 2013).
25. Economic Report of the President (Washington: United States Government Printing Office, 1997), available at http://www.presidency.ucsb.edu/economic_reports/1997.pdf (accessed 18 May 2015).
26. Joseph Fishkin, *Bottlenecks: A New Theory of Equal Opportunity* (Oxford: Oxford University Press, 2014).
27. Gøsta Esping-Andersen, *Social Foundations of Postindustrial Economies* (Oxford: Oxford University Press, 1999).
28. See concluding chapter in this volume.
29. See John Gray, *The End of Social Democracy* (London: Demos, 1996).
30. Wren, *The Political Economy of the Service Transition*.
31. *Ibid.*
32. *Ibid.*
33. Hacker, 'The institutional foundations of middle class democracy'.
34. Michael Corak, 'Income inequality, equality of opportunity, and intergenerational mobility', *Journal of Economic Perspectives* 27/3 (2013), pp. 79–102.
35. Patrick Emmenegger, Silja Häusermann, Bruno Palier and Martin Seeleib-Kaiser (eds), *The Age of Dualization: The Changing Face of Inequality in Deindustrializing Societies* (New York: Oxford University Press, 2012).
36. British Social Attitudes Survey (2014).

37. Stephen Nickell, 'Poverty and worklessness in Britain', *The Economic Journal,* 114/494 (2004), pp. C1–C25.
38. OECD Centre for Educational Research and Innovation, 'Education at a Glance' (Paris: OECD, 2013).
39. *Ibid.*
40. Rebecca Allen and Simon Burgess, 'Can school league tables help parents choose schools?', *Fiscal Studies* 32/2 (2011), pp. 245–61.
41. Lorraine Dearden, Stephen Machin and Anna Vignoles, 'Economics of education research: a review and future prospects', *Oxford Review of Education* 35/5 (2009), pp. 617–32.
42. Anne West, 'Poverty and educational achievement: why do children from low-income families tend to do less well at school?', *Journal of Poverty and Social Justice* 15/3 (2007), pp. 283–97.
43. Kitty Ussher, 'What is predistribution?' (London: Policy Network, 2012).
44. Gøsta Esping-Andersen, *Social Foundations of Postindustrial Economies* (Oxford: Oxford University Press, 1999).
45. Jen Lexmond and Richard Reeves, *Building Character* (London: Demos, 2009).
46. Dearden et al., 'Economics of education research'.
47. Allen and Burgess, 'Can school league tables help parents choose schools?'.
48. See Chapters 12 and 13 in this volume.
49. HM Revenue and Customs, 'Measuring Tax Gaps' (London: Gov.uk, 2013).
50. See Chapter 1 in this volume.
51. Wren, *The Political Economy of the Service Transition.*

Welfare States after the Crisis

Andrew Gamble

The 2008 financial crash and the recession which followed are widely seen as aspects of the gravest economic and financial crisis since the 1930s.[1] Swift coordinated action by governments, however, prevented the crash from turning into the kind of financial meltdown which characterised that earlier crisis. Partly as a result, the political effects of this crisis have been much more muted, and the resilience of political systems and policy regimes has been marked, even in those countries in the eurozone where the impact of austerity has been most severe. Here the contrast is not just with the 1930s, but with the 1970s. After the suspension of the Bretton Woods monetary regime in 1971, the world economy was plunged into a lengthy period of political and economic restructuring. The Keynesian order of embedded liberalism in the 1950s and 1960s became discredited. It had become, according to one influential commentator at the time, Peter Jay, 'an amalgam of unstable forces', because of the difficulty of reconciling stable prices with full employment, strong trade unions and democracy. The neoliberal order which ultimately replaced the Keynesian order has been dominant through the last three decades but has now also revealed itself as similarly flawed and unstable. But the ideological and political pressures for change appear much weaker than they were in the 1970s. There is no sign of any Polanyian double movement, and little evidence for the emergence of a clear alternative model of growth or new institutional dispensation.

The depth of the crisis is indicated by the slow, protracted recovery – the longest since 1945 – and even now almost seven years after the crash it is not yet securely established. Interest rates remain at record low levels, quantitative easing has still not been phased out, and the fear is no longer of inflation, but deflation. As in the 1970s, the Western economies are gripped by stagflation, only now the fear is of falling rather than rising prices. The sharp falls in output in 2009 (up to 10 per cent of GDP in some countries) meant that public spending increased sharply as a proportion of GDP, creating pressure for an equally sharp fiscal adjustment. Most countries, the US being the exception, adopted austerity programmes or had austerity programmes imposed upon them, which were followed through with varying degrees of severity. Welfare spending in all of them was identified as a prime target. The politics of the recession became focused on where the cuts should fall, and which groups should bear the main costs of restoring balance in the public finances.

European welfare states survived the advent of neoliberalism in the 1970s, although several of them were subject to sustained attack, and many of their features changed. The general ambition of neoliberalism was to scale back welfare states to a social minimum, a residual welfare state, where spending was targeted primarily on need, and universalism rejected. In the neoliberal era, some progress was made in this direction, although some welfare states were able to strengthen their provision. What the neoliberal era did was to accentuate the different underlying logics which lay behind different welfare states, but even the most residual welfare states were still recognisably welfare states, and most welfare states were hybrids, like the UK, with a mixture of universal and residual programmes. The functional necessity of providing some kind of welfare support in modern economies was understood, but to this was now added the analysis of political scientists like Paul Pierson who examined the record of the Thatcher and Reagan governments' attempts to cut back welfare, and how this proved much more difficult in some areas than others because of the strength of political resistance and institutional inertia. Universal welfare programmes with strong support from voters proved difficult to cut openly, and most neoliberal governments abandoned the attempt.

The question raised by the present crisis and its aftermath is whether this pattern will be repeated. The welfare states might suffer general cuts, which are then restored once economies start growing again. The longer the recovery is delayed, however, the greater the possibility that some of the cuts may prove enduring, and may lead to attempts to scale back welfare states permanently. Each national situation will be different, with particular factors and circumstances. But there will also be some common features. Two in particular are worth emphasising. The first is that while there appears to be no new growth model available, the neoliberal growth model has revealed some fairly deep flaws which have not been fixed. There are signs in several countries of a return to debt-fuelled growth, relying on pumping up credit once more through private and corporate households, but this is likely to meet constraints quite quickly. If it is allowed to proceed unchecked, it will end in another financial crash. The gloomy prospects for growth are related to the fragility of the international economy and the difficulty of finding ways to renew the international institutional architecture that can incorporate the rising powers of the East into its governance arrangements. But they are reinforced by the problems associated with technology and productivity to which a number of economic historians have recently drawn attention. There is also the alarming prospect of the need to divert increasing quantities of resources to tackling the effects of climate change, since agreement to reduce carbon emissions on anything like the scale needed is proving elusive.

A third obstacle which must be overcome for sustainable long-term growth to be restored is some answer to the problems of the tax state. There is a deepening problem of legitimacy and consent in Western states, which has many indications – the fall in support for mainstream parties, the growth of new populist, anti-system parties, the declining levels of trust in politicians and the processes of government, coupled with great ignorance about them. The restlessness and unhappiness of many voters has, at its root, a disjunction between the different elements of the tax state. The oft-cited paradox is that voters simultaneously want Swedish-style public services and US levels of personal taxation. For rich countries, there is no crisis of affordability of the welfare state since programmes could be properly funded if taxes were raised sufficiently. The problem arises because governments want to spend more than they can raise in taxes. The increasing unwillingness of voters to pay existing taxes let alone increase them, helps to create a new fiscal crisis, whose root is this disjunction between the quality of services voters want, and their willingness to pay for them through taxes. The basic social contract which underlies the welfare state, treats them as an efficient way to spread risk and protect every individual against a number of well-known contingencies which everyone faces. But there is increasing anxiety about the affordability of many welfare state programmes, particularly because of the continuing growth in entitlements and therefore in expectations, and because of demographic trends, particularly the way that populations are ageing in so many countries, potentially increasing the number of dependants and reducing proportionately the number of working age, tax-paying adults.

The fiscal deadlock is seen at its most dramatic in the USA, with fundamental decisions on the budget constantly postponed because of the difficulty of reaching compromises over the balance of taxation and spending in a highly partisan Congress. But the problem has become endemic in all Western economies. There is both an urgent need to increase taxes and broaden the fiscal base in order to fund the programmes and entitlements which citizens expect, and a strong resistance to additional taxes needed to fund them. Governments resort to taxation by stealth to increase the resources available, or they resort to borrowing, but neither provides long-term stability. The other option is to cut spending drastically, ending public provision of many services, and reducing the welfare state to a simple safety net for the very poorest. This would allow public spending as a proportion of GDP to be brought down below 25 per cent. The Cato Institute advocates adoption of the Rahm curve, which recommends that public spending should be kept within the range of 15 to 25 per cent of GDP to maximise economic growth.

Why has there been so little movement in that direction? Such proposals may still seem improbable, and unlikely to be realised, but we need to ask why that is so. Why has spending on welfare states in the neoliberal era been maintained, and will that continue in the present period of austerity, when the easy gains from neoliberal growth have disappeared? What is preventing a race to the bottom developing now that there is increasing competition from rising powers, and the displacement of labour from so many established occupations, and the ability of so many transnational companies to avoid paying tax in the countries in which they trade? The stagnation of living standards for the majority of citizens in Western economies reaches back to the beginning of this century, before the financial crash. It is not yet clear whether this will increase support for welfare states, as citizens come to value even more the security which welfare states provide, or whether it will prepare the ground for a new assault on welfare states, as citizens come to resent more the level of taxes required to fund welfare states. In the struggles around austerity, new political coalitions are forming which may sustain present levels of spending on welfare states, or even increase them.

Sustaining welfare states in this new era will not be easy. Issues that need addressing are given below.

Broadening the Tax Base

At present, the tax base is contracting. This is because of the trend to lower rates for many taxes, including income tax and corporation tax, and proposals to abolish certain types of tax altogether, such as inheritance tax. Increasing reliance is being placed on indirect taxes to generate revenue for the state. One of the main sources of tax resistance in the neoliberal era has been the increasing indebtedness of households to sustain their consumption. This has the effect of making the tax burden more visible, and makes it easier to attract voters with tax-cutting pledges. There is also the phenomenon of tax avoidance, again aided by another prominent feature of the neoliberal era, the abolition of capital controls and the multiplication of off-shore financial centres. The freer movement of capital has posed new challenges to national tax jurisdictions. Some concerted international action against tax havens and money laundering has been undertaken, but much more needs to be done if the fiscal basis of the state is to be protected. Campaigns against companies like Amazon, Google and Starbucks, which pay little or no tax, have helped raise the political salience of this issue.

Constructing Electoral Coalitions

The rapid pace of social change has removed some of the old political bases of support for welfare states, and weakened some of the solidarities which used to underpin it. But many universal benefits remain popular. The predistributive agenda, focused on market reforms and social investment in health, education, skills, and parenting, retains strong political support, which is reflected in the reluctance of politicians to challenge spending in these areas. The focus for spending cuts has been welfare benefits, including unemployment benefit and disability benefit. In general, the attack on selective benefits has targeted the working poor rather than pensioners. The intergenerational divide between young workers and pensioners has become much more marked in many countries, with the benefits of pensioners receiving greater protection. This reflects an electoral logic (pensioners are more likely to vote than young people), and is an unintended consequence of the way policies have been designed in this area. New divides have also emerged based on gender and on skills. Finding ways to resist the politicisation of these divides is essential since the scapegoating of these groups is a favoured tactic on the right seeking to frame austerity agendas. The language of strivers and shirkers, makers and takers, are new versions of the much older deserving and undeserving poor. The stigma which is attached to being on benefits is proving powerful, as stories in the media abound about benefit fraud and the corrupting effects of dependency.

The ideal tax state would be one in which there was collective insurance against risks, individual self-reliance, full employment, low inequality and high social cohesion. The Nordic model is the nearest approximation to this, although it is showing some strain. At the other end of the spectrum are those tax states in which the scope and scale of public services is being reduced, welfare recipients stigmatised, and inequality is increasing. It is easy to see how such a political economy then develops its own logic. A conflict develops between services where the quality is uneven but the provision is free, and services where the quality is high, but they are provided only to those able to pay. The exit of the more affluent citizens to purchase their own welfare through the market further weakens public provision and can become self-fulfilling, with support weakening for universal welfare programmes and the taxes needed to support them.

To counter these trends it will not be enough to reiterate the value of collective welfare programmes to everyone in society. What is required is a much more focused attempt to identify different groups which benefit from the welfare state, and to seek ways to join them with other groups in campaigns to preserve and strengthen key features of the welfare state. A priority should be finding ways to end the damaging intergenerational conflict. If the young working poor come to feel that the welfare state is no longer there for them, this could have long-term negative consequences.

Institutional Reforms

Throughout the neoliberal era, welfare states have been subjected to institutional reforms, aimed at increasing efficiency and improving quality of services. These reforms have been viewed very differently, seen on the one hand as undermining the essential ethos of non-market public services dedicated to meeting human needs, and preparing the way for privatisation, and on the other as essential improvements to increase the choices available to citizens and ensure continuing support for the principle of collectively-funded welfare programmes. Sometimes the debate has not been helped by oversimplified and reductionist accounts of neoliberalism, and the merging together of privatisation, marketisation and deregulation as a unified strategy pointing in a single direction. The different strands of the new public management need to be unpicked. The tendency for costs in labour-intensive public services to rise faster than costs elsewhere means that just to stand still, welfare states either have to raise additional revenues (for example, through taxation or charging) or they have to operate more efficiently, changing working practices and re-organising services. The imperative to improve efficiency frequently conflicts with responsiveness to the preferences of citizens as to how services should be delivered. An example of this is the strong desire of communities to retain their local hospitals, while health service managers identify major savings (and often superior care) by closing smaller units, and concentrating services and expertise in a few large centres.

Similar problems have arisen following the adoption of the principle of the purchaser/provider split, which then allows the outsourcing of services to private companies and third sector organisations. Welfare states have never been self-contained public services; they have always relied on contracts with private companies and non-state bodies for the supply of particular services. But the purchaser/provider split has taken this to new levels, fuelling anxieties that the core principle of welfare states – in particular the commitment to collective security allowing many services to be free at the point of use – is being compromised. Equally, the fear is that the more individualised services become, the more the ground is being prepared for full privatisation. That possibility does exist, and there is no doubt that the scope of welfare states has contracted in the neoliberal era as the state has ceased to provide certain services such as housing, and has begun charging much more for others, such as higher education. But strong political support still remains for the principle of free at the point of use, and this is not directly affected by the choice of supplier. The big dividing line for the future of welfare states is switching from public funding of services through collective taxation to individual funding of services through private insurance or other means. The political obstacles to effecting that switch remain high. The argument of institutional reformers is that it will stay high so long as the quality of services which are provided publicly continues to improve and broadly matches what the private sector can offer. If the private sector and the third sector can be utilised to provide that quality, then on this view that helps to maintain political support for welfare states and the taxes necessary to underpin them. But the contrary view is that the public sector is poor at negotiating with private companies, leading to the perception that welfare states become easy pickings for boosting corporate profits, and weakening public accountability and public responsibility, and the ethos of public service.

Another key area of institutional reform and innovation is balancing the different pillars of welfare states – the basic income agenda of providing income support to all citizens through transfer payments and tax credits, as well as the predistribution and social investment agenda of providing direct services to boost human capital and ensure equal opportunities. Both are redistributionist in intent, aimed at reducing and smoothing inequalities between social groups and over the life cycle. In recent times, greater attention has come to be paid to the predistribution agenda, in part because of the difficulties of maintaining political support for some forms of income support. But both will remain vital to any successful welfare state. To these can be added the third pillar of asset-based welfare, which is also predistributive in intent, seeking to equip all citizens with assets they can draw on at key stages of their career, and to counter one of the most persistent sources of inequality. Opening up new strategies to develop welfare states which take into account the changing character of societies will be important in building new coalitions of support, and weathering the impact of austerity in the aftermath of the crash.

Note

1. This chapter draws on themes and arguments developed in Andrew Gamble, *Crisis Without End? The Unravelling of Western Prosperity* (Basingstoke: Palgrave Macmillan, 2014).

Part I

Future Changes in Welfare Societies

CHAPTER 1

Public Opinion, Predistribution and Progressive Taxation

Distributional Politics and Voter Preferences after the Financial Crisis

Lucy Barnes

In the long run context of dramatically rising inequalities in income and wealth, the financial crisis and ensuing 'great recession' pose a dual challenge to egalitarian policy. Low growth and fiscal constraints provide technocratic constraints on feasible policies, as well as looming large in the ideational spaces occupied by policy-makers. But more subtly, hard economic times may provide political challenges for egalitarian policies if they undermine trust in government intervention, or promote a 'hunkering down' in policy mood.[1] This chapter examines public attitudes, focusing on two particular tools for shaping the distribution of income: the size of government and the progressivity of its tax structures. The news on the former is bad, for egalitarians. But in both public opinion and in economic reality, I argue that progressive tax structures provide a feasible policy response to inequality in hard times. Furthermore, the importance of the role of progressivity in combating inequality is not redistributive, but predistributive. That is, the confiscatory element of progressive taxation does not yield high enough revenues to effect much fiscal redistribution. But in contributing to the shape of market income inequality, progressive taxation constitutes an important predistributive policy tool.

Public opinion appears to have hardened against egalitarian policy following the financial crisis. This is certainly true with regard to the size of government spending and the overall level of taxation. However, this does not imply a retreat from redistribution with regard to the structure of taxation (and possibly spending). In general, attitudes towards progressivity are both different and more favourable than those towards large government. But can progressive taxes actually achieve meaningful egalitarian progress? There is some truth in the argument that progressive tax structures do not do much to reduce inequality. However, evidence on this score considers only the mechanical effects of taxation on the difference between market and disposable income inequality; where in fact the larger effect may be on the distribution of market income itself.

First, I present the results from some work in progress on the impact of the crisis on public attitudes to state intervention in Britain. In the context of hard times, public attitudes militate against high levels of taxation and spending, beyond any economic constraints. However, and second, there are important differences between public attitudes towards the overall size of government, and the shape it takes in terms of targeting different income groups. How does the public assess progressive tax structures? By 'progressive' we denote tax structures in which the share of income contributed to the state is an increasing fraction of income, as income increases. I present data from the UK that reflects my previous findings that progressivity is viewed more favourably than large government. Third, I show that if anything, support for progressivity has increased in the context of the great recession. These findings on progressivity paint a more optimistic picture for egalitarian policy.

But does this leave us with the dilemma of having effective tools for redistribution (high levels of taxation and spending) that receive little public support, and ineffective tools (progressive tax structures) that are popular? In the final section, I argue that this is not the case, based on the impact of progressive taxation on the distribution of incomes before government intervention. Recent economic research indicates not only that the progressivity of (income) taxation reduces income inequality, but also that this comes essentially at the expense of bargaining rents for top managers rather than productive activity. Public reactions to this kind of tax policy are less well explored, but the data that do exist seem to point in a favourable direction.

Preferences over the Size of the Government Budget in Hard Times

Support for redistributive policies declined precipitously with the financial crisis and subsequent recession after 2007. Some have argued that the financial crisis discredited Labour's economic policies, as they came to be seen as incompetent by virtue of presiding over the crisis. However, in recent research with Timothy Hicks, I have found that a large part of the turn away from redistributive policies can be accounted for by the material interests of voters as aggregate economic conditions changed.

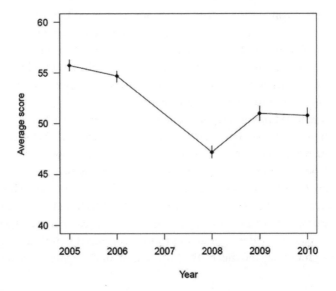

FIGURE 1.1   The effect of aggregate income changes on preferences for government intervention.
Source: British Election Study (2010); Barnes and Hicks (2014).

Figure 1.1 shows the impact of the recession in raw data from the British Election Study that asks respondents whether the government should spend more on health and social services and increase taxation, or should cut taxes and spend less on health and social services. The clear drop in the recession is partly recovered in 2009 and 2010, but attitudes towards government intervention are much more wary in hard times.

This seems to suggest a new 'Robin Hood paradox': when Robin Hood is most needed to redistribute from rich to poor, he is least likely to gain support. It seems this may be true not only in times of high inequality (as originally formulated), but also in times of high unemployment and low growth. Recessions look bad for egalitarian policy-making.

The Size versus the Shape of Government

The size of government taxes and spending are not the only policy dimension that governments might vary according to their preferences over equality. The structure of taxation – its overall progressivity in particular – and the way that publicly financed benefits are distributed will also affect levels of disposable income. This is true in the pre-crisis period, but importantly, when not only public opinion but also economic circumstance militate against high levels of spending, redistribution via the shape of government remains popular.[2] In recent work, I find that across the advanced industrial countries, the general attitude towards taxation is one of resistance to higher levels but support for higher progressivity.[3]

This general finding is replicated in the UK and illustrated in Figure 1.2. First, in the middle column we see an immediate discrepancy between views on taxes overall and taxes on the rich. Compared to the original 60 per cent, only 25 per cent of respondents think that taxes on the rich are too high. A plurality, 37 per cent, think that taxes on the rich are about right. However, this acceptance of taxes paid by the rich hides a much higher demand for relative progressivity in tax policy changes. That is, most of those who think the rich pay about the right amount in taxes think that low and middle income groups pay too much. The final column of the figure takes this into

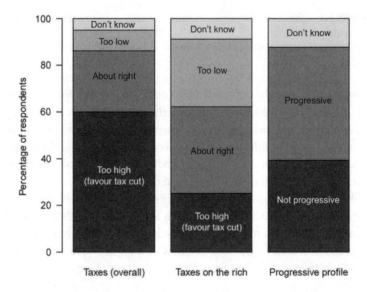

FIGURE 1.2   Attitudes towards the structure of taxation in the UK, 2006.
Note: Progressive type compares the attitude towards tax on the rich with the respondent's attitude to taxes on other income levels. Overall, 48 per cent of respondents, or 55 per cent of those with substantive responses, have response profiles indicating preferences for relatively higher taxes on those with high incomes than those with middle and low incomes.
Source: ISSP Research Group (2006).

account in creating a variable that captures whether the profile of responses that an individual makes when responding about the level of tax paid across income groups is progressive. For example, if we ask about taxes on high, middle and low incomes, and the response is that they are 'too low; about right; too high', this constitutes a progressive profile, as does 'about right, too high, too high'. In contrast, saying that taxes on all groups are too low – or more realistically, too high – is not a progressive profile.

Under these definitions, support for progressive taxation stood at a majority 55 per cent in the UK in 2006. Thus, even before the crisis drop in support for large government, changes to the structure of taxation were already a more favoured type of redistributive change.

Support for Progressivity in Hard Times

Just as we saw change in support for large government in response to the economic crisis, we might expect to see changes in attitudes towards progressivity. In fact we do, but these changes are in the opposite direction as far as taxes on the rich are considered. Further, progressive tax policies remain popular when made as concrete policy proposals with real income brackets specified, such that not all of the support for progressive policies relies on misconceptions about what counts as 'high income'.

Figure 1.3 replicates the results for attitudes on taxing the rich from the 2006 ISSP, and compares them to a similar question asked by YouGov in 2012. The questions are not identical, as the ISSP asks about taxes on 'those with high incomes', while the YouGov poll asks about 'the richest people in Britain'. Thus, the implicitly higher incomes of 'the richest' rather than merely 'high' incomes may explain some of the discrepancy. Nevertheless, it is certainly not the case that support for progressive taxes on the rich declined with the crisis in the same way as support for tax and spending levels.

Progressive tax policies also remain popular in more concrete terms, rather than the abstract notion of 'taxes on the rich'. Over the past four years, the introduction, elimination and re-proposal of the 50p rate for the highest income tax bracket has kept a concrete, progressive reform on the political agenda. In April 2009, Chancellor of the Exchequer Alistair Darling announced an increase in the top rate of tax to be paid by very high income earners: above a £150,000 threshold, income would be taxed at a rate of 50 per cent. This additional rate compares to the previous top rate of 40 per cent, which in 2010 (when the 50p rate was introduced) applied to

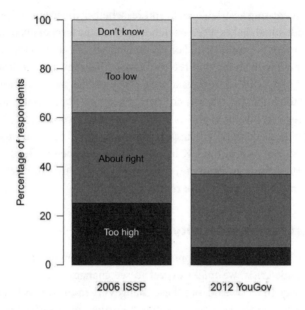

FIGURE 1.3   Attitudes towards the level of taxes paid by those with high incomes before and after the financial crisis.
Note: The share of respondents thinking that the rich pay too little in tax increased to 55 per cent in 2012.
Source: YouGov (2012), ISSP Research Group (2006).

incomes above £37,400. After the election of the coalition, the 2012 budget announced the reduction of the additional rate to 45p. The 50p top rate made headlines, if not a reality, again in January 2014 when the shadow Chancellor promised that a Labour government would restore the higher top rate.

As well as ensuring that the question of progressivity remained in the public eye – and in pollsters' surveys – this history provides some useful background variation against which to gauge support for progressive taxation. First, over the full period it is symmetrical in including both tax increases (the 2009 change and 2014 proposal) and a tax cut (in 2012). There are two reasons why this might be important. First, having policy proposals on both the introduction and elimination of the 50p rate means that we should be able to identify if blanket support for generic 'tax cuts' or increases drives opinion. In this case, we would see lower support for the progressive rate in response to George Osborne's 2012 budget. Alternatively, the policy status quo may have an impact on preferences. The 2009 introduction of a new tax rate might be expected to provoke more resistance on the grounds of novelty.[4] This would drive our expectations in the opposite direction: once the tax is in place it would be more popular. However, the lifetime of the 50p tax may have been too short to generate any real path dependence of this sort.

Second, asking about a concrete tax change also mitigates concerns that everyone is in favour of taxes on 'the rich', as long as that group is defined as those with higher incomes than themselves. By explicitly stating the cut-off at £150,000, the concrete policy question avoids this ambiguity. It is worth noting that this threshold is very high in the context of UK income distribution: for an individual without children, this amount of income is well within the top 1 per cent of the distribution in 2013. As such, most people will not be personally affected by the additional rate. The constant bracket in a period of moderate inflation (an average of just over 3 per cent in the five years from 2009 to 2014) means that the number affected may have increased somewhat since the initial introduction of the top rate, but it is still a tiny share of the population who are counted as 'rich'.

Figure 1.4 shows support for the 50p rate in four polls taken over the five years between April 2009 and January 2014 (the precise question wording in each case is given in the Appendix), and coincides with the events in the history of the 50p rate outlined above. The drawback of these questions is that none of them precede the financial crisis, thus they give us no indication as to whether hard times increase support for progressive taxes; but what they do show is consistently strong support for the 50p top rate over the crisis period.

Although the sample sizes in each poll are not so large as to give extremely precise estimates of the proportion supporting progressive taxation, in every poll the 50p top rate easily receives majority support – from around 55 to 60 per cent of respondents. The estimates are not precise enough to rule out that this support is entirely constant across the period; but to the extent that the minor variation estimated is systematic, it is at least consistent with expectations in the sense that support for the 50p rate is lowest when the proposal is to reduce the top rate to 45 per cent in 2012. That is, a bias in favour of tax cuts could explain the dip in support to the extent that it is not a matter of sampling variability.

Thus, it is not only in the abstract that progressive tax policies receive popular support. Even (or perhaps especially) in economic hard times, disproportionate taxes on the rich garner broad approval from voters. The contrast with general resistance to high rates of taxation and high levels of

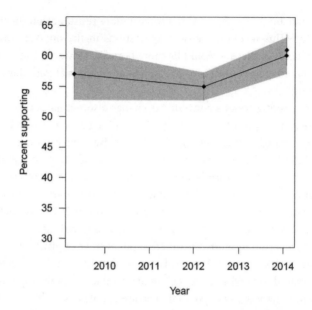

FIGURE 1.4   Support for the the 50p tax rate on incomes above £150,000.
Note: The grey shaded area represents uncertainty around the estimates, denoting 95 per cent confidence intervals for the estimated proportions. Since 2009, support for the policy has remained high and effectively unchanged, with a majority of voters in favour. Note that this is true despite the different status of the tax in relation to the status quo during this period.
Source: YouGov (2014), Survation (2014), Populus (2009), YouGov (2012).

government activity overall is pronounced. It is also important if both the size and the structure of the government budget can be used as tools to achieve distributional goals. Whether progressive tax policy can play such a role is the subject of the next section.

Progressive Taxes as Egalitarian Policy

Public support for progressive taxation is all very well, but the scholarly consensus is that progressive structures generally do not do that much to reduce inequality.[5] The amount of redistribution that governments do depends more on the overall size of government – raising lots of tax revenue – than the details of the tax structure. There are two related reasons for this: first, existing tax structures overall are simply not very progressive. Although marginal rates within the income tax are progressive, the distribution of the tax bases across income groups undermines this effect. Second, even proportional taxes can do a lot of redistribution as long as the goods they fund are distributed more equally than the initial distribution of income. In the case of many (most) government services, even with a slightly regressive structure in their uptake the distributive 'gap' between outlays and (proportional) taxation is much larger than the gap between slightly progressive and proportional systems.

Progressive Taxes as Predistributive Policy

However, redistribution in the instantaneous distribution of income – the measured difference between market and disposable incomes – is not the only way in which progressive tax policies affect inequality. In fact, there are a number of good reasons to think that highly progressive income taxation will reduce inequality in market incomes themselves. Since higher tax rates tend to reduce the size of the base they are levied on, more strongly increasing rates should reduce the difference between higher and lower incomes. This argument might be used on both sides of debates about progressivity. Lower market income inequality as the result of more progressive taxation points to behavioural responses to the tax code which might undermine economic growth (to the extent that they suppress valuable productive activity). Even if falling incomes at the top only undermine rent-shifting activities,[6] they will nevertheless reduce government revenues to the extent that they are successful in diminishing top incomes.

I follow Piketty, Saez, and Stantcheva[7] in outlining three behavioural mechanisms underlying an expectation that high marginal tax rates should reduce market income inequality. The first mechanism – and one which is commonly used as an argument against strongly progressive taxation – is that high taxes disincentivise effort. Since expending effort on productive activities (which generate income) is costly, reducing the returns to that effort by taxing them more strongly will cause individuals to substitute out of productive activities, and into leisure, at the margin.[8]

The second possibility, which also tends to weigh against high marginal rates, is that more onerous taxation may lead to more active tax avoidance. The underlying economic activity may be exactly the same, but by taking remuneration in fringe benefits, by pursuing business forms that are advantageous only for tax purposes, and so on, reported income may decline with high rates. This mechanism points primarily to the futility of high tax rates – any observed reduction in inequality is a statistical artefact rather than a true effect. It also points to some 'real' effects to the extent that energies are wasted avoiding taxation which could be more fruitfully targetted elsewhere.

Finally, high top marginal tax rates may reduce the incentives to economically inefficient abuses of managerial power in the form of rent-seeking. To the degree that managerial compensation is the outcome of wasteful bargaining efforts rather than objective performance, then high taxes on the returns of this activity have a positive, corrective effect.

Beyond a focus on purely individual incentives, progressive taxation may affect the market income distribution of incomes indirectly via its influence on norms of equality and fair pay. Progressive taxation may play a role in maintaining attitudes towards the link between merit and value, and financial reward. That is, by reducing the financial returns to success, progressive taxation may help prevent success from being measured in solely financial terms. If the rewards of success come in other forms (perhaps such as social esteem) the incentives to earn large incomes as a signal of success may be reduced, and thus inequality at the top limited.[9]

The first empirical question, then, is whether higher marginal tax rates do in fact lead to lower levels of inequality. Figure 1.5 shows the association between the income share of the top 1 per cent of taxpayers and the marginal tax rates paid by those with incomes equal to five times GDP per capita, an income level approximately equal to the 99th income percentile. This is a better measure than just a top marginal rate as it keeps constant the number of people who will be affected by the rate in question. Panel (b) shows the

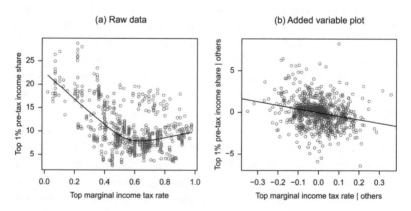

FIGURE 1.5 The relationship between progressive taxation and market income inequality.
Source: Calculations based on Roine, Vlachos, and Waldenström (2009).

relationship between the two variables once the independent effects of country, year, GDP, population and their interaction have been averaged out via regression analysis.

The results are clear: higher marginal tax rates do seem to be associated with lower levels of inequality (as measured by the top 1 per cent share). Although these effects cannot strictly be thought of as causal, most confounding factors will be accounted for via the country and year fixed effects. They also replicate the findings of Roine, Vlachos, and Waldenström, who consider a broader range of potential confounders and also use some alternative strategies to make a causal interpretation more credible.[10]

The impact of progressive taxation on inequality may operate less through the mechanical impact of the tax structure on fiscal redistribution, and more through its predistributive effects. Just as other contributions to this volume emphasise the importance of government policy in raising incomes at the lower end of the distribution,[11] progressive taxation may be one of the few tools available to governments seeking to rein in inequality at the top. This is not achieved by confiscation per se, but by changing the incentives to accumulate huge market incomes.

In this context we may be concerned by the potential impact of high top tax rates on economic growth. If the effect of highly progressive taxation on incentives to earn high incomes operates through the first channel identified by Piketty, Saez, and Stantcheva[12] progressivity may have an adverse effect on growth. This relationship, in figures analogous to those above for inequality, are shown in Figure 1.6. Here, there is no evidence in

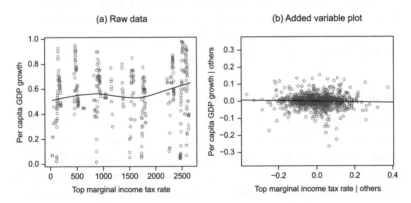

FIGURE 1.6 The non-relationship between progressive taxation and economic growth.
Source: Calculations based on Roine et al. (2009).

the data that high tax rates undermine economic performance. This is also consistent with recent work by IMF economists who found no evidence that redistribution is harmful to growth, unlike inequality itself.[13]

How are these ideas reflected in public opinion? Unfortunately, to my knowledge there are no sources of data that ask respondents explicitly about whether they would be prepared to trade off growth to see income more equally distributed.

Alternatively, the idea that highly progressive tax rates may not maximise tax revenues is one on which the British public are surprisingly sanguine. In the same YouGov poll analysed above, when faced with the question:

> Imagine it was the case that a top tax rate of 50p did not bring in any extra money. Which of the following would best represent your view?

Forty per cent of respondents thought that 'A 50p top tax rate should be introduced regardless of what it brings in – it is morally right that the rich should pay higher taxes', as against only four percentage points more (44 per cent) who thought that such a tax should not be levied.

Progressivity, Revenues and the Predistribution Agenda

The two preceding sections suggest that progressive taxation should be seen as a policy with which to regulate the supply side rather than a motor for revenue generation. In this sense, taxation should be at the centre of predistributive as well as redistributive government policy.

However, taxation is the way in which countries raise revenues to pay for traditional redistribution as well as any spending on new social risks, or investments in education and skills. Thus taxation must play a dual role in the broader predistributive agenda.

Conclusion

Progressive taxation thus fits the broader redistributive agenda in acting as a regulatory, as well as a revenue-raising tool. The ways in which private actors respond to the changed incentives and social norms that more progressive tax structures generate may have a more significant impact on inequality than their pure redistributive impact. These taxes tend not to raise large amounts of revenue, in part because they apply only at very high levels of income. To the extent that these changed incentives have limited detrimental effects on growth, they should be considered positively.

Moreover, the political popularity of progressive taxation cannot be gainsaid. In this chapter, I have focused on the UK, but as Figure 1.2 in this chapter shows, general support for tax progressivity is replicated across the developed world. In this regard, progressive taxation may have a key place in the broader redistributive agenda. While education spending is generally popular as a priority within government spending categories (in 2013, 30 per cent of people advocated prioritising education),[14] the first section of this chapter showed that popular support for government spending in general may be closely constrained. Moreover, the specific predistributive policies most strongly advocated in this volume may be those which struggle to gain popular support: when choosing between recipients of social transfers, only 22 per cent of respondents favour increases for single parents and children combined – compared to 48 per cent support for prioritising pensions. Within the education sector, the news is yet worse: only 3.7 per cent of respondents favour spending on students' further education – the locus for vocational policies of the type advocated as a key driver of predistribution. Early years intervention fares somewhat better, but there is little evidence of any groundswell of support for this kind of predistributive programme of the sort enjoyed by progressive taxation.

The empirical evidence presented here supports the notion that tax policy in general – and progressive taxation in particular – is a tool that not only has strong popular support but can also have an important effect on the distribution of incomes. Considering three arguments against this position with reference to the empirical record and the state-of-the-art research, I can reject the arguments (a) that progressive policy is unpopular; (b) that progressive taxation does little to help inequality; and (c) that to the extent that it helps combat inequality, progressive taxation also undermines growth. Tax policy could thus play an important role in a predistributive agenda oriented towards greater equality.

Appendix: A.1 Survey Question Texts

TABLE 1A.1   Survey question texts and responses coded as support for progressive taxation for Figure 1.4 on the 50p top tax rate.[15]

Date	Firm	N	Question	Responses coded as support for 50p rate
Apr-09	Populus	518	I am going to read out some measures that were announced by the Chancellor of the Exchequer in this afternoon's budget statement. Please say in each case if you think it is a positive measure or a negative measure, or if you think that it won't have much effect either way, please say so. An increase from next year in the top rate of tax from 45% to 50% for those earning over £150,000.	Very positive, fairly positive (versus no real effect, fairly negative, very negative).
Mar-12	YouGov	1835	Do you support or oppose the following policies announced by the Chancellor: Cutting the top rate of income tax for people earning over £150,000 from 50p to 45p?	Oppose (versus support).
Jan-14	YouGov	1381	Currently the top rate of income tax is 45p in the pound for earnings over £150,000. Would you support or oppose increasing the top rate of income tax on earnings over £150,000 to 50p in the pound?	Support (versus oppose).
Jan-14	Survation	1045	Shadow Chancellor Ed Balls annnounced today that if Labour wins power it will raise the top rate of income tax from the current 45p in the pound to 50p in the pound for those with earnings over £150,000. To what extent do you agree or disagree with this policy?	Agree strongly; agree somewhat (versus neither agree nor disagree; disagree somewhat; disagree strongly).

Notes

1. James Alt, Ian Preston, and Luke Sibieta, 'The political economy of tax policy', in *Dimensions of Tax Design: The Mirrlees Review* (Oxford: Oxford University Press, 2010), pp. 1204–79; James Alt, *Politics of Economic Decline: Economic Management and Political Behaviour in Britain since 1964* (Cambridge: Cambridge University Press, 1979).

2. I focus primarily on the tax side of the budget, but it is worth noting that the so-called 'paradox of redistribution' on the spending side – where more targeted programs undermine redistribution due to their lack of popular support – appears to have been historically limited to the pre-1990 era. See Lane Kenworthy, *Progress for the Poor* (Oxford: Oxford University Press, 2011) and Ive Marx, Lina Salanauskaite and Gerlinde Verbist, 'The paradox of redistribution revisited: and that it may rest in peace?', IZA Discussion Paper Series, 7414 (May 2013). Available at http://ftp.iza.org/dp7414.pdf (accessed 21 March 2015).

3. Lucy Barnes, 'The size and shape of government: Preferences over redistributive taxation', *Socio-economic Review* 10 (2014).

4. Martin Daunton, *Trusting Leviathan: The Politics of Taxation in Britain, 1799–1914* (New York: Cambridge University Press, 2001), p. 15; Richard Rose and Terence Karran, *Taxation by Political Inertia: Financing the Growth of Government in Britain* (London: Allen and Unwin, 1987).

5. Monica Prasad and Yingying Deng, 'Taxation and worlds of welfare', *Socio-economic Review* 7 (2009); Thomas R. Cusack and Pablo Beramendi, 'Taxing work', *European Journal of Political Research* 45 (2006); Steffen Ganghof, 'Tax mixes and the size of the welfare state: Causal mechanisms and policy implications', *Journal of European Social Policy* 15 (2006).

6. Facundo Alvaredo, Antony B. Atkinson, Thomas Piketty, and Emmanuel Saez, 'The top 1 percent in international and historical perspective', *Journal of Economic Perspectives* 27/3 (2013), pp. 3–20.

7. Thomas Piketty, Emmanuel Saez, and Stefanie Stantcheva, 'Optimal taxation of top labor incomes: A tale of three elasticities', *American Economic Journal: Economic Policy* 6/1 (2014), pp. 230–71.

8. There is also likely to be an income effect whereby higher taxes would induce greater effort, but we ignore this for now.

9. Carola Frydman and Raven Molloy, 'Pay Cuts for the Boss: Executive Compensation in the 1940s', NBER Working Papers 17303 (2011). Available at http://www.nber.org/papers/w17303 (accessed 21 March 2015); Frank S. Levy and Peter Temin, 'Inequality and institutions in 20th century America', MIT Department of Economics Working Paper 07-17 (2007). Available at http://www.nber.org/papers/w13106.pdf (accessed 21 March 2015).

10. Jesper Roine, Jonas Vlachos, and Daniel Waldenström, 'The long-run determinants of inequality: What can we learn from top income data?' *Journal of Public Economics* 93/7–8 (2009), pp. 974–88.

11. Marius Busemeyer; Rémi Bazillier, both this volume.
12. Piketty, Saez, and Stantcheva, 'Optimal taxation of top labor incomes'.
13. Jonathan D. Ostry, Andrew Berg, and Charalambos G. Tsangarides, 'Redistribution, Inequality, and Growth', IMF Staff Discussion Note, SDB/14/02 (Feb 2014). Available at http://www.imf.org/external/pubs/ft/sdn/2014/sdn1402.pdf (accessed 21 March 2015).
14. British Social Attitudes, Series EDSPEND1C, SPEND1, SOCBEN1 (2013). Available at http://www.britsocat.com (accessed 25 October 2014).
15. Populus, Post-Budget poll – April 2009. Available at http://populus.co.uk/Poll/PostBudget-Poll-April-2009/; YouGov. Yougov/*The Sun* Survey 21–22 March 2012. Available at http://cdn.yougov.com/cumulusuploads/document/yp5s1ymci9/YG-Archives-Pol-Sun-results-220312.pdf; YouGov. YouGov/*Times* Survey, 24–27 January 2014. Available at http://d25d2506sfb94s.cloudfront.net/cumulusuploads/document/c1rz7jiy8q/YG-Archive-140127-50p-Tax.pdf; Survation, Survation economic policy poll for the *Mail on Sunday*, 25 January 2014. Available at http://survation.com/wp-content/uploads/2014/04/Economic-Policy-Poll-Tables.pdf. (accessed 24 March 2015).

CHAPTER 2

Progressive Social Policies for Intergenerational Justice in Ageing Societies
Demography is not Destiny

Pieter Vanhuysse

Population ageing across the advanced welfare states has led not only to a renewed popular awareness of the notion of justice between the generations but also to renewed academic interest.[1] However, efforts to measure intergenerational justice empirically have largely lagged behind. How can we improve policies when we do not know the state of affairs in terms of intergenerational justice in practice? At the request of the Bertelsmann Stiftung in Germany, I have therefore developed a simple four-dimensional snapshot indicator to improve the cognitive toolkit of academics, journalists and policy-makers. This chapter reports on this Intergenerational Justice Index (*IJI*).[2] I shall conclude by arguing that combating presentism (i.e. a focus on the short-term) in social policies is needed to safeguard the future of ageing welfare states in a globalised world economy.[3] Predistributive social policies, especially in the form of early human capital investment to empower young and future generations, ought to play a key role in this endeavour.

Sustainability is the moral intuition behind this approach. The UN Brundlandt Commission famously made the case for why this notion is intimately linked to intergenerational relations: societies need to 'meet the needs of the present without compromising the ability of future generations to meet their own needs'.[4] In terms of the available opportunities for social security, education, the environment, and other valued rights, capabilities and resources, this means that 'enough and as good' ought to be left by each generation to the next.[5] Contrary to some recent political theories,[6] I argue that it is typically not a priori morally problematic when at one given point in time different *age groups* receive an unequal treatment from the state. But when it appears that, even after taking into account socio-economic controls and reasonable income growth over time, such inequalities are perpetuated across different *birth cohorts* over the entire life cycle, then we end up with lucky and unlucky generations – or insider and outsider cohorts – within the same country, implying intergenerational inequities.[7]

Furthermore, a society – or cohorts within it – need not be morally blamed for lower fertility and still less so for longer life expectancy. Clearly, living longer lives (of quality) is an undeniable yardstick of social progress. Moderately low levels of fertility may actually imply improvements in living standards.[8] In fact, they may even be desirable as long as human capital levels increase,[9] as well as from an environmental point of view. But crucially, the way in which a society's public policy models react to these demographic changes is *not* neutral from an intergenerational justice perspective.

Four Dimensions of Empirical Intergenerational Justice

My aim with the *IJI* is pragmatic and empirical: to compare intergenerational justice across rich, ageing welfare states. The analysis is synchronic not diachronic. The unit of analysis is countries, and the *IJI* reflects a macro-level notion of justice as linked primarily to government activity rather than private behaviour. The snapshot was taken based on the years for which the most complete recent data was available for 29 OECD countries: the end of the 2000s or the start of the current decade, depending on the dimension. Three of the *IJI* dimensions, two of which are strongly policy-determined, measure outcomes that leave legacy burdens towards younger and future generations: the ecological footprint created by all generations alive today; early-life starting conditions as measured by child poverty levels; and the fiscal burdens on the shoulders of currently young generations, as measured by public debt levels per child. The fourth *IJI* dimension measures policy effort in the form of a new synchronic indicator of the overall pro-elderly bias in social spending (henceforth *EBiSS*).[10]

First, the intuitive appeal of the ecological footprint is that it captures in a single figure (measured in global hectares per capita of the population) the general pressure put by human societies on their natural environment. Within Europe, Denmark and Belgium produced the biggest environmental pressure in the late 2000s, followed by countries such as the Netherlands, Finland, Ireland, and Sweden. On the environmentally friendly side of the spectrum, European societies such as Hungary, Poland, and Portugal all produced relatively small ecological footprints, as did the UK. But once one compares the ecological pressure put on the environments with the environment's capacity to absorb that pressure, only Finland and to a lesser extent Baltic and Nordic countries such as Sweden, Estonia and Norway (all of which have vast sea and forest surfaces) turn out to be net environmental creditor countries in Europe, in the sense that they impose less pressure than they can absorb. By far the largest environmental debtor countries in Europe were Belgium and the Netherlands, followed by other high-density countries such as Italy, Spain, Greece, Denmark and the UK.

Child poverty, the second dimension, is important for intergenerational justice as it can create dynamic knock-on effects reaching far into poor children's subsequent lives and which start from birth onward – indeed, even before birth. These range from lower levels of school readiness and early educational outcomes, to lower cognitive and behavioural skills and lower high school completion rates, and later still to lower wages and home ownership rates and higher rates of adult unemployment, welfare dependency and poverty, and so on. Using a relative measure of child poverty, southern countries such as Portugal, Spain, Italy, and Greece, as well as Poland and the UK, performed worst within Europe. Nordic countries as well as Austria and Slovenia, occupied the bottom five (best) ranks.[11] To be sure, we must not forget that many elderly Europeans live in poverty – especially in the new EU member states. But in most European countries, elderly poverty rates are lower than child poverty rates.[12]

Third, to measure the public debt burden weighing on the shoulders of the currently young, I calculated the total general government debt for each country in 2011 per person aged 0–14. The variance in debt per child within the EU was large. Italy and Greece occupied the highest ranks, followed by Belgium, Germany, Norway, Austria, and Ireland. At the other end of the spectrum, poorer central and eastern European countries such as Estonia, the Visegrad-4 and Slovenia currently saddle their youngest generation with comparatively low levels of government debt.

The fourth dimension of *IJI* measures welfare states' overall pro-*EBiSS*.[13] On the *elderly*-oriented spending side, the *EBiSS* numerator includes old-age-related benefits in cash and in kind, survivors benefits in cash and in kind, disability pensions, occupational injury and disease-related pensions, and early retirement for labour market reasons. On the *non-elderly*-spending side, the *EBiSS* denominator includes family benefits in cash and in kind, active labour market programmes, income maintenance cash benefits, unemployment compensation and severance pay cash benefits, and all education spending. To control for demographic structure, the resulting elderly/non-elderly social spending ratio has been adjusted by means of each country's old-age support ratio (the number of persons aged 20–64 over the number of persons aged 65 or more). Since public health spending, a major elderly-oriented spending item everywhere, has not been incorporated into these *EBiSS* calculations, the *EBiSS* as defined here almost certainly *underestimates* the pro-elderly bias of welfare state spending.[14]

Pro-elderly Social Policy Bias: Demography is not Destiny

As Figure 2.1 shows, the least pro-elderly biased welfare states around the start of the global economic crisis were South Korea, Ireland, and New Zealand. Europe is more strongly represented at the other end of the spectrum. EU member states occupy eight of the nine highest *EBiSS* positions. Poland was the most pro-elderly-biased welfare state in the sample. The Polish welfare state spent 8.6 times as much on each elderly Pole as it spent on each non-elderly Pole in the late 2000s. Following at some distance, Greece and Italy (*EBiSS* values around 7 or more), Slovakia, Japan, the Czech Republic, and Portugal (between 6 and 7), and Slovenia and Austria (above 5.5) all have

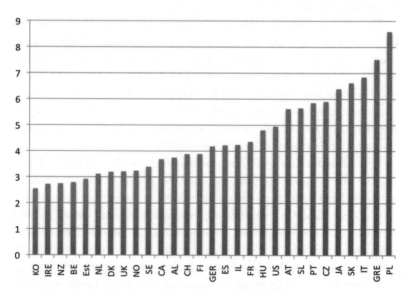

FIGURE 2.1   Elderly Bias Indicator of Social Spending (*EBiSS*).
Source: Vanhuysse (2013: 27).

very high *EBiSS* values as well. The UK, by contrast, has a relatively low *EBISS* value, at just above 3.

The equity question here too is essentially a matter of sustainability.[15] In theory, one could argue that any particular value of the *EBiSS*, which is a snapshot of how different *age groups* are treated at one point in time (today), is morally unproblematic. Unproblematic, that is, as long as the same value applies to successive *cohorts* over time (unless of course successive younger cohorts explicitly agree to reduce their expected lifecycle benefit/cost ratio compared to older cohorts). But the burden of proof then falls on those making such a seemingly Panglossian argument for the case of, say, Poland, Greece, or Italy in Figure 2.1. They must then demonstrate that the high Polish, Greek, or Italian *EBiSS* values really reflect democratically desired 'Spartan childhood for luxury old age' tradeoffs, *and* that such values are sustainable over time.

As it happens, mounting evidence indicates that younger age groups today increasingly doubt the intergenerational equity of current policy patterns – with good reason.[16] Moreover, National Transfer Accounts indicate that in all European countries studied (but in few other countries), public transfers already tend to flow from non-elderly to elderly groups today.[17] Non-snapshot age-period-cohort analyses similarly show that in continental-conservative Europe (first and foremost in France) and in all of southern Europe, disposable income after taxes and transfers of some unlucky generations (typically those born before World War II and after 1955) are significantly lower than those of the lucky cohorts born between 1945 and 1950.[18]

Of course, *EBiSS* figures refer purely to public spending efforts. Working-age groups spend very significant time and resources caring for both older and, much less visibly, younger generations within family settings.[19] And net private financial transfers everywhere in Europe still flow from older to younger age groups. But, of course, there is an obvious regressive element about such private transfers, especially in today's world of ever-increasing wealth inequalities and reduced income mobility.[20] What is more, in a number of countries, these private transfer flows are no longer large enough to offset the public transfer flows in the other direction. For instance, in Germany, Austria, and Slovenia the net direction of *total* transfers is now from non-elderly to elderly groups. As Ronald Lee points out, this amounts to 'a sea change in human history'.[21]

Demography is not destiny as regards the pro-elderly bias of European welfare states. Instead, it is policy choices as determined by longstanding governance cultures that drive *EBiSS* patterns.[22] Figure 2.1 shows that of the

OECD's four demographically oldest societies, Italy and Japan had a high level of pro-elderly social spending bias at the end of the 2000s, whereas Germany showed only a moderate and Sweden relatively low pro-elderly bias. Conversely, the Irish, Belgian, and Estonian welfare states all spent roughly 2.5 to three times as much per elderly citizen as per non-elderly citizen, even though Ireland was a demographically young society (old-age support ratio 5.6) whereas Belgium and Estonia are much older societies (3.5 and 3.6).

The spurious connection between demographic structure and pro-elderly policy bias can also be illustrated differently. In the demographically old Greece, the state spent seven times more for every elderly Greek as it spent for every non-elderly Greek. But in comparably old Sweden, the state spent only 3.4 times more. In the absence of evidence indicating that they truly reflect legitimate 'Spartan childhoods for luxury old age' tradeoffs agreed to by successive cohorts in Greece but not Sweden, the higher Greek *EBiSS* values appear unsustainable, hence intergenerationally inequitable. This impression is further strengthened by analysis of the distributional impact of the radical social policy reforms and cutbacks implemented in Greece after the severe post-2009 recession. Poverty rates have gone up more among young and working-age than among 65+ age groups after 2009. And while older age groups have shouldered some of the post-2009 austerity through the abolition of 13th and 14th pension months and the introduction of pensioners' solidarity taxes, social reforms have also favoured powerful lobby groups that defend privileged social benefits (not least pensions) for unionised workers in nationalised industries and for professions such as judges, engineers and medics, as against younger age groups and recession losers such as the unemployed (especially youth) and young families.[23]

Together with three 'usual southern suspects' (Greece, Italy, and Portugal), Slovakia, the Czech Republic, Hungary, Slovenia and (especially) Poland have the most pro-elderly biased welfare states according to the *EBiSS* measure.[24] Six of these eight countries (Poland and the Czech Republic excepted) have also registered among the highest levels of young people not in employment, education or training (NEETs) in Europe in the past decade.[25] This is likely to lead to lifelong scarring effects for hundreds of thousands of young southern and eastern Europeans. The evidence on high *EBiSS* levels in central Europe is also congruent with a different measure specifically on children – UNICEF's five-domain, 26-dimensional indicator of child well-being for 29 countries. Slovakia, Hungary, and Poland also occupy bottom-third ranks on this measure, with the Czech Republic and Slovenia occupying 14th and 12th rank.[26]

Pairwise comparisons are illuminating on the *EBiSS*. The welfare state in 'middle-aged' Hungary (old-age support ratio of 3.9) spent 4.8 times more on every elderly as on every non-elderly citizen in the late 2000s. But in slightly older Estonia (with a lower old-age support ratio of 3.6), the welfare state spent only 2.9 times more. The 'young-to-middle-aged Czech Republic (old-age support ratio 4.5) spent 5.9 times more on every elderly as on every non-elderly citizen, but equally young-to-middle-aged Australia spent just 3.7 times more. In the same vein, the welfare state in 'young' Slovakia (old-age support ratio 5.5) spent 6.6 times more on every elderly citizen, but in the equally young Ireland it spent only 2.7 times more. And as we have seen, Poland still occupied prime position on the *EBiSS* in the late 2000s – a decade after the implementation of a significant systemic pension reform in 1999. In this 'young-to-middle-aged' society (old-age support ratio 4.8), the state spent 8.6 times as much on every elderly Pole as on every non-elderly Pole in the late 2000s. Yet in the equally young New Zealand, the state spent only 2.7 times as much.

Here too, in the absence of evidence of democratically expressed rolling contract agreements between successive cohorts to trade off low state spending early in life for generous spending later on, these higher central European *EBiSS* values strongly indicate, but do not conclusively demonstrate, unsustainable policy patterns. They can be explained largely as a result of legacies of early post-communist transition, such as the need to compensate pensioners for the loss of their savings through (hyper-) inflation in the early 1990s, 'familialising' state approaches towards mothers and children, and policy-induced, historically unprecedented exit into early and disability pensions.[27] For instance, in the first seven years of democracy alone, literally hundreds of thousands of working-age Hungarians and Poles, but not Czechs, were incentivised to exit into early and disability pensions by means of more generous and better protected pension benefits relative to 'younger' programs such as unemployment and family benefits.[28]

These policies led to an immediate reversal of poverty trends for pensioners (downward) relative to other age groups (upward) after 1989, and to great abnormal pensioner booms. Whereas the number of 60-plussers remained stable in Hungary and grew by 10 per cent in Poland between 1989 and 1996, the number of old-age pensioners increased by respectively one-fifth and 46 per cent. In the same period of just seven years, the number of disability pensioners also increased by one-half in Hungary and by one-fifth in Poland.[29] At least in Poland, sustained high levels of economic growth and a dynamic economy over the past decade, including in the post-2008 crisis years, have served to alleviate immediate fiscal and sustainability worries. So has a more recent refocusing on education investment and significant improvements in both the share of NEETs and in the Programme for International Student Assessment (PISA) results.[30] By contrast, in Hungary, pension spending remained subject to electoral business cycles throughout the late 1990s and early 2000s. In 2011, the two-thirds majority FIDESZ government even renationalised a previously privatised pensions pillar worth around 10 per cent of GDP.[31]

Health technologies and healthy lifestyles also appear to lag behind in central European countries. One way to show this is by remeasuring old-age dependency ratios by aggregating people's remaining or *prospective* life expectancies (that is, how many birthdays they will still celebrate) rather than their chronological ages, as is usually done (how many birthdays they have already celebrated). In terms of physical fitness, for instance, a chronological age of 70 today does not mean the same thing as it did three or four decades ago. It turns out that using these alternative (prospective) old-age dependency rates actually produces far less dramatic trends in current and projected levels of population ageing for most EU countries. But there is one notable exception to this observation: the central European democracies. These latter countries show fast-worsening trends also in prospective old-age dependency for the near future.[32]

The lack of preparedness of central Europe is also evident in the European Centre Vienna's four-domain, 22-dimensional Active Aging Index (AAI) for Europe. Slovakia, Hungary, and Poland occupy the bottom three positions in the 27-country sample on the overall AAI, whereas the Czech Republic ranks in 11th and Slovenia in 21st position. In addition, these same three Visegrad countries occupy three of the bottom five positions on the AAI's four-dimensional 'elderly workers' employment' domain index, with the Czech Republic in 14th and Slovenia in 19th position. And they also occupy three of the bottom five positions on the AAI's six-dimensional 'capacity and enabling environment for active ageing' domain, with the Czech Republic and Slovenia again ranking 14th and 19th.[33] In sum, adverse labour market, lifestyle, and health policy cultures from the past decades, combined with fast population ageing in the next two decades, add up to a bleak 'generational politics' picture for central Europe, not just southern Europe.

The Intergenerational Justice Index: Implications for Predistributive Social Politics

The four *IJI* dimensions discussed above were then normalised and aggregated into an overall *IJI* value ranging from 0 (least equitable) to 1 (most equitable), using a 'benefit-of-the-doubt' weighting method to respect the (revealed) preferences of democratically elected governments. As Figure 2.2 shows, among the most intergenerationally just countries by this four-dimensional measure were Estonia and all of Nordic Europe (in addition to South Korea and New Zealand). By contrast, among the least intergenerationally just countries were Italy, Greece, and the Czech Republic (but even more so, the USA and Japan). The UK, in 11th position, had a benefit-of-doubt *IJI* value of about 0.8. Clearly, these snapshot findings are only indicative, and they are best viewed as focusing a laser beam in order to highlight best-case and worst-case examples, thereby inviting more thorough case study analysis. More research needs to be done, ideally involving lifecycle data and cohort approaches to enrich the snapshot analysis presented here.[34] But it seems plausible to state that unless low-*IJI* countries such as the USA, Japan, Italy, and Greece can somehow guarantee

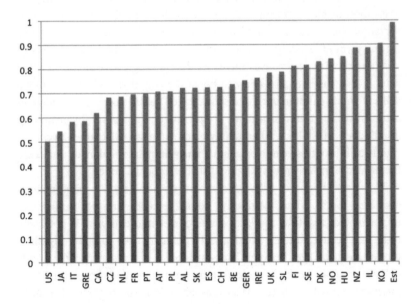

FIGURE 2.2 Intergenerational Justice Index with benefit-of-the-doubt weighting. *Source*: Vanhuysse (2013: 37).

fast economic and productivity growth and rapid technological innovation (including in environmental technology) in the near future, not reforming current policy patterns would most likely mean that a high degree of injustice continues to be inflicted upon currently young and future citizens.

On the policy supply side, seemingly 'obvious' measures that merit a new look in light of this perspective include fiscal and social security benefits or credits to reward family members for raising younger and caring for elderly generations (often expending substantial private cost for societal benefit), the adjustment of official pension ages and pension benefits to rising life expectancy, and ecologically motivated tax frameworks such as carbon taxes. But predistributive social policies can also be key here. One promising target group is socially disadvantaged adolescents and youth; another is secondary school age adolescents in modernised vocational schooling.[35]

But there is a particularly strong case for mobilising political coalitions for spending more on high quality *early childhood* education and similar social investment policies that increase the human capital of the smaller-sized younger generations – and bolster the fiscal basis of ageing welfare states in the process.[36] Such investments are a way to boost the skill levels of young people preparing to enter future labour markets in which much will be uncertain – but not the increasing returns to marketable skills.[37] They are a readily available way to marry economic efficiency (in the form of very high social returns throughout the later lifecycle) with intergenerational justice (in the form of levelling the playing field for all citizens across barriers of class and cohort).[38] Such investments are doubly progressive on the outcome side, in that they are also likely to boost the cognitive and non-cognitive skills of young children born in disadvantaged families. And, if provided on a universal basis, they can be made progressive on the cost side by instituting a sliding fee schedule based on family income. This is what James Heckman rightly calls progressive universalism.[39] Early human capital investments are therefore a singularly promising predistributive social policy.

However, the hard *political economy* of population ageing matters crucially, too.[40] When 'obviously' sound policies are not sufficiently implemented, wishfully thinking such policies into existence is not likely to be an effective strategy. Political entrepreneurs need to better highlight the inherent *linkages* between backward-looking intergenerational goods (BIGs) such as health care and long-term care and forward-looking intergenerational goods (FIGs) such as education – or 'why social security is good for the environment'.[41] And they need to acknowledge that rearing children is a resource-intensive and only partly visible activity that is highly valuable to *society*. Children themselves are also *public* goods.[42] The resources involved in raising children need to be better valued by public policies (that is, socialised) to safeguard the sustainability of ageing welfare states. Asset-based predistributive policies such as child trust funds or baby bonds, to be set up by government for each newborn baby and potentially topped up by parents, which could be made accessible with compound interest rates upon reaching legal voting age, are one example of an intergenerationally progressive policy.[43]

Similarly, the time is ripe for at least reopening an empirically informed democratic debate about predistributing *political rights*, for instance in the form of giving each parent an additional half-vote, to be used on behalf of each under-age child until that child reaches legal voting age.[44] These child proxy votes for parents could be made conditional on parents guaranteeing minimum standards of child welfare, and they could otherwise be regulated according to a host of civic requirements deemed desirable in an open democratic debate. I argue that such proxy votes for children can be defended on deontological grounds as a consistent and symmetric, yet pragmatic, application of the quintessentially democratic one-person, one-vote principle. And proxy votes could also be justified on instrumental grounds, as they internalise through political rights the positive social externalities of raising children in societies with low fertility and large elderly cohorts, for instance those implied by the future contributions of children to the pensions and health costs of non-parents.[45] The latter argument would hold even if parents did *not* use these proxy votes to vote in the children's interest. On the policy demand side, proxy votes would add hard power to the claims of younger generations in ageing societies, as they could significantly alter the incentive structure and the temporal horizons of elected policy-makers. Like predistributive human capital policies, they constitute an intergenerationally progressive political idea.

Notes

1. For example, Axel Gosseries and Lukas Meyer (eds), *Intergenerational Justice* (Oxford: Oxford University Press, 2009); Clara Sabbagh and Pieter Vanhuysse, 'Intergenerational justice perceptions and the role of welfare regimes: a comparative analysis of university students', *Administration and Society* 42/6 (2010), pp. 638–67; Dennis Thompson, 'Representing future generations: political presentism and democratic trusteeship', *Critical Review of International Social and Political Philosophy* 13/1 (2010), pp. 17–37; Pieter Vanhuysse and Achim Goerres (eds), *Ageing Populations in Post-Industrial Democracies:*

Comparative Studies of Policies and Politics (Abingdon: Routledge/ECPR Studies in European Political Science, 2012); Juliana Bidadanure, 'Treating young people as equals: Intergenerational justice in theory and practice', Doctoral dissertation (University of York, 2014); Martin Kohli, 'Aging and justice', in R. H. Binstock and L. K. George (eds), *Handbook of Aging and the Social Sciences*, 6th edition (London: Academic Press, 2006).

2.   Pieter Vanhuysse, *Intergenerational Justice in Aging Societies: A Cross-national Comparison of 29 OECD Countries* (Gütersloh: Bertelsmann Stiftung, 2013). The present chapter is a revised version of Pieter Vanhuysse, 'Intergenerational justice and public policy in Europe', European Social Observatory (OSE) Paper Series, Opinion Paper No.16, (2014). Available at http://papers.ssrn.com/sol3/papers.cfm?abstract_id=2416916 (accessed 21 March 2015).

3.   For a longer treatment, see Pieter Vanhuysse, 'Skills, stakes, and clout: early human capital foundations for European welfare futures', in Bernd Marin (ed.), *The Future of Welfare in a Global Europe* (Farnham: Ashgate, 2015). On presentism, see furthermore Mark Thompson, *Now for the Long Term*, Oxford Martin Commission for Future Generations (Oxford: Oxford Martin School, 2013); Inigo Gonzalez Ricoy and Axel Gosseries (eds), *Institutions for Future Generations* (Oxford: Oxford University Press, 2015).

4.   Brundlandt Commission, *Our Common Future* (Oxford: Oxford University Press, 1987); see also Amartya Sen, 'The ends and means of sustainability', *Journal of Human Development and Capabilities* 14/1 (2013), pp. 6–20; Eric Neumayer, *Weak versus Strong Sustainability* (Cheltenham: Edward Elgar, 2010).

5.   Brian Barry, 'Sustainability and intergenerational justice', *Theoria* 45/89 (1997), pp. 43–65; Philippe Van Parijs, 'The disfranchisement of the elderly, and other attempts to secure intergenerational justice', *Philosophy and Public Affairs* 27/4 (1998), pp. 292–333.

6.   Dennis McKerlie, *Justice between the Young and the Old* (Oxford: Oxford University Press, 2013).

7.   Louis Chauvel and Martin Schröder, 'Generational inequalities and welfare regimes', *Social Forces* 92/4 (2014), pp. 1259–83.

8.   Ronald Lee, 'Is low fertility really a problem? Population aging, dependency, and consumption', *Science* 346 (2014), pp. 229–34.

9.   Erich Striessnig and Wolfgang Lutz, 'Can below-replacement fertility be desirable?', *Empirica* (2013).

10. Vanhuysse, *Intergenerational Justice in Aging Societies*.

11. See also UNICEF, 'Child Well-being in Rich Countries', Innocenti Report Card 11, UNICEF Office of Research, Florence (2013). http://www.unicef-irc.org/publications/pdf/rc11_eng.pdf (accessed 21 March 2015).

12. See also Karen M. Anderson, this volume.

13. See Julia Lynch, *Age and the Welfare State* (Cambridge: Cambridge University Press, 2006); Markus Tepe and Pieter Vanhuysse, 'Elderly bias, new social risks, and social spending: change and timing in eight programs across four

worlds of welfare, 1980–2003', *Journal of European Social Policy* 20/3 (2010), pp. 218–34; Haya Gamliel-Yehoshua and Pieter Vanhuysse, 'The pro-elderly bias of social policies in Israel: a historical-institutional account', *Social Policy and Administration* 44/6 (2010), pp. 708–26.

14. Vanhuysse, *Intergenerational Justice in Aging Societies*.

15. Vanhuysse, 'Intergenerational Justice and Public Policy in Europe'.

16. For instance, in a study of more than 2,000 undergraduate university students from eight democracies across four worlds of welfare, younger working-age adults (aged 18–35) are systematically perceived to be treated worse than either older working-age adults or the elderly. See Sabbagh and Vanhuysse, 'Intergenerational justice perceptions and the role of welfare regimes'. On perceived *pension* injustice specifically, see Clara Sabbagh and Pieter Vanhuysse, 'Perceived pension injustice: a multidimensional model of attitudes in two most-different cases', *International Journal of Social Welfare* 23/2 (2014), pp. 174–84.

17. Ronald Lee, 'Intergenerational transfers, the biological life-cycle, and human society', in G. McNicoll, J. Bongaarts, and E. Churchill (eds), *Population and Public Policy: Essays in Honor of Paul Demeny* (New York: The Population Council, 2013), pp. 23–35; Ronald Lee and Andrew Mason (eds), *Population Aging and the Generational Economy: A Global Perspective* (Cheltenham: Edward Elgar, 2011).

18. Chauvel and Schröder, 'Generational inequalities and welfare regimes'. A similar fate predicted for US cohorts who entered the labour market after 2000, see Paul Beaudry, David A. Green, and Benjamin M. Sand, 'The declining fortunes of the young since 2000', *American Economic Review* 104/5 (2014), pp. 381–86.

19. Robert Gal, Endre Szabo, and Lili Vargha, 'The age-profile of invisible transfers: the true size of asymmetry in inter-age reallocations', *Journal of the Economics of Aging* (2014). See also Nancy Folbre, 'Children as public goods', *American Economic Review* 84/2 (1994), pp. 86–90.

20. David Autor, 'Skills, education, and the rise of earnings inequality among the "other 99 percent"', *Science* 344/6186 (2014), pp. 843–51. See also Peter Hall, this volume.

21. Lee, 'Is low fertility really a problem?', p. 33; Lee and Mason, *Population Aging and the Generational Economy: A Global Perspective*.

22. Lynch, *Age and the Welfare State*; Achim Goerres and Pieter Vanhuysse, 'Mapping the field: Comparative generational politics and policies in ageing democracies', in Pieter Vanhuysse and Achim Goerres (eds), *Ageing Populations in Postindustrial Democracies* (Abingdon: Routledge/ECPR Studies in European Political Science, 2012).

23. Manos Matsaganis and Chrysa Leventi, 'The distributional impact of the Greek crisis in 2010', *Fiscal Studies* 34/1 (2013), pp. 83–108; see also Manos Matsaganis, 'The crisis and the welfare state in Greece: A complex relationship', in Anna Triandafyllidou, Ruby Gropas, and Hara Kouki (eds), *The Greek Crisis and European Modernity* (Palgrave Macmillan, 2013), pp. 152–77.

24. Vanhuysse, 'Intergenerational justice and public policy in Europe'.

25. Vanhuysse, 'Skills, stakes, and clout'.

26. UNICEF, 'Child Well-being in Rich Countries: A comparative overview', Innocenti Report Card 11, UNICEF Office of Research, Florence (2013). http://www.unicef-irc.org/publications/pdf/rc11_eng.pdf (accessed 21 March 2015).

27. Pieter Vanhuysse, *Divide and Pacify: Strategic Social Policies and Political Protests in Post-Communist Democracies* (Budapest: Central European University Press, 2006); Pieter Vanhuysse, 'Power, order, and the politics of social policy in central and Eastern Europe', in Alfio Cerami and Pieter Vanhuysse (eds), *Post-Communist Welfare Pathways: Theorizing Social Policy Transformations in Central and Eastern Europe* (Basingstoke: Palgrave Macmillan, 2009), pp. 53–70.

28. Pieter Vanhuysse, 'The pensioner booms in post-communist Hungary and Poland: political sociology perspectives', *International Journal of Sociology and Social Policy* 24/1/2 (2004), pp. 86–102; Pieter Vanhuysse, 'Czech exceptionalism? A comparative political economy interpretation of post-communist policy pathways, 1989–2004', *Czech Sociological Review* 42/6 (2006), pp. 1115–36.

29. Vanhuysse, 'Skills, stakes, and clout'; Vanhuysse, 'Power, order, and the politics of social policy in central and Eastern Europe'.

30. Vanhuysse, *Divide and Pacify*.

31. Jan Drahokoupil and Stefan Domonkos, 'Averting the funding-gap crisis: East European pension reforms since 2008', *Global Social Policy* 12/3 (2012), pp. 283–99.

32. Warren Sanderson and Sergei Scherbov, 'Remeasuring aging', *Science* 329 (2010), pp. 1287–78. *Prospective* old-age dependency ratio is defined here as the number of people in age groups with life expectancies of 15 or fewer years, divided by the number of people of at least 20 years old in age groups with life expectancies greater than 15 years.

33. European Centre Vienna, *Active Ageing Index 2012*. 'Concept, Methodology, and Final Results', Report submitted to the European Commission's DG Employment (2013).

34. Chauvel and Schröder, 'Generational inequalities and welfare regimes'; Gal, Szabo and Vargha, 'The age-profile of invisible transfers'; Lee and Mason, *Population Aging and the Generational Economy: A Global Perspective*; Lee, 'Is low fertility really a problem?'.

35. Marius R. Busemeyer, this volume.

36. In economics, see especially Pedro Carneiro and James Heckman, 'Human capital policy', in James Heckman and Alan Krueger (eds), *Inequality in America* (Cambridge: MIT Press, 2003); Fernando Cunha and James Heckman, 'The economics and psychology of inequality and human development', *Journal of the European Economic Association* 7/2–3 (2009), pp. 320–64; James Heckman, *Giving Kids a Fair Chance* (Cambridge: MIT Press, 2013). In public policy, see for instance Goesta Esping-Andersen, 'Childhood investments

and skill formation', *International Tax and Public Finance* 15 (2008), pp. 19–44; Pieter Vanhuysse, 'The new political economy of skill formation', *Public Administration Review* 68/5 (2008), pp. 955–9; Vanhuysse, 'Skills, stakes, and clout'. See also Peter Hall, this volume. In demography, see Striessnig and Lutz, 'Can below-replacement fertility be desirable?'.

37. Alan Manning, this volume; David Autor.

38. Vanhuysse, 'Skills, stakes, and clout'.

39. Heckman, *Giving Kids a Fair Chance.*

40. Markus Tepe and Pieter Vanhuysse, 'Are aging OECD welfare states on the path to gerontocracy?' *Journal of Public Policy* 29/1 (2009), pp. 1–28 (2009); Vanhuysse and Goerres, *Ageing Populations in Postindustrial Democracies.*

41. Antonio Rangel, 'Forward and backward intergenerational goods: why is social security good for the environment?', *American Economic Review* 93/3 (2003), pp. 813–43.

42. Gal, Szabo, and Vargha, 'The age-profile of invisible transfers'; Folbre, 'Children as public goods'.

43. David Nissan and Julian Le Grand, *A Capital Idea: Start-up Grants for Young People* (London: Fabian Society, 2000).

44. Paul Demeny, 'Pronatalist policies in low-fertility countries: patterns, performance and prospects', *Population and Development Review* 12 (1986), pp. 335–58; Achim Goerres and Guido Tiemann, 'Kinder an die macht? Die politischen konsequenzen des stellvertretenden elternwahlrechts' *Politisches Vierteljahresschrift* 50 (2009), pp. 50–74; Van Parijs (1998); Warren Sanderson and Sergei Scherbov, 'A near electoral majority of pensioners', *Population and Development Review* 33/3 (2007), pp. 543–54.

45. See Vanhuysse, *Intergenerational Justice in Aging Societies.*

Part II

Welfare States after the Crisis:
A Predistribution Agenda?

CHAPTER 3

Predistribution and Redistribution
Alternative or Complementary Policies?

Evelyne Huber and John D. Stephens[1]

At least since the Lisbon summit, support for the social investment approach has been near hegemonic within social democracy and beyond. The language is now familiar: 'prepare rather than repair', activation rather than passive receipt of benefits. What made social investment attractive as a new social democratic strategy was not that it was an alternative to promoting income equality but rather it seemed to be an alternative way to promote lower income inequality and poverty to traditional tax and transfer redistribution. By distributing market resources more equally, in this case, marketable skills, less income inequality would result. Thus, 'predistribution' would reduce the need for 'redistribution'.

However, from the beginning, there has been a rift in social democracy about social investment. It overlaps with the earlier debate about activation in social policy, though in that debate, there was a clear neoliberal pole that emphasised cutting benefits to the unemployed to push them back into the labour force and a social democratic pole that emphasised job training and job creation, negative and positive activation in Kananen, Taylor-Gooby, and Larsen's[2] formulation. Even within social democracy, few academics and even fewer politicians were willing to defend unlimited access to the passive benefits, as the labour reduction strategies of the continental welfare states in response to the increased unemployment in the 1970s and 1980s were widely seen as failures. After 1990, social democratic governments sometimes lowered benefit levels and frequently tightened qualifying conditions for unemployment benefits, especially the requirement to seek and accept employment. On the other side, investments in education and training were, and arguably still are, uncontroversial within social democracy, but there has been wide variability in the extent to which social democratic governments actually prioritise education and training.

We see a similar divide between those who see social investment and predistribution as alternatives to redistribution and those who view redistribution as a necessary complement to a social investment strategy. Predistribution, that is, policy measures to equalise market income, is not limited to social investment. Minimum wages and legislation to tip the balance in collective bargaining toward labour, such as making unionisation easier or affording labour a greater range of conflict measures, obviously also affect market distribution. However, what makes social investment particularly attractive is the strong evidence, based theoretically on endogenous growth theory, that human capital has a very large positive effect on economic growth, larger, in fact, than investment in physical capital.[3] Thus, we concentrate our discussion here on social investment, particularly investments in early childhood education and care, in primary, secondary and tertiary education, in vocational education, and in adult labour market training. These investments affect income distribution by increasing the quality of labour at the bottom of the distribution and by increasing the quantity of educated labour at the top, thus lowering the education wage premium.

In the extreme, the position that sees social investment as a substitute regards traditional social democratic redistribution as a mistake, perhaps not in the heyday of the postwar welfare state but certainly in the current post-industrial knowledge society. Among academics, Giddens[4] is often cited as advancing this position, but in truth his argument is much more nuanced than that. At a political level, this view is best exemplified by the discourse of New Labour, especially in the drive to take power and the first few years in office. The rhetoric surrounding the New Deals and the view that poverty was a problem but not inequality per se (if it was just a matter of the rich getting richer) are exemplary of this view. Moreover, again in the practice of social democratic governments faced with scarcity of resources, redistributive policies and social investment policies may appear to be viable alternatives.

The other point of view, that redistribution is a necessary complement to successful social investment, was clearly articulated by Esping-Andersen[5] in the volume that arose directly from the Lisbon agenda. Esping-Andersen[6] argued that parental poverty was a barrier to children's educational success that even the most well-intentioned and well-funded early childhood education and care and further primary and secondary education would find almost impossible to surmount. Academically, this is a very difficult argument to challenge because it is backed up by a large body of research in the sociology of education summarised below, which shows strong links between children's educational achievement and parents' social-economic standing, especially mother's education, neighbourhood effects, peer group effects, and in some cases like the USA, varying tax bases of different school districts.

Drawing on our recent analysis of the causes of income inequality in post-industrial democracies,[7] we will present evidence which supports the proposition that investing in skills does result in lower pre-tax and transfer (market) income inequality. However, we will also show that post-tax and transfer income inequality in the parental generation is a powerful predictor of average skill levels in their offspring's generation independent of social investment in that period. This finding indicates that there is a limit to how much one can reduce market income inequality without equalising post-tax and transfer income inequality. Moreover, we show that, without redistribution, income inequality would be high in even the most egalitarian countries with the strongest record of social investment, the Nordic countries.

Social Investment and Market Income Inequality

In *The Race between Education and Technology*, Goldin and Katz[8] argue that the long-term development of inequality in the USA can be explained by the relationship between technological change which creates ever growing demand for skilled and educated workers, and educational expansion which creates a greater supply of skilled and educated workers. For the first three-quarters of the twentieth century, the pace of increase in the supply of educated workers exceeded the increase in demand created by technological change. Thus, the education wage premium and the level of inequality declined in this period. In the last quarter of the twentieth century, the opposite happened; the USA failed to expand education fast enough and the supply of educated workers fell relative to the demand created by technological change, so the education wage premium and the level of inequality increased. Thus, Goldin and Katz show that the familiar refrain that skill-biased technological change has led to increasing inequality is only true if one ignores the supply side – the supply of educated workers.

In Huber and Stephens,[9] we test the Goldin-Katz hypothesis on the causes of variation in market income inequality through time and across countries. Our dependent variable is the Gini index of pre-tax and transfer household income inequality among the working age (household head 25–59) households measured by Luxembourg Income Study (LIS) surveys.[10] The data cover 18 post-industrial democracies from the late 1970s to 2010.

Figure 3.1 shows the order of magnitude of the variables that were significant in the second model of Table 3.2 of the article.[11] The fit of the model is very good as indicated by the R^2 (0.66). In almost all of these countries, market income inequality has been rising in recent decades. The figure shows that deindustrialisation, deunionisation, rising unemployment, and family structure change are prime reasons for these trends. Employment (measured by the percentage of the population age 15–64 employed), which has been increasing in all of these countries, has been a countervailing force. The effect of education spending varies: Where it has been declining, as in the Anglo-American countries, it has contributed to increasing inequality; where it has been increasing, as in the Nordic countries, it has dampened the increase in inequality.

Let us focus on education spending as investment in human capital as one of the keys to our argument. The effect of education spending on market income inequality would appear to be modest. There are good reasons to believe that education spending is an underestimate of the effect of level and distribution of human capital among the adult population on market income inequality. The best measures of the level and distribution of adult skills are the OECD studies, the International Adult Literacy Study (IALS) carried out in the mid-1990s and the Study of Adult Skills (SAS) carried out 2008–13. In both studies, a standardised test of general skills in three areas (literacy, mathematics, and document handling) was administered to random samples of the adult populations of the participating countries. Columns 5 to 7 of Table 3.1 show the scores of the 5th, mean, and 95th percentile on the IALS.[12] As one can see from the table, most of the variation

Pre-tax and transfer Gini

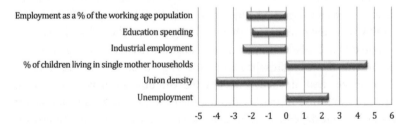

FIGURE 3.1 Estimated effect of a two standard deviation change in the independent variables on pre-tax and transfer Gini.
Source: Huber and Stephens (2014a), see note 7.

TABLE 3.1 Social investment, human capital stock, and wage dispersion.

	Education spending	Spending	Public spending	ALMP total	Daycare 5th percentile	Mean	Score on OECD literacy test 95th percentile	Wage dispersion 90–10 ratio
Nordic Countries								
Denmark	8.2	1.6	1.9	11.7	213	289	353	2.5
Finland	6.3	0.9	1.0	8.2	195	288	363	2.3
Norway	7.0	0.6	0.8	8.4	207	294	363	2.0
Sweden	7.0	1.3	1.6	9.9	216	304	386	2.2
Mean	7.1	1.1	1.3	9.5	208	294	366	2.3
Western Continental Europe								
Belgium	6.2	1.1	0.8	8.1	163	277	359	2.2
Germany	4.6	1.0	0.4	6.0	208	285	359	3.1
Netherlands	5.4	1.3	1.0	7.7	202	286	355	2.8
Switzerland	5.4	0.6	0.3	6.3	150	271	349	2.8
Mean	5.4	1.0	0.6	7.0	181	280	356	2.7
Southern Europe								
Italy	4.6	0.6	0.6	5.8	114	237	325	2.4

(Continued)

TABLE 3.1 (Continued)

	Education spending	Spending	Public spending	ALMP total	Daycare 5th percentile	Mean	Score on OECD literacy test 95th percentile	Wage dispersion 90–10 ratio
Portugal	5.3	0.6	0.4	6.3	96	229	334	4.0
Mean	5.0	0.6	0.5	6.1	105	233	329	3.2
Anglo-American countries								
Australia	4.8	0.3	0.4	5.5	146	274	359	2.9
Canada	5.1	0.3	0.2	5.6	145	280	372	4.2
Ireland	4.8	0.7	0.1	5.6	151	263	353	4.1
New Zealand	6.4	0.4	0.7	7.5	158	272	361	2.3
UK	5.2	0.3	0.9	6.4	145	267	360	3.5
USA	5.5	0.1	0.3	5.9	133	272	371	4.6
Mean	5.3	0.4	0.4	6.1	146	271	363	3.6

Source: Huber and Stephens (2001).[14]

in the IALS scores is at the bottom end of the distribution and the variation in the mean is largely a product of variation in the bottom half of the distribution. The table also includes various measures of social spending on skills and education. One can see that spending on human capital is related to the stock of human capital.

One can also see from the table that the adult literacy scores co-vary with the degree of wage dispersion as measured by the ratio of the wage and salary income of the wage earner at the 90th percentile of the distribution to the wage earner at the 10th percentile. In fact, Nickell[13] has shown that the 95–5 ratio on the IALS test is a more important determinant of wage dispersion than union density or bargaining centralisation, a finding which we were able to replicate on more recent data. Thus, it would appear that 'predistribution', a strategy to equalise market income by raising skill levels at the bottom and raising the supply of skills at the top (and thus lowering the education wage premium), is very promising.

Disposable Income Inequality in the Parents' Generation and Children's Educational Chances

This strategy, however, has limits. We have argued elsewhere that a major cause of skill levels, above all at the bottom end, was the degree of poverty and inequality in the parental generation.[15] Poverty and social exclusion reduce the capacity of students to take advantage of educational opportunities offered. The disadvantage of young children from poor households at the point of entering formal education is well documented. Much research 'has found a pervasive tendency for children born in socially disadvantaged families to have poorer health, education, and general welfare'.[16] Researchers have found social-emotional factors that account for the achievement gap of disadvantaged students, such as academic and school attachment, teacher support, peer values, and mental health.[17] Socialisation tends to continue to work against educational success, both through inadequate support for learning and peer pressure to reject compliance with expectations and self-discipline. Family-based factors have been found to be the most powerful in predicting achievement and delinquency, followed closely by influence from 'best friends'.[18] However, school and neighbourhood composition matter as well; Van Ewijk and Sleegers[19] performed a meta-regression analysis of 30 studies that found varying degrees of impact of peers' socio-economic status on students' test scores.

These micro-level relationships manifest themselves at the macro-level in relationships between levels of poverty and inequality and the level and distribution of cognitive skills. The nature of the school system, tracked versus comprehensive and overwhelmingly public versus strong private participation, can reduce or reinforce the impact of class inequality on educational inequality. Cross-national differences in inequalities in educational achievement have been explained with the level of inequality in the society, the level of modernisation of the society, and school systems.[20] Where school systems are tracked, social selection is biased towards privileged groups and perpetuates or increases class inequality. The same argument can be made about school systems with strong reliance on private schooling.

The analysis in Table 3.2 shows that, in fact, inequality in the parents' generation is a very strong determinant of the mean level of skills (and the distribution of skills, given what we know about the relationship between the mean and the scores at the bottom) in the offspring's generation. We regress the mean SAS score on post tax and transfer inequality in LIS Waves I or II (early to mid-1980s) and average human capital spending 1980–2010 and then average years of education of the adult population in 2010. The 25–30 year difference in the time point at which inequality and adult skills were measured is roughly equivalent to a generation. In both regressions, the coefficients for inequality are much larger than the ones for human capital investment and average years of education. A two standard deviation decrease in disposable income Gini results in a 12.5 point increase in average test score, which is substantial given that a standard deviation in the test score is 12.0. This finding argues that there are limits to how much one can raise the average level of human capital without decreasing inequality.

TABLE 3.2 Determinants of mean adult skills (PIAAC/SAS 2008–2013).

Gini working age LIS Wave I or II	−1.380**	−1.932***
Average spending on human capital 1980–2010	2.161	
Average years of education of adult population		1.163
Constant	288.091***	304.411***
R^2	0.67***	0.62***
Observations	15	15

*Significant at 0.05; **significant at 0.01, ***significant at 0.001.

A final point in our argument is that one cannot reach the low levels of inequality necessary to complement social investment effectively by lowering market income inequality alone. This is shown by Table 3.3. One can see that, in a hypothetical situation of no tax and transfer redistribution, the Nordic countries would be as unequal as the Anglo-American (Liberal)

TABLE 3.3   Inequality and redistribution.

	Market income inequality	Disposable income inequality	Redistribution
Nordic countries			
Denmark 2004	33.8	20.7	38.8
Finland 2004	36.0	23.4	35.1
Norway 2004	36.3	24.1	33.5
Sweden 2005	36.1	21.9	39.4
Mean	35.6	22.5	36.7
Continental Europe			
Austria 2004	36.3	26.5	27.2
Belgium 2000	37.5	26.1	30.6
France 2005	37.6	27.1	27.9
Germany 2007	37.7	32.7	13.3
Netherlands 2004	35.4	25.7	27.3
Switzerland 2004	29.8	25.8	13.5
Mean	35.7	27.3	23.3
Southern Europe			
Italy 2004	38.9	34.3	11.8
Spain 2004	39.3	31.0	21.1
Mean	39.1	32.7	16.5
Anglo-American countries			
Australia 2003	41.0	30.2	26.5
Canada 2007	47.6	32.7	31.3
Ireland 2004	44.1	30.6	30.5
UK 2004	43.9	34.2	22.1
USA 2004	43.5	36.2	16.8
Mean	44.0	32.8	25.4

countries are after their welfare state redistribution. A stark illustration of this is that, in 2005, 48 per cent of single mother families in Sweden fell below the poverty line in terms on their market income. After taxes and transfers, the figure was 10 per cent. Vulnerable groups like single mothers and their children need welfare state redistribution to give them a chance in life.

Conclusion

In this chapter, we have shown that redistribution of income through taxes and transfers cannot be dispensed with in social democracies' policy packages. Not only is redistribution essential to producing low levels of inequality and poverty, it is also an essential element of a strategy to produce high levels of skills and an equal distribution of skills. Still, we fully agree that the social democratic turn to social investment is of major importance. Social investment has a major effect on skill distribution, which in turn has a major effect on wage distribution and market income distribution. In addition, social investment is a key component of social democratic growth strategy. Finally, as Busemeyer[21] argues, social investment helps to cement coalitions between working and middle class voters, which is increasingly politically important to social democracy in the post-industrial knowledge economies. By the same token, it also brings women into the coalition as they increasingly attain higher levels of education than men and thus are increasingly dependent on high quality public education.

Notes

1. An earlier version of this chapter was delivered at the Harvard Multidisciplinary Program in Inequality and Social Policy, 22 September 2014, and the Policy Network's conference on 'Predistributive Social Policy: Future Changes in Welfare Societies' at St Catherine's College, University of Oxford, 30 June–1 July 2014. We would like to thank the participants at that conference and Nathalie Morell for helpful comments.

2. Johannes Kananen, Peter Taylor-Gooby, and Trine P. Larsen, 'Public attitudes and new social risk reform', in Klaus Armingeon and Giuliano Bonoli (eds), *The Politics of Post-Industrial Welfare States: Adapting Post-War Social Policies to New Social Risks* (London: Routledge, 2006), pp. 83–99.

3. Eric A. Hanushek and Ludger Woessmann, 'Do better schools lead to more growth? Cognitive skills, economic outcomes, and causation', *Journal of Economic Growth*, 17 (2012), pp. 267–321; Peter Evans, Evelyne Huber, and

John D. Stephens, 'The political foundations of state effectiveness', in Miguel Centeno, Atul Kohli, and Deborah Yashar (eds), *State Building in the Developing World*, (Princeton: Princeton University Press, forthcoming. Evelyne Huber and John D. Stephens, 'Social investment in Latin America', paper delivered at the World Congress of the International Sociological Association, Yokohama, Japan, 14–19 July 2014. Available at https://www.sas.upenn.edu/dcc/sites/www.sas.upenn.edu.dcc/files/Huber%20-%20Social%20Investment%20in%20Latin%20America.pdf (accessed 21 March 2015).

4. Anthony Giddens, *The Third Way: The Renewal of Social Democracy* (Cambridge: Polity Press, 1998).

5. Gøsta Esping-Andersen, 'A child-centered social investment strategy', in Gøsta Esping-Andersen (ed.), *Why We Need a New Welfare State* (Oxford: Oxford University Press, 2002), pp. 26–67.

6. *Ibid.*, pp. 49–50.

7. Evelyne Huber and John D. Stephens, 'Income inequality and redistribution in post-industrial democracies: demographic, economic, and political determinants', *Socio-Economic Review*, 12 (2014a), pp. 245–67.

8. Claudia Goldin and Laurence F. Katz, *The Race between Education and Technology* (Cambridge: Harvard University Press, 2008).

9. Huber and Stephens, 'Income inequality ans redistribution in post-industrial democracies'.

10. Luxembourg Income Study Database. Available at: http://www.lisdatacenter.org. Available at http://www.lisdatacenter.org (accessed 15 May 2015).

11. This article is available from the authors on request.

12. We show the IALS data rather than the more recent SAS data because the SAS data for the 5th and 95th percentile published in OECD (2013) do not adjust for literacy related non-responses (basically respondents who were not literate enough to take the test), which vary greatly across countries (e.g. from 0 per cent in Sweden to 5 per cent in the US). The means for IALS and for the adjusted SAS data are very highly correlated (.85).

13. Stephen Nickell, 'Poverty and worklessness in Britain', *Economic Journal* 114 (2004), C1–C25.

14. See note 16. David Brady, Evelyne Huber, and John D. Stephens. Comparative Welfare States Data Set, University of North Carolina and WZB Berlin Social Science Center (2014). Available at http://www.unc.edu/~jdsteph/common/data-common.html (accessed 21 March 2015).

15. Evelyne Huber and John D. Stephens, *Development and Crisis of the Welfare State: Parties and Policies in Global Markets* (Chicago: University of Chicago Press, 2001), p. 95.

16. David M. Fergusson, L. John Horwood, and Joseph M. Boden, 'The transmission of social inequality: Examination of the linkages between family socio-economic status in childhood and educational achievement in young adulthood', *Research in Social Stratification and Mobility* 26 (2008), pp. 277–95.

17. Bronwyn E. Becker and Suniya S. Luthar, 'Social-emotional factors affecting achievement outcomes among disadvantaged students: closing the achievement gap', *Educational Psychologist* 37 (2002), pp. 197–214.
18. Greg J. Duncan, Johanne Boisjoly, and Kathleen Mullan Harris, 'Sibling, peer, neighbor, and schoolmate correlations as indicators of the importance of context for adolescent development', *Demography* 38 (2001), pp. 437–47.
19. Reyn van Ewijk and Peter Sleegers, 'The effect of peer socioeconomic status on student achievement: a meta-analysis', *Educational Research Review* 5 (2010), pp. 134–50.
20. Gary N. Marks, 'Cross-national differences and accounting for social class inequalities in education', *International Sociology* 20 (2005), pp. 483–505.
21. Marius R. Busemeyer, 'Social democrats and the new partisan politics of public investment in education', *Journal of European Public Policy* 16/1, (2009) pp. 107–26.

CHAPTER 4

The Potential and Limits of Predistribution in the UK
Tackling Inequality and Poverty

Paul Gregg

The UK labour market produced increasingly unequal outcomes across working-age families through the 1980s and 1990s. The distribution of work and earnings amongst those in work became ever more polarised. For employment in households this polarisation was evident through more dual earner couples and no earner households. By 1997, employment rates had recovered close to levels seen in 1979 before the deep 1980s recession, and indeed in 1989 before the 1990s recession. However, there were more than one million more workless households combined with a similar greater number of dual earner couples.[1] This polarisation of work with excess levels of workless households was particularly marked for families with children. By 1997, one in five children was living in a family without a worker present and among the growing number of lone parents, under 40 per cent were in work. Even among parent couples, over one in ten had no one in work. This was broadly twice the numbers that would be expected given levels of employment prevailing at the time.

At the same time, the distribution of earnings widened dramatically from 1978 onwards. By the late 1990s, real wages adjusted for inflation for the lowest paid tenth of men had risen by just 10 per cent over 20 years, whereas for the highest paid tenth they had grown by well over 60 per cent. This huge increase in inequality emanating from the labour market placed a major burden on a welfare state built on full employment and limited earnings inequality, although rapid growth in top incomes did provide substantial increases in tax revenues. More recently, a new dimension has emerged over the last decade where earnings growth for the typical British worker first slowed prior to the great recession and then fell dramatically, such that real average wages have fallen by 10 per cent in the last five years, which has only just ended. Thus the story of the 1980s and 1990s was one of rising living standards, but growing inequality. The last decade has seen stagnation and then recently-falling living standards, although the rise in inequality has largely stopped.

Told another way, the story of the last 15 years or so was that initially, median wages stopped rising in line with improvements in the productive efficiency of the economy. Then since the recession, improvements in productive efficiency stopped and wages started to fall.[2] The implications of this are profound. Since around 1850, when the industrial revolution was firmly established, technological and organisational improvements meant there have been steady productivity gains in the economy. A worker armed with bigger and better machines and improved organisations could achieve greater outputs; the benefits from this increased efficiency were broadly shared across society so that living standards of all, not just the owners or managers of factories, increased. Workers' wages were said to be coupled to productivity gains and grow in tandem, greater economic efficiency created the returns for wages to rise, and rising wages created the incentives for firms to invest and improve efficiency to save on more expensive labour. From the early 1990s, but more markedly from the early 2000s, the wage increases of typical British workers started to lag behind improvements in productivity. This de-coupling of median wages from productivity first occurred 30 years ago in the US, some 20 years ago in Canada and a decade ago in the UK.

Furthermore, there has not been a big increase in share of national output going in profits, rather a growing share of the proceeds of productive efficiency went to top earners (hence rising wage inequality) and more recently, to fund pension commitments. Firms had committed to these deals in periods where stock market returns were stronger, but with sustained weak stock market returns since the 1990s and more rapid increases in longevity than were expected, firms had to pay a greater share of the total compensation package to meet these pension costs. It is worth noting that much of these pension costs were largely paid to workers who were already retired and the more generous Defined Benefit schemes, which pay a proportion of earnings on retirement, have largely closed to new workers. Defined Contribution schemes pass the risk of stock market returns fluctuations and longevity onto the worker. It is also worth noting that distribution of firms' pension contributions have favoured top earners even more than was the case for wages, so there was an inequality issue here too.[3]

Faced with these challenges emerging from the labour market, there are two broad classes of policy response. These are not contradictory, and in some cases they can be mutually reinforcing, but the distinction is helpful. The first is to understand and counter the forces that are driving these patterns in the labour market. These are policy-driven attempts to change the primary distribution of work, wages, pensions and so on. that represent the dominant sources of income for households apart from state transfers. This strategy is sometimes referred to as predistribution, as it comes before the second major state response, which is the secondary redistribution of the market incomes of families through a well-established set of institutions behind taxation, welfare benefits, tax credits and freely accessible services such as education, and in the UK, the NHS. The recent policy interest in predistribution stems in part from a perceived sense of limitation to the secondary redistribution strategy. These are the limits of political acceptance of higher taxation on the well off to give to the poor: redistribution creates disincentives to work, get a better education and save if the proceeds of these activities are then heavily taxed or benefits aggressively means-tested. The extent of these incentive concerns is central to the left–right political discourse, with the right arguing that they are so important as to make redistribution ineffective, leading to the outcomes they are seeking to help. The argument for the existence of the pervasive culture of welfare dependency is an example here. Finally, the current large budget deficits in most Western economies arguably place major constraints on the redistribution strategy, though this will also be true of some of the tools for primary or predistributive policy options.

It is worth noting that generally societies with high inequality in the primary distribution of work and wages tend to redistribute more, including the USA. The extent of this redistribution only dampens, but does not smooth out the higher inequality in primary distribution of incomes.[4] The same is true within a society as inequality rises; the tax and welfare institutions tend to work harder to reduce inequality but never by enough to fully offset the rise. The success of Scandinavian countries in producing low inequality is that relatively low inequality in the primary distribution of work and wages is combined with levels of redistribution normally seen in more unequal countries.

The key policy areas for predistribution in the UK are:

A) Work, which here means unemployment and especially the high number of households without any workers, who are hence reliant on one of the major out-of-work benefits that grew rapidly up to the mid-1990s.[5] Over the last 20 years, there has been a key focus on reducing worklessness in families with children, and especially among lone parents as part of the drive to reduce child poverty, with marked success. In addition to household worklessness, low levels of employment among marginalised groups such as the young, the less educated and especially those with health issues and disabilities are a focus here.

B) Low wages, especially for those who are aged over 20 years and are thus expected to make a significant contribution to the upkeep of households or to establish new households when leaving the parental home.

C) The high cost of living, which is the other side of the coin of the low value of wages, in that it asks how inflation remains high (substantively higher than wages growth) when it should reflect the costs of production where wages are the major cost.

D) Debt and savings behaviours and the implications for families to protect themselves against adverse shocks (discretionary saving) and over the life course (personal pension saving).

Policy Tools for Predistribution

The policy tools for predistribution are quite varied and not always directly under the control of government, but may also be influenced by wider societal pressures. They cover legal restrictions or close relatives like regulation and license to practice. The most obvious is the national minimum wage (NMW), though we might also think of staffing levels regulations and required qualifications in the childcare, and even security, industries, which have made a big difference to wages paid to security staff. It would also cover rules around bank or pay day loan lending, bank and pension management charges. The requirements on firms to offer sick and holiday pay and, most recently, minimum pension offers under the national employment savings trust (NEST) regulations would also come here.

A very important area for legal and regulatory influence that makes the argument well on how predistribution can be influential concerns gender and maternity regulation. Equal pay legislation, combined with paid and unpaid maternity leave, giving the right to return to the same job and right to request part-time working have led to a huge rise in not only women's pay and employment, but also productivity and output in the economy.[6] Predictions at the time, from free market thinktanks, on how this would discourage employers from hiring women were hopelessly wrong: they missed the fact that there was a huge loss of productive potential that occurred when women left the workforce for periods of time when children were young and returned to lower status, lower paid and lower productivity jobs. Allowing women to ease the massive tension between career and children has been one of the biggest social policy wins over the last 30 years, substantively because it married gender equity goals with improving economic efficiency. Harkness also shows how women's increased earnings and employment have reduced household inequality because they are only weakly correlated with that of men in the same households, and thus dampen inequality patterns.[7] It remains true that increasing women's employment in the UK and reducing the gender pay gap further would reduce household inequality and child poverty.

The effects of regulating the primary distribution of work and wages need not be direct. The weak performance of wages at the bottom half of the wage distribution has been widely linked to two factors: first, technological change with declines in workers' bargaining power through unions, second, high unemployment and less clearly through growing employment insecurity. Hence, regulations that effect the ability of trade unions to organise and gain bargaining rights will indirectly influence the distribution of wages. Likewise, employment protection regulations may help shield workers from employment insecurity and reduce their sensitivity to local unemployment levels. However, there are issues here as to whether this aids employed workers at the expense of the unemployed. But strategies that support lowering unemployment will have knock-on effects on wages as workers' employment options improve. Central here is high youth unemployment across Europe. It has been established in numerous studies[8] that young people experiencing protracted unemployment or cumulatively a large number of months out of work go on to have higher future unemployment risks and lower wages when in work (and almost certainly, though it has not been shown formally, lower productivity). Furthermore, these scarring effects, as they are called, continue well into a person's forties. Policy interventions, such as the Youth Guarantee in Europe (Job Guarantee in the UK), have the potential, if effective, to thus reduce these scarring effects and the key drivers of low wages amongst adults, especially for men.

The second major area for predistributive policy interventions are social norms and consumer campaigns. There are a large number of campaigns which use social norms of fairness as a motivator of consumer behaviour or that of other actors. The Living Wage Campaign or Fair Trade logos on goods sold in supermarkets are prominent examples. The amount that behaviour actually moves may understate their impact if firms respond to avoid censure or being out of line with norms. The recent moves by UK retail firms to start worrying about their suppliers' employment conditions following deaths of garment workers in Bangladesh is an important example. The firms' response was to avoid or reduce negative publicity. More than that, it has established the principle that UK retail firms have a responsibility for the conditions in which their goods are produced and the wages workers receive, even though they do not work directly for the retail firm. Another example would be the horse meat scandal for meat sold in the UK labelled as beef.

Supply chains and the rules firms can impose on their suppliers have a huge potential impact on industry behaviours. The Living Wage Campaign has relatively few workers covered, but some, mainly large finance firms, have applied the living wage not just to their direct employees but also to those of catering and security staff employed under contract to work in their offices. This use of business-to-business contracting to influence wages and other conditions thus has substantial potential where firms are sensitive to reputational costs. A recent report published by the Resolution Foundation into the potential for increased minimum wages argues that higher levels of minimum wages, which are not legally binding, could be applied to sectors or groups of major employers.[9] The argument is that the Low Pay Commission, calling for a higher value minimum wage that could be afforded by major firms would create the reputational pressure on firms to act collectively to pay higher wages. By acting in unison, it would eliminate the risks from the competition gaining a price advantage from lower wages, which is a key brake on firms paying more. Thus, in this case, through a non-statutory body, reputational effects might be harnessed to raise pay for a large portion of the workforce. Reputational effects need not always be negative; corporate social responsibility is the use of reputational gain as a device to encourage desired firm behaviours.

The next major group of mechanisms concerns incentives to produce behavioural responses that influence the distribution of work and wages. These can again be direct or indirect. Incentives systems are widely used as a public policy tool to encourage people to work, save, invest in education among individuals or training, or invest in research by firms. An example of effective social policy in this area has been the spread on private pension saving where firms and workers receive tax or social insurance based incentives to fund such systems. The spread of private pensions saving 30 years ago has produced falling poverty rates among older people over the last two decades. The incidence of poverty amongst the old used to be the highest of any group before 1980 or so, but in the UK at least, this has been replaced by childhood. As noted above, though, the extent of pension contributions from employers is steadily becoming less generous for those not close to retirement. An interesting variant on incentives to save for pensions is the new NEST pensions system. This requires firms to offer a pension package to its employees with minimum contributions from the firm. But the novelty is that workers are automatically enrolled unless they choose to opt out, rather than as with other previous schemes, to opt in. The hope is this will raise the extent of pension coverage, especially among the young.

Incentives are also central to the design of welfare systems and welfare to work programmes. In response to the growing evidence of levels of workless households, especially with children, for given levels of aggregate employment, the incoming Labour government set about introducing three major welfare reforms which used incentives in two very different ways. The first was the financial support through tax credits of low-paid employment in families with children. These are transfers to address low income. In addition, especially in the first few years, they were designed to improve incentives to work. To put it in the language of New Labour, 'to make work pay'. The system had minimum hours rules such that a parent in these families had to be working for at least 16 hours to receive the tax credits. This was designed to incentivise a minimum number of hours, which for lone parents would be enough to generally escape poverty. For single parents, this was supplemented by extra financial support for childcare. Around 1994, only 34 per cent of lone mothers were in work; today this stands at 60 per cent, and the timing of the changes supports the view that these incentives matter.[10] In addition to financial carrots, the welfare system also increasingly used sticks, in the form of behavioural conditions for the receipt of out of work benefits.

This then is the second main incentives variant, and it is being widely used throughout the world, perhaps most commonly as conditional cash transfers. Here financial payments for children in many developing countries are made conditional on the child attending school and health clinics for very young children. In the UK, unemployment benefits became conditional on proof that a person meets certain minimum job search requirements with the onset of job seekers allowance (JSA) replacing unemployment benefit. This model was extended to lone parents on social assistance benefits, initially by requiring attendance at work focused interviews. From 2008, those without young children were migrated onto JSA. The other major use of conditions was in mandated participation in welfare to work programmes where those who had been unemployed for a given period were required to join New Deal programmes, which included work experience. This was a precursor to the EU's youth guarantee programme. The central point in incentives can include such conditions being attached to the receipt of financial payments from the state.

Such conditions attached to financial transactions can also apply to firms. Governments, central and local, commission a large array of services from businesses. These contracts can have conditions, sometimes called 'riders', which mean that as well as providing the core service, certain other criteria need to be met. In construction projects, especially large ones like the London Olympics or the new high speed rail link from London to the north of England, such riders have been used extensively to require, for instance, a set number of apprenticeships to be created for young people. The use of public sector contracting in this way has strong parallels with earlier discussions around the use of supply chains to initiate the spread of best practice or industry norms.

Policy Options for Predistribution

Given the above discussion on the range of policy tools, it is worth engaging in some illustrative predistribution policy ideas. These are UK-focused and are broken down into two groups below: those that are plausible, but generally minor, and a set of more ambitious ideas/agendas. The more challenging set are likely to come with some significant wider costs, borne by some part of society, but this is largely inevitable with predistribution. However, compared to taxation and redistribution, these costs are less transparent and perhaps less likely to create political resistance. To the extent that there are employment issues attached to policy changes, the UK is in a very different space than much of Europe. Unemployment is falling rapidly and so creating jobs per se is not the problem; the challenge is getting employment to marginal groups and improving the quality and pay of jobs that are the dominant issues of the day.

Plausible

Employment of Marginal Groups

While employment is recovering well in the UK, after the moderate fall through the 'great recession', there are still groups struggling to gain a foothold in the labour market. Employment has mostly risen by a fall in job leaving, especially (early) retirement among the over-60s, than through new hires. This means that the long-term unemployed and the young – groups looking for (re-)entry into the labour market – are still struggling. For those with ill-health or a disability, employment remains low and hiring rare. The government's Work Programme is proving broadly effective, that is in line with past policy initiatives, in helping the first two groups. However, it is having no beneficial effects for the sick and disabled.[11] For all three groups, the absence or lack of a recent work record and good references act as a major barrier to employment. For the sick and disabled, there is an additional issue that the person may not know the limits of what they can do, let alone a potential employer. A programme with a proven track record in this area, at least for the young, is a period of work experience supported by the government. This was used in the New Deal programmes, as well as for the young through the recession in the future jobs fund (FJF).[12] There was considerable room for improvement on FJF as it was developed in a mad rush and lacked some basic quality controls, especially about employment outcomes. However, the evaluation strongly suggests that it added value and such programmes do help those with no or poor recent employment records.

For those with lower levels of disability and health-related work limitations, this approach has not been tried extensively in the UK, though there are a number of charitable businesses which provide stepping stones to employment for similar groups such as the ex-homeless. The core idea is to encourage employment in part-time transitional jobs, meaning employment in businesses paying at least the minimum wage, but supported by the government with a clear focus on supporting people into regular employment. There are a number of funding models, including large outcome-related payments on a successful transition. Here then there are few upfront costs to the government. Gaining experience, references and confidence can help people into sustained employment and reduce welfare reliance and hence inequalities in access to employment records.

For those developing health problems whilst currently working, far more could be done to hold people in employment. The contrast with maternity leave rights is illuminating. When a person becomes ill they are normally placed on statutory sick pay. This lasts for six months, after which the person's employment contract ends and they typically flow onto the main disability benefit, employment support allowance. There is rarely any attempt to support a return to work through workplace adaptation or re-deployment into different functions and also rarely any occupational rehabilitative efforts. For mothers going on maternity, by contrast, their leave paid by employers continues for just six weeks, but they then go onto maternity allowance up until nine months, followed by unpaid leave for another three. The point here is that the ending of maternity pay does not end the employment contract and there is a right of return to the same employer for the first year. There is also a right to request part-time working and financial support for childcare in the welfare system in the low to middle parts of the family income distribution. This has been a huge success for employment, wages, gender equality and productivity. This broad model could be extended to those with health issues, such as: a far longer right of return to the employer, well beyond the end of statutory sick pay; a right to return part-time, a right to request redeployment if the previous job is no longer appropriate; a right to workplace adaptation, and, after say three months of work, a person should be seen by an occupational rehabilitation specialist. A financial support package to the firm should reflect some of the extra costs. This would be funded from lower numbers on disability benefits. But it should be recognised that firms will benefit in the same way as they do with mothers. The loss of skills and knowledge from such separations has a large cost to the employee, as most will never get back to the same levels of seniority in new jobs, as well as to firms and to society in the form of lost potential productivity.

Low Wages

The NMW should be raised as part of this broad agenda. The constraint of potential employment losses will diminish as an issue as unemployment falls to historically low levels over the next few years. However, for any real bite except at the very lowest wages, there needs to be traction on wages beyond the NMW. Living wage campaigns, backed by more extensive use of public procurement conditions in contacts and through firms requiring the Living Wage from suppliers, offer ways of spreading expectations of higher pay levels than the NMW. The Low Pay Commission, which sets the NMW, could do more here to push large sectors where firms are sensitive to reputational issues, such as major retail firms. The aim would be for a non-legally binding higher rate to be set and to challenge major firms to meet it. Pressure to move collectively is easier for firms as it reduces the risk of being undercut by rivals.

Pensions

The NEST pension scheme requires all firms to offer access to pension savings pots with a minimum degree of employer contributions. These are modest to date, with just a minimum 3 per cent of earnings contribution from employers required after 2018, and less before. Management fees are set at 1.8 per cent of new contributions and 0.3 per cent of the fund. This second element is low by industry standards, but generally more could be done to keep management fees down for the now dominant defined contribution pension funds. Raising the minimum employer contribution for employees in NEST schemes looks like a sensible predistribution idea. Expanding the coverage of occupational pensions through NEST-type schemes, backed with restrictions on management fees to make them better value to the low waged and self-employed, should be considered. A bolder idea would be to prevent firms from offering higher levels of employer pension contributions to executives than the rest of the workforce. A one-size model for all the workforce would perhaps encourage firms to offer a better pension deal or induce them to restrict pension payments for their executives. If firms switched from pension payments for executives to regular executive pay, it would generate large revenues for the exchequer.

Charges by Energy Firms

Energy firms charge higher prices to poor customers who do not have resources to pay by direct debits. These are especially marked payment systems such as charge keys for those who have insecure or unstable incomes. Such varying prices for payment systems are increasingly common and penalise the less well off. For energy firms, such pricing policies could be addressed by government-set restrictions. Most likely, this would have a small knock effect for regular customers, but would make a big difference to the poor.

More Challenging

Reducing Britain's Long Tail of School Underachievement

High levels of educational inequality – attainment gaps between high and lower achievers and, all too often, large attainment gaps between rich and poor children – are strongly associated with high levels of earnings inequality.[13] Britain in particular has a long tail of low attainment on international tests. Reducing this long tail and narrowing educational inequalities, thus, offers a strong route to reducing inequality in the labour market. London has achieved astonishing success in narrowing these educational gaps between rich and poor since the late 1990s. Research suggests this is only partly due to high parental aspirations of immigrants who represent a large slice of London's population, but also a marked improvement in London schools in raising educational achievement of poor children.[14] It is not entirely clear what started to go right in London from the late 1990s, but it does suggest that it is possible to reduce educational inequalities over relatively short time periods, that is, under a decade. It is also clear that the lowest attainment of poor (free school meals-eligible) children is not in our deprived northern cities, but in affluent leafy areas like Surrey and Kent. A number of places are launching initiatives to reduce this weakness, and Ofsted is now specifically charged with monitoring poor children's educational performance in schools, not just overall achievement. Furthermore, the pupil premium is giving schools resources to address low attainment for poor children, even though to date it is not hypothecated for addressing this issue. It is the pressure on schools to address this which is rising. Clearly, this is not a quick policy win as it takes years to flow through to lower wage inequalities, but getting it right offers serious hope of transformational change.

Raise Worker Bargaining Power on Wages

More immediate effects could be achieved by raising the bargaining power of workers over wages. Lower unemployment does this naturally, but we saw rising wage inequality in the UK when unemployment was under 5 per cent in the 2000s. Unemployment would have to fall far further for this alone to narrow earnings gaps between high and low earners. Raising bargaining power might be addressed more directly by increasing employment protection legislation, making workers more secure, or increases in the presence of trade unions. However, it is not clear how this might be achieved politically. Furthermore, increased employment protection may well not help the most marginal groups of workers. More plausible, but less ambitious, is restricting the ability of firms to use zero hours and temporary contracts to avoid paying sick and holiday pay, as well as limiting semi-voluntary self-employment, which passes all risks onto workers.

Training in Low Wage Sectors

Low wage sectors are characterised by high job turnover, which discourages both firms and workers from training, as workers are likely to move on too quickly for either party to see returns from the training. Pushing low wage sectors towards long-term and investment-focused employment contracts has long been discussed, but little progress has been made. Rather, the rise of zero hours contracts is symptomatic of instability in low-wage sectors. Low unemployment and the introduction of the NMW and its subsequent increased coverage did not change this pattern in the 2000s, and is unlikely to be any different over the next decade. Most low wage sectors do offer career advancement paths with rungs on the pay ladder, but they involve typically small wage gains and have been subsequently squeezed by the NMW. For a long time, training levies have been a proposed solution, where firms have to pay a wage-related contribution to industry training boards, who then pay firms to train their workforces. These obviously raise wage costs and may lead to valueless or low-quality training, though the boards should seek to prevent that. But they smack of old style tri-partite bodies, from an almost forgotten era. On the other hand, regulations around a trained workforce have transformed the security industry in recent years.

Conclusion

Predistribution offers a framework for policy thinking to address inequality in the primary distribution of work and wages rather than after the fact through taxes and transfers. The policy options in this area are not new, however. Most plausible policy levers in this space have been used to varying degrees and in many cases with some success. What the framework offers, therefore, is not individual policy innovations, though there are some possible angles here, but rather an attempt to construct a broad and coherent policy agenda all focused on the same goals. Yet this is not cost free. Although many policies are not costly in terms of government spending, there are costs borne by some other groups. Importantly, though, is that with predistribution these are more opaque than taxation and thus potentially attract less political resistance. Yet it remains the case that predistribution policies are likely to be far broader in terms of winners and losers than taxes and transfers which can be targeted quite well in terms of the poor or affluent. For instance, a NMW raises earnings for all the low-paid, many of whom are not poor. Tax credits paid to low-income families are targeted on low pay that results in low incomes and as a result can address poverty among a far larger group of the lower paid than a minimum wage ever could. Given this, if there are wider costs, such as lessening economic efficiency that flow from predistribution policies, then this is probably not the optimal strategy. It is where there are wider social benefits or improvements in education, skills and productive potential that such a strategy should focus.

Notes

1. Paul Gregg and Jonathan Wadsworth, 'Unemployment and inactivity in the 2008–2009 recession', in *Economic and Labour Market Review* (London: Office for National Statistics, 2010).
2. Paul Gregg, Stephen Machin, and Mariña Fernández-Salgado, 'The squeeze on real wages – and what it might take to end it', *National Institute of Economic Review*, (2014), *vol. 228, no. 1*. pp. R3-R16.
3. See Gregg et al., 'The squeeze on real wages' or, for a more detailed discussion on these issues, see John Van Reenen and Joao P. Pessao, 'The UK Productivity and Jobs Puzzle: Does the Answer Lie in Labour Market Flexibility?', Special Paper No. 31 (London: Centre for Economic Performance, 2013). Available at: http://cep.lse.ac.uk/pubs/download/special/cepsp31.pdf (accessed 15 March 2015).
4. For example, see Jonathan D. Ostry, Andrew Berg, and Charalambos G. Tsangarides, 'Redistribution, inequality, and growth', IMF Staff Discussion Note, SDB/14/02 (February 2014). Available at http://www.imf.org/external/pubs/ft/sdn/2014/sdn1402.pdf (accessed 21 March 2015).
5. Paul Gregg, Kristine Hansen, and Jonathan Wadsworth, 'The rise of the workless household', in Paul Gregg and Jonathan Wadsworth (eds), *The State of Working Britain* (Manchester: Manchester University Press, 1999).
6. Alan Manning, 'The equal pay act as an experiment to test theories of the labour market', *Economica* 63/250 (1996), pp. 191–212.
7. Susan Harkness, 'Women's employment and household income inequality', in Janet C. Gornick and Markus Jäntii, *Income Inequality: Economic Disparities and the Middle Class in Affluent Countries* (Chicago: Stanford University Press, 2013).
8. Paul Gregg, 'The impact of youth unemployment on adult unemployment in the NCDS', *Economic Journal* 111/475 (2001), pp. 626–53.
9. James Plunkett, Alex Hurrell, and Conor D'Arcy, 'More than a minimum: The review of the minimum wage', Resolution Foundation (2014).
10. See Gregg et al., 'The rise of the workless household'.
11. Centre for Economic and Social Inclusion, Work Programme statistics: Inclusion analysis (2014). Available at http://www.cesi.org.uk/sites/default/files/response_downloads/WP_stats_briefing_SEPT14_MASTER.pdf (accessed 21 March 2015).
12. See Department of Work and Pensions, 'Impacts and costs and benefits of the future jobs fund' (2012) available at http://www.gov.uk/government/uploads/system/uploads/attachment_data/file/223120/impacts_costs_benefits_fjf.pdf (accessed 15 May 2015).
13. Stephen Nickell, 'Poverty and worklessness', *Economic Journal* 114/ 494 (2004), pp. C1–C25.
14. Ellen Greaves, Lindsey Macmillan, and Luke Sibieta, 'Lessons from London schools for attainment gaps and social mobility', Social Mobility and Child Poverty Commission (2014). Available at https://www.gov.uk/government/uploads/system/uploads/attachment_data/file/321969/London_Schools_-_FINAL.pdf (accessed 21 March 2015).

Part III

Predistributive Labour Market Policies

CHAPTER 5

Fostering Equitable Labour Market Outcomes
A Focus on Raising Employment

Paul de Beer

P redistributive policies with respect to the labour market essentially boil down to policies fostering a high employment rate and low unemployment and vacancy rates, that is, a good match of supply and demand. However, even if the labour market is functioning well in this sense, the outcome may still be sub-optimal from a societal point of view if there are large earnings disparities, and/or if career opportunities vary greatly. Consequently, in addition to policies that improve the functioning of the labour market, policies should be put in place that address the outcomes of the labour market in terms of wages and careers. Put differently, predistributive labour market policies should address both the efficiency and the equity of the labour market. Policies that enhance a well-functioning labour market can focus either on fighting unemployment or on raising the employment rate. The former policies mainly address cyclical factors, while the latter concentrate on structural factors. In this contribution, predistributive policies are those that are intended to affect the functioning of labour markets, in particular the interaction of supply and demand and the wage distribution, instead of policies aimed at correcting the unfavourable outcomes of a malfunctioning labour market.

Fighting Unemployment

Fighting unemployment has always been the main goal of labour market policies. Since the 1990s, the OECD and the EU have encouraged their member states to tilt the balance in the field of social policy from passive, protective measures, such as unemployment compensation, to active labour market policies, such as training, counselling and job subsidies.[1] However, despite the broad agreement among scholars and policy-makers that a shift from passive to active measures is indispensable, the evidence that it works is still remarkably scarce. Most evaluation studies of active labour market policies (ALMPs) find only weak positive effects, and sometimes no significant effects or even adverse effects, due to the problems of deadweight loss, lock-in effects and displacement.[2] Moreover, even if specific active measures are shown to be effective for individuals or for small groups, they may not be effective if scaled-up to larger groups. Since most measures contribute primarily to improving the relative labour market position of an individual unemployed person vis-à-vis other unemployed, it is dubious whether such measures would be effective if applied to all unemployed. For example, training may enhance an individual's chance of being hired by an employer, but if all applicants for a vacancy have followed a course, still only one will be hired. Only in case cases where there are skill mismatches, which cause some vacancies to be difficult to fill even in the case of high unemployment, training may contribute to reducing unemployment. However, this seems to be a rather exceptional scenario.

During a downturn, when there is a lack of job openings, most active labour market policies that focus on the supply side are not effective in reducing the total number of unemployed. Only measures which increase the total number of job openings by boosting labour demand will help in reducing the unemployment rate. But few measures are effective in creating more jobs. The main exception is direct job creation in the public sector. However, these measures have been strongly criticised, for example, by the OECD, since they often have a strong lock-in effect, that is, they discourage workers on a subsidised job to seek a regular job in the open labour market.[3] Nevertheless, as long as the recession continues, subsidised jobs at least prevent the unemployed from losing their attachment to the labour market by providing them with the opportunity to maintain their skills and work routine. Moreover, since the workers on subsidised jobs would otherwise have received an unemployment benefit, the additional costs of creating subsidised jobs are relatively modest.

For this reason, it is regrettable that few European countries used direct job creation as a measure to reduce unemployment during the current crisis. According to OECD data, only Finland, Hungary, Ireland, Luxembourg, and Portugal increased the number of participants in the category of direct job creation between 2008 and 2012. In seven countries, the number of subsidised jobs was even reduced.[4]

Apart from the measures taken immediately after the outbreak of the financial crisis in 2008 and 2009, remarkably few efforts have been made in the current crisis to stimulate employment directly. Due to the strong emphasis on financial consolidation and reduction of budget deficits, EU countries have failed to take anti-cyclical macroeconomic measures that might have

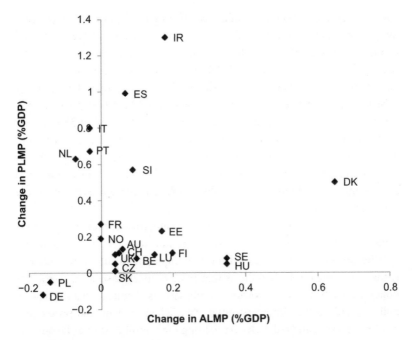

FIGURE 5.1 Change in expenditure on active labour market policies (ALMP) and passive labour market policies (PLMP) as % of GDP from 2008 until 2012. IR (Iran), ES (Spain), IT (Italy), PT (Portugal), NL (Netherlands), SI (Slovenia), DK (Denmark), FR (France), NO (Norway), EE (Estonia), AU (Australia), CH (Switzerland), UK (United Kingdom), CZ (Czech Republic), SK (Slovakia), BE (Belgium), LU (Luxembourg), FI (Finland), SE (Sweden), HU (Hungary), PL (Poland), DE (Germany)
Source: OECD Statistics (Labour market programmes).

cushioned the crisis aftershocks in the labour market. As a consequence, a sharp rise in unemployment increased the need for redistributive policies, such as unemployment compensation and poverty alleviation. Figure 5.1 shows that in many European countries, public expenditure on passive measures, in particular unemployment compensation, increased considerably more between 2008 and 2012 than expenditure on active measures. Denmark, Sweden, and Hungary are the main exceptions to this rule.

Raising Employment

In the long term, increasing the employment rate is a more important goal of predistributive labour market policies than fighting unemployment.

Even though the Lisbon target of an overall employment rate of 70 per cent by 2010 has not been achieved, most EU member states have succeeded in raising the employment rate over the last 15 years. However, this was mainly due to a rise of the female labour participation rate. Between 2000 and 2010, the overall employment rate in the EU (excluding Croatia) was raised from 62 to 64 per cent of the population aged 15–64. This was entirely due to the increase of the female employment rate from 54 to 58 per cent, since the male employment rate declined slightly from 71 to 70 per cent.[5] The rise of female labour participation was, however, largely an autonomous development, related to the rise of educational attainment of women and socio-cultural developments. The role of government policies has probably been moderate, at best.

The large cross-country differences in the employment rate nevertheless show that policy matters. However, it is not easy to pin down which policies are most effective in raising the employment rate. Most likely, it is the appropriate mix of policies that matters most, instead of particular policies as such. Therefore, various combinations of education and training policies, childcare facilities, parental leave schemes, dismissal protection, minimum wages and collective bargaining may result in similar favourable outcomes, as the experiences of Denmark, Sweden, the Netherlands, and Austria have shown.

In the past ten years, it has become vogue to characterise a successful policy mix as a 'flexicurity' strategy. Denmark and the Netherlands have repeatedly been presented as examples of effective flexicurity policies. However, one should realise that flexicurity is not a coherent policy concept, but rather a term that stresses two important goals of effective labour market policies – a flexible (although I would prefer to use the term adaptable) labour market, and sufficient employment and income security. Denmark and the Netherlands show that quite different policy mixes might result in similar outcomes in terms of employment and unemployment rate. Thus, instead of being a recipe for improving labour market performance, the term flexicurity points to the need to address both the adaptability of the labour market and the security of workers at the same time. The problem is, however, that most policy advice under the guise of flexicurity stresses the first element – flexibility – much more than the second element – security. This is partly understandable, since governments can increase labour market flexibility, for example by relaxing employment protection legislation, while it is much more difficult to ensure employment security. Since a more flexible labour market will not automatically create more employment security – that is exactly why the flexicurity concept stresses both components – it is essential that flexicurity policies do not at the same time reduce income protection (i.e. passive, redistributive measures) and employment protection. A really successful flexicurity mix should enhance labour market adaptability while at the same time enhancing employment and income protection.

A comparison between the Netherlands and Denmark is illustrative in this respect. Dutch labour market policies are characterised by a large discrepancy between employment protection for permanent and for temporary contracts and by a relatively generous system of unemployment compensation, including unemployment benefits with a maximum duration of 38 months (although this will be reduced to 24 months in the near future). Dutch employment protection legislation has stimulated a strong increase in the use of flexible contracts. In the Netherlands, 20 per cent of Dutch employees are employed on a fixed-term contract (including temp agency work), the third highest figure in the EU, after Poland and Portugal.[6] This has created a flexible labour market in which employers can quickly adjust their workforce to changing circumstances. At the same time, employees on a permanent contract are well protected. In the event they are dismissed nevertheless, they receive a relatively generous unemployment benefit of 70 per cent of their former wage for a period of up to three years and two months. However, flexible workers who lose their job are often entitled to only a short-term unemployment benefit or no unemployment benefit at all since they do not comply with the qualifying period. So, the flexibility of the labour market and strong employment and income protection for the majority of employees comes with a price for the group of flexworkers.

In Denmark, the flexibility of the labour market is the result of relatively weak employment protection for all employees, both on permanent and on temporary contracts. As a result, employers do not seek refuge in using flexible contracts, but trust that they can quickly adjust their workforce by dismissing permanent staff. As a consequence, only 9 per cent of Danish employees are employed on a temporary contract. Just as in the Netherlands, the Danish unemployment compensation system is relatively generous, although the maximum duration of unemployment benefits is limited to two years. Due to intensive active labour market programmes, most unemployed succeed in finding a new job relatively quickly. Thus, in contrast to the Netherlands, Denmark spreads the flexibility of the labour market more evenly among the whole labour force.

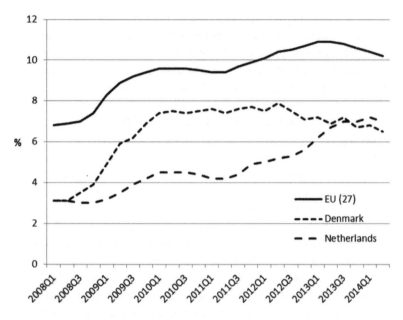

FIGURE 5.2 Quarterly unemployment rates (seasonally adjusted) from 2008 until 2014 for Denmark, the Netherlands, and the EU (excluding Croatia).
Source: Eurostat Statistics (Labour Market; LFS Main Indicators).

As Figure 5.2 shows, a disadvantage of the flexible Danish labour market is that unemployment rose very quickly at the beginning of the economic crisis in 2009. However, the unemployment rate started to decline in 2012 as the Dutch and the average European unemployment rate were still rising. As a consequence, the Dutch and the Danish unemployment rate were almost equal again at the end of 2013, just as they were on the eve of the crisis. Nevertheless, the average unemployment rate over the past five years was much lower in the Netherlands than in Denmark.

A closer examination shows that the strong increase of Danish unemployment in 2009 was not due to a larger inflow of dismissed workers into unemployment, but to a smaller outflow out of unemployment. In other words, employers did not increase their layoffs, but simply reduced the number of hirings. As a consequence, the share of long-term unemployed (unemployment duration of more than 12 months) increased sharply in Denmark, from less than 10 per cent in the beginning of 2009 to over 30 per cent at the end of 2012. It was only in 2013 that the number of people who left unemployment started to grow again. In the Netherlands, the unemployment rate initially increased in 2009 due to a small increase in the inflow into unemployment. From 2012 onwards, the further increase of the unemployment rate was mainly due to a drop in the outflow from unemployment to work.

This comparison between Denmark and the Netherlands shows that different labour market institutions can cause different dynamics regarding employment and unemployment, but nevertheless result in a similar performance with respect to labour market outcomes.

Fostering Equitable Labour Market Outcomes

Even if a labour market functions well, in the sense that employment is high, unemployment is low and the labour market adjusts quickly to a changing environment, the outcome can still be undesirable or even unacceptable in terms of income inequality and/or career opportunities. The question I address in the second part of this chapter is to what extent predistributive policies can redress or prevent these unfavourable labour market outcomes.

The difficulty with respect to earnings differentials is that they are partly efficient and productive and partly inefficient and unproductive. A well-functioning labour market needs earnings differentials as an incentive mechanism to allocate workers efficiently among the available jobs. Moreover, performance-related earnings can foster productivity and stimulate workers to invest in education and training. However, whereas some incentives are indispensable, others may have adverse or even perverse effects. The roots of the financial crisis have rightfully been traced partially to perverse incentive mechanisms in the banking sector. As Robert Frank and Philip Cook have already shown in their 1995 book *The Winner-Take-All-Society*, increasing reliance on pay schemes that are based on relative performance can give the wrong incentives, that is, incentives which are economically inefficient. If workers are paid according to their relative performance, they may be able to raise their pay by improving their own performance as well as by hindering the performance of their colleagues who at the same time become their competitors. Individual performance pay may be detrimental to cooperation, which is an important source of innovation.

Moreover, it may result in excessive investment in competences which have a small societal (aggregate) payoff, but a high expected individual payoff, since individuals do not take account of the negative effect of their own effort towards the (expected) returns of their competitors' efforts.

This is a case of negative externalities, which are best addressed by taxing them. Consequently, progressive taxation of incomes is not just a matter of redistribution, but may also have a favourable predistributive impact by discouraging very high executive pay. Indeed, Piketty et al. find a negative correlation between the top income tax rate and the share of (before-tax) top incomes in total income, which demonstrates that higher taxation of top incomes may also affect the market incomes of top executives.[7] Indeed, they argue that a top rate of over 80 per cent may be optimal from the perspective of social welfare.

Predistributive policies may also be directed at the other end of the earnings distribution, that is, the minimum wage. Although there is general agreement that a mandatory minimum wage reduces earnings inequality, there is much more debate on the impact on low-wage employment and, therefore, on the total income distribution. If raising the minimum wage would raise the wage of part of the minimum wage employees, while making another part of them jobless, the total impact on the income distribution is ambiguous. The lower the current minimum wage relative to the median wage, the smaller the likely negative impact on low-wage employment. Thus, for countries with a comparatively low minimum wage, raising the minimum wage is a rather innocuous way of reducing earnings differentials. Countries with a relatively high minimum wage probably have to pay a price for raising the minimum wage by accepting some job loss among the low paid. Unfortunately, it is not clear above which level raising the minimum wage will have a detrimental effect on low paid unemployment.

In addition to focusing on top incomes and low paid workers, one could consider policies that affect middle income groups. There is evidence that wage differentials within occupational groups or within educational categories have grown, too. This may be due to a growing importance of individual performance pay. Gradually, trade unions seem to have accepted that annual pay rises are (partially) conditional on individual performance assessment. In addition, profit-related remuneration and bonuses may also play a role, which can cause wage differentials between similar workers in different companies to increase. There does not seem to be a role for governments to intervene directly in such remuneration systems. However, unions should consider to what extent they are willing to accept such schemes in collective agreements. Of course, if performance or profit-related pay gives the right incentives, it may enhance productivity and, thus, benefit both the workers and the company.

A more promising alternative might be the introduction of profit-sharing schemes which are not paid out in cash but in shares. If these shares are deposited in a fund which is collectively managed by the employees of the firm, they may gradually accrue an increasing share in the equity of the company. In this way, they may gain more control over the management of the company and may thus, for example, influence the pay of top executives. Moreover, employee stock ownership reduces the dependence of the company on external investors and may, consequently, tilt the balance from short-term to long-term interests. Actually, employee share ownership would imply that the sharp dividing line between labour and capital is blurred, since the workers also become capital owners. After more than a century of struggle between labour and capital, this might usher in a new phase of capitalism, in which employees gradually conquer control over capital and, consequently, over the management of private companies. In view of the much discussed prediction of Piketty[8] that the relative size and concentration of capital will grow in the future, this strategy would be an attractive alternative for Piketty's plea for a global progressive wealth tax.[9] After all, the problem is not the size of wealth, but its highly lopsided distribution across the population. For social democrats, the question should therefore be how a more balanced wealth distribution can be achieved, without impeding the growth of wealth. Remarkably enough, progressive politicians have only recently considered this question. Assuming that direct dispossession ('socialisation') of private wealth is not an option (because it represents a breach of private ownership rights), wealth should be distributed by promoting the accrual of wealth among employees who currently have little or none.

A Dualisation of Labour Markets

A final issue that should be addressed is the (increasing) dualisation of labour markets between insiders and outsiders – the cleavage between workers with a well-protected permanent job, and temporary contract and self-employed workers. The latter category not only lacks protection against dismissal, but in many cases is not entitled to unemployment compensation or sick pay either. Labour economists who point to this cleavage usually recommend relaxation of the employment protection legislation for workers on permanent contracts. Indeed, in some countries the permanent workforce may be so well-protected that it discourages employers to offer a permanent contract to new staff. However, in most countries, relaxing dismissal protection for permanent workers may simply mean that job security for the insiders is weakened without improving career opportunities for the outsiders.

The main problem does not seem to be the strict protection of workers with long tenure as such, but the sharp dividing line between temporary contracts and permanent contracts. As a consequence, employers are forced to make an explicit decision whether to offer a worker a temporary contract or a permanent contract. In a time of economic uncertainty and volatile demand, most employers are reluctant to offer a permanent contract to a new worker to avoid the risk of having to pay redundancy or severance pay in case they need to downsize their staff. A more attractive alternative would be to abolish the distinction between permanent and temporary contracts, and introduce a new kind of indeterminate or indefinite contract. Dismissal protection and the right to severance pay would then gradually increase with tenure, so that employees are better protected the longer they have been working for the same employer. However, there would be no sharp dividing line between a temporary and a permanent contract any more, so the employer would no longer have to choose between offering a newly-hired employee a temporary contract or a permanent contract. Newly-hired employees would then get the opportunity to show their capacity and develop their competences within the same company. Still, the employer would be able to dismiss a worker if s/he does not function well or if demand falters, without excessive dismissal costs.

Conclusion

The idea of creating the preconditions for a well-functioning labour market instead of correcting and compensating the unfavourable consequences of a malfunctioning labour market is attractive. However, on closer inspection, it is not so easy to determine which predistributive policies are effective in raising employment, lowering unemployment, increasing the adaptability of the labour market and reducing disparities in the distribution of wages and career opportunities. There is not one specific labour market instrument that is clearly superior to others. In general, the effectiveness depends on the specific policy mix, the combination of different measures. Different policy mixes may result in similar labour market outcomes, although each has its specific trade-offs, as the examples of Denmark and the Netherlands have shown. So there is not one best predistributive policy that can be copied by other countries. Moreover, even in the countries with the highest employment rate and the lowest unemployment rate, a significant proportion of the labour force can still be out of work, in particular during a recession. Therefore, predistributive labour market policies will never make redistributive policies, in particular unemployment compensation, redundant.

When it comes to predistributive policies for reducing the inequality of earnings, raising the mandatory minimum wage is the most obvious measure, but it is only effective up to a certain point. With respect to top incomes, progressive taxation – actually a kind of redistributive measure – may also have the desired predistributive effect of reducing before-tax top incomes. A very different but promising predistributive policy may be the introduction of collective employee share ownership. This may help in levelling the very unequal wealth distribution and at the same time give employees more control over management.

Finally, in order to close the gap between labour market insiders and outsiders, the introduction of a new indeterminate employment contract is a credible option. If employment protection gradually increases with tenure, employers no longer have to decide between offering a temporary contract or a permanent contract to their employees. Thus, there will no longer be a sharp dividing line between flexworkers and permanent workers.

I conclude that there is not a clear distinction between predistributive and redistributive labour market policies. Some redistributive policies, such as progressive taxation of top incomes, may have favourable predistributive consequences. Some predistributive policies may, if they are effective, reduce the need for redistributive policies, such as unemployment compensation, but they will never be able to replace these compensatory measures completely. Ultimately, the best policy mix will be a balanced combination of both predistributive and redistributive measures.

Notes

1. John P. Martin, 'What works among active labour market policies: evidence form OECD countries' experience', *OECD Economic Studies* 30 (2000), pp. 79–113.

2. David Card, Jochen Kluve, and Andrea Weber, 'Active labour market policy evaluations: a meta-analysis', *The Economic Journal* 120 (2010), pp. 452–77.

3. Martin 'What works among active labour market policies', Card et al., 'Active labour market policy evaluations'.

4. OECD StatExtracts. Available at http://stats.oecd.org/ (accessed 15 May 2015).

5. Eurostat Statistics. Available at http://epp.eurostat.ec.europa.eu/portal/page/portal/statistics/search_database (accessed 15 May 2015).

6. *Ibid.*

7. Thomas Piketty, Emmanuel Saez, and Stefanie Stantcheva, 'Optimal taxation of top labor incomes: A tale of three elasticities', NBER Working Paper 17616 (Cambridge, MA: NBER, 2011). Available at http://www.nber.org/papers/w17616 (accessed 21 March 2015).

8. Thomas Piketty, *Capital in the Twenty-First Century* (Cambridge: Harvard University Press, 2014).

9. Paul de Beer, 'What can we learn from Piketty?', in Paul de Beer and Wiemer Salverda, *Piketty in the Netherlands: the first reception*, AIAS Paper Series on the Labour Market and Industrial Relations in the Netherlands 2014–16 (Amsterdam: Amsterdam Institute for Advanced Labour Studies, 2014), pp. 9–20.

CHAPTER 6

Labour Market Flexibility and Income Security in Old Age

The Policy and Political Challenges of Pension Reform

Karen M. Anderson

L abour market and pension system reform have been important items on national political agendas across Europe for three decades. Governments have recalibrated, and sometimes slashed, pension benefits not only to reduce public expenditure, but also to increase incentives for individuals to retire later and sometimes even to continue working beyond the statutory retirement age. Similarly, policy-makers – encouraged by policy expertise from organisations like the OECD – have targeted 'rigid' labour markets for reform. A key rationale behind both reform trends is the belief that reform is necessary to make both pension systems and labour markets 'fit' for demographic change and globalisation.

Most analyses of labour market and pension reform emphasise the neoliberal direction of recent policy changes[1] and their negative consequences for inequality and social inclusion.[2] To be sure, many recent reforms have reduced pension benefit generosity and employment protection, but there is considerable variation in the extent to which reforms have targeted 'vices' (social policies that generate unintended inequities) and attempted to turn them into 'virtues' (increased protection for excluded groups).[3] This chapter focuses on national reform trajectories that draw on the 'vice into virtue' strategy and thereby promote a predistributive agenda. A predistribution approach emphasises the prevention of inequality before it occurs, for example, by investing in education and skills, creating inclusive labour markets, and providing adequate income during periods outside of the labour market, especially retirement.

In hindsight, the three decades following the end of World War II were unusual, with their high birth rates, steady economic growth, and high levels of employment for full-time breadwinners. The introduction and/or expansion of generous, pay-as-you-go (PAYGO) pensions were plausible policy choices in the context of economic growth and favourable old-age dependency ratios. Indeed, in 1960, the average total fertility rate (number of children per woman) in Europe was 2.59.[4] Analysts also viewed the old-age dependency ratio with indifference: in 1960, the standard cut-off between work and retirement was age 60, yielding an old-age dependency ratio of 29.3 per cent. The mid-1970s saw the first signs that the high fertility, high employment, high growth equilibrium had begun to give way to a period of economic and demographic uncertainty. By 2012, the total fertility rate had fallen to 1.58 in the EU-28.[5] Developments in the labour market were equally dramatic: persistent unemployment and widespread labour-shedding threatened to become permanent features of many European economies, especially on the continent. In keeping with the widespread repudiation of labour-shedding policies in the 1990s and 2000s, analysts began using a cut-off of 65 years to calculate the old-age dependency ratio. Even with this new definition, the trend was no less dramatic: the old-age dependency ratio increased from 20.6 per cent in 1990 to 26.1 per cent in 2010.[6]

The comparative welfare state literature has been slow to recognise the interactive effects of labour market and pension reform. There are important exceptions to this,[7] but it is fair to say that most analyses have focused on the political and economic drivers of reform or the distributional effects of *either* pension reform or labour market reform. An emerging literature shows, however, that the interaction of labour market flexibility and pension system recalibration generates very different distributional and political effects. And one of the most important causes of variable effects concerns institutional design. As recent research shows, the countries that have been most successful in combining labour market flexibility (albeit at different levels) and old age income security have, first, a generous, flat rate basic pension, quasi-mandatory, contractual occupational pensions and, secondly, a mix of labour market policies that emphasise dual or one and a half earner households and active labour market policies.[8] The Nordic countries (especially Denmark and Sweden) and the Netherlands have been particularly successful at combining flexible labour markets and security in old age. The following sections will discuss the reform trajectories of these 'success stories' in the European context. I will highlight aspects of policy design that may be transferable to other countries, paying particular attention to the political challenges associated with labour market and pension reform.

The Keys to Success in Northern Europe

Although most European countries face similar demographic and fiscal pressures, there has been large variation in policy responses because of different national institutional starting points and the role of electoral politics in translating reform pressures into concrete reforms. It is important to emphasise that Denmark, the Netherlands and Sweden now benefit handsomely from policy choices made decades ago for political reasons in vastly different economic contexts.[9] All three countries introduced flat-rate basic pensions more than 50 years ago. These institutional choices shaped the subsequent development of pension provision: contractual occupational pensions emerged early in the Netherlands and developed parallel to the basic pension introduced in 1957. In Denmark, political stalemate surrounding contractual pensions left a policy vacuum in the 1960s and 1970s, creating incentives for governments to expand basic pension provision. The extensive system of collectively bargained 'labour market pensions' that has emerged since the 1980s was layered on top of a generous basic pension. In Sweden, the 1957 ATP (*allmänna tilläggspensionen*, or supplementary pension) reform created statutory earnings-related pensions to supplement the existing basic pension. Swedish reforms since the 1990s preserve this general orientation, but benefits are more actuarial and there are mandatory individual investment accounts in the statutory system.[10]

All three countries also benefit from early institutional choices concerning active labour market policy (ALMP). Sweden is a well-known pioneer in this area: ALMPs have been a core component of economic policy since the 1950s. Denmark and the Netherlands joined the ALMP bandwagon somewhat later, adopting 'flexicurity' reforms in the 1990s and 2000s that aimed to tap unused labour reserves (Dutch women) and activate the unemployed and disabled.[11]

Despite these favourable starting points, governments in all three countries have somewhat scaled back their commitment to active labour market policy in the last decade, especially Sweden. As Ingrid Esser shows in her contribution to this volume, Sweden devoted approximately 75 per cent of its pre-1990 spending on labour market policy to active measures such as training. Between 1990 and 2010, spending on active measures has decreased by one-third, and this has occurred in the context of a general decrease in expenditure on active labour market policies. The Netherlands and Denmark have also retreated somewhat from their commitment to active labour market policies (these are called 're-integration policies' in the

Netherlands). Although spending as a percentage of GDP remains relatively high (between 1 and 2 per cent of GDP) in both countries, governments have tightened eligibility, reduced cash benefits, and now place more emphasis on the job search itself rather than training.[12]

The key point here is that all three countries made institutional choices decades ago that have turned out to be effective policy responses to the demographic and economic uncertainty of the 2010s. Moreover, all three countries have been able to adapt these core institutions to economic and demographic trends, although this is somewhat less true of the Netherlands. I return to this point below. To summarise the central elements of this strategy: a basic pension[13] provides minimum income security for all residents, and quasi-mandatory contractual pensions that cover most workers' top-up statutory benefits. Labour market outsiders are thus guaranteed minimum income security, and middle and higher income groups enjoy benefits related to their standard of living in employment. Moreover, the tax system, social service programs, and labour market policy combine to create very strong incentives for paid employment: households can rely on tax-financed, high quality day care and elder care in Denmark and Sweden (social services such as day care are less developed in the Netherlands compared to Sweden and Denmark). The Danish and Swedish tax systems are based on individual taxation (tax benefits in the Netherlands for non-working spouses will not be phased out until 2024) and an extensive system of training and re-integration programs aims to speed the re-entry of the unemployed and sick/disabled into paid employment. In short, the complex of social security, labour market and tax policies in all three countries is intended to maximise employment, and there is adequate (even generous: the Dutch and Danish basic pensions) pension provision for those with atypical employment biographies. Women, especially mothers, face very strong work incentives in Denmark and Sweden, and the extensive child care system facilitates full-time or near full-time work.[14] In contrast, Dutch women tend to work few hours, even if their aggregate labour market participation rates are high. Women are thus more likely to be economically independent in Sweden and Denmark than in the Netherlands.

A glance at poverty statistics for different age groups demonstrates the strong performance of all three models. Figure 6.1 below shows the proportion of those people aged 65 and over at risk of poverty according to Eurostat data (income below 60 per cent of equalised median income after taxes and transfers in 2012). The social democratic welfare regimes are grouped at the left of the figure. Among the affluent European democracies, the Netherlands achieves a very low level of poverty risk in old age (about 5 per cent of households are at

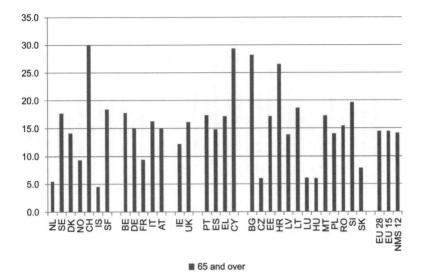

FIGURE 6.1   A.r.o. poverty rates for those aged 65 and over, 2012 (60 per cent of equalised median income).
Note: EU 28 – all 28 EU countries; EU 15 – 15 original EU countries; NMS 12 – 12 New Member States.

risk of poverty). This is an impressive achievement, and it is largely due to the effects of the generous basic pension. Denmark and Sweden's performances are less impressive, but nonetheless respectable. Figure 6.2 compares at risk of (a.r.o.) poverty rates among those over 65 to those of working age and Figure 6.3 shows the difference in a.r.o. poverty rates between both groups. There is considerable heterogeneity across Europe in terms of the effectiveness of labour market institutions and pension schemes in generating incomes above the poverty line, both during employment and during retirement.

The results do not support the conclusion that pensioners are consistently worse off in terms of income than the working population across Europe. Figure 6.3 demonstrates this most clearly because it shows the percentage point difference in poverty rates between the two groups. A negative score indicates the extent (in percentage points) to which pensioners as a group are worse off than the working population. A positive score (in percentage points) indicates the extent to which pensioners, as a group, are better off than the working population. For example, the a.r.o. poverty rate for the Dutch working population was 10.1 per cent while the rate for those aged 65 and over was 5.5 per cent. This yields a difference in a.r.o. poverty rates of 4.6

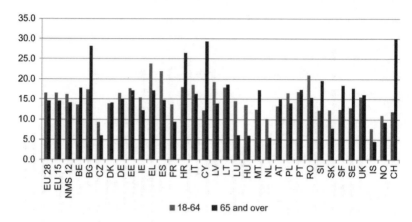

FIGURE 6.2   A.r.o. poverty rates of 18–64 yr olds and 65+, 2012 (60 per cent of median equalised income).

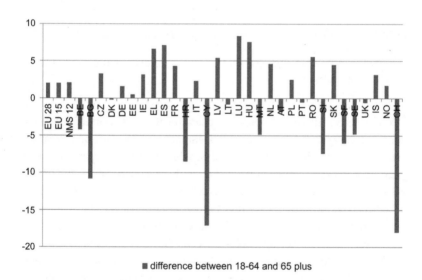

FIGURE 6.3   Difference in a.r.o. poverty rates between 18–64 yr olds and 65+, 2012.

percentage points; Dutch pensioners as a group face considerably less poverty risk than the working population. The opposite trend is visible for Sweden. The a.r.o. poverty rate for the working population was 12.9 per cent while the rate for those aged 65 and over was 17.7 per cent , yielding a difference of −4.8 percentage points. In Denmark, the difference in a.r.o. poverty rates is nearly zero. These results suggest that we should be wary of general statements concerning intergenerational conflict fuelled by differences in income security between workers and pensioners.

Will these current trends hold for the future? OECD data makes it possible to forecast trends in pension income decades into the future. The forecasts are based on pension rules for 2012, and they obviously depend on assumptions about the rate of return in pension systems and inflation, so the results should be viewed with caution. Figures 6.4 and 6.5 show the projected net pension replacement rates for single earners entering the labour market in 2012 with a full career, that is, retiring around the year 2057. The OECD calculated replacement rates for three types of earner: 50 per cent of average wages, and 150 per cent of average wages for both men and women. Figure 6.4 shows that in social democratic pension regimes, the Danish model will continue to provide strong coverage for male and female less-than-average earners (a replacement rate well over 100 per cent); the Dutch system will provide high replacement rates for all three groups (for both men and women); the Swedish results are more mixed. Low income earners and high income earners have higher replacement rates than those with average wages. Figure 6.5 shows results for the same groups in conservative/corporatist regimes. Two things are surprising: the Belgian pension system is notably redistributive (higher replacement rate for those earning half of average wages), and the German pension system provides consistently low (50–60 per cent of average wages) replacement rates for all groups.[15] These

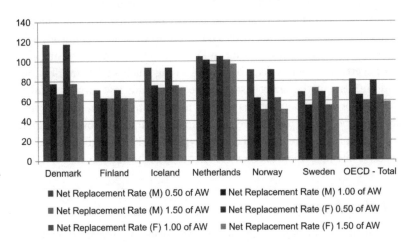

FIGURE 6.4 Net replacement rates (M/F) in SD regimes with full career (2012 labour market entrants).

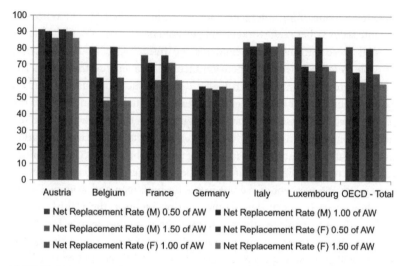

FIGURE 6.5   Net replacement rates (M/F) in conservative regimes (2012 LM entrants).

data suggest that there is considerable variation in terms of the income security provided by different types of pension regimes, and even within these regimes, there is heterogeneity.

Figures 6.4 and 6.5 do not consider those with atypical employment biographies, so analysts can only rely on forecasts carried out by country specialists that consider different typical and atypical biographies. Research in this area shows very clearly that labour market reforms that increase atypical employment at the lower end of the wage scale in countries with conservative/Bismarckian pension systems are a recipe for increasing old-age poverty.[16] Pension systems based on a strong link between contributions and entitlements naturally disadvantage those with low earnings, unless the state or industrial relations steps in to repair these gaps. Thus, even if the conservative/corporatist welfare regimes continue to provide adequate protection for those with a full career, atypical workers and those with long spells of unemployment are likely to fall below the poverty line.

A Policy Agenda

As noted, the northern European success stories are difficult to emulate. However, the experiences of Sweden, Denmark, and the Netherlands suggest several lessons that are potentially transferable to other countries.

1. The single most important way to provide income security in retirement for labour market outsiders (atypical workers, those with outdated skills, those with long spells of unemployment) is to guarantee a minimum income in old age. This is obviously costly, and it is not clear that, for example, the Netherlands can sustain the levels of spending required to keep its basic pension at its current level as the number of retirees grows. Reform of the public pension has been on the political agenda since the 1990s, but it is extremely unpopular. The most likely policy response is to continue the trend toward 'fiscalising' the pension by increasing the general revenue share of financing relative to the share financed by earmarked income taxes which pensioners do not pay.

   The Danish and Swedish approaches offer more possibilities for emulation. The mix of policies in both countries maximises employment so that earnings-related pensions provide a large (Sweden) or growing (Denmark) share of retirement income, thereby decreasing the importance of basic pension provision for many retirees. This is more true of Sweden than it is for Denmark. The Swedish basic pension (the 'guarantee pension') is pension-tested in the sense that it is payable only when an individual has little or no other pension income. The earnings-related public pension and collectively bargained, quasi-mandatory occupational pensions provide the bulk of income for a large majority of pensioners. To the extent that the Swedish approach to employment maximisation is successful, the importance of the guarantee pension decreases. The Danish basic pension pays a fairly generous amount, but pension-tested supplements are very important, especially for those with atypical earnings profiles or no contractual pension.

   In short, the key to the success of all three countries in reducing poverty in old age and maintaining the standard of living of retirees is their reliance on generous state pension provision combined with collectively organised occupational pensions.

2. Maximising employment (as in the Nordic countries) means strengthening work incentives. This sounds neoliberal, but the Swedish/Danish approach is to limit or phase out derived social security rights (in public schemes) and tax benefits and to base statutory social security on employment history. These policies are flanked by education and training policies that aim to train and re-train workers in response to technological and economic change. Despite some deterioration in the scope and content of ALMPs, they continue to perform a vital function. Moreover, as discussed earlier, the very high labour market participation

rates among men and women in Sweden and Denmark result in adequate entitlement to social security and pension benefits, thereby reducing the likelihood of poverty among the working-age population and retirees.

3. Move away from the intergenerational contract. Both the Swedish and Danish pension provision approaches are based on intragenerational solidarity rather than intergenerational solidarity. Basic pension provision is tax-financed, and occupational pensions are a notional defined contribution (NDC) scheme (Sweden) or a collective defined contribution scheme (Denmark). In contrast, Swedish contractual occupational pensions are defined contribution (DC). This approach implies more income inequality in retirement than in a statutory system like the old Swedish ATP pension scheme. Indeed, there are rumblings of political conflict concerning the unequal pension outcomes generated by the reformed Swedish pension system.[17] The lesson here is that a collectively designed, mandatory DC scheme has the potential to produce acceptable distributional outcomes in the context of progressive taxation. Moreover, it decreases the potential for intergenerational conflict.

4. Introduce DC schemes that include non-standard workers. The Swedish, Danish, and Dutch pension systems already do this (although Dutch contractual pensions are still largely *defined benefit*) to a large extent. Wide collective bargaining coverage is a prerequisite for these models. In countries lacking wide collective bargaining coverage, the answer may be to require employment contracts to include mandatory pension savings accounts administered within a statutory framework that limits administrative fees. Here the Swedish, Danish, and Dutch approaches are instructive because the financial sector's profit-making opportunities are limited. Collective actors in all three countries, as well as the state in Sweden, negotiate the terms under which financial institutions market their products, and use their negotiating power to keep administrative costs low. Germany's Riester pensions are an example of a model that should not be emulated because there are fewer limits on the activities of financial institutions offering Riester products.

Conclusion

The central argument of this chapter is that it is possible to combine labour market flexibility with income security in old age. The experiences of Sweden, Denmark, and the Netherlands demonstrate that one effective approach is to combine employment-maximising policies with multi-pillar pension provision. This approach rests on several integrated elements: individual taxation and social security entitlement, active labour market policies that provide training and coaching to those outside of the labour market, a basic pension that provides an adequate income in retirement, and collectively organised occupational pensions that provide income related to previous earnings. This policy mix is predistributive because it creates the conditions under which individuals can earn an adequate income during their working life and retire with a pension that, at a minimum, provides a basic level of income protection regardless of their employment history, and at a maximum, pays a benefit that mirrors their standard of living while in employment.

However, this particular policy mix is not easily transferred from the small states of northern Europe to other countries. First, active labour market policies and basic pension provision require extensive financial resources. Even governments with the political will to enact such policies may find themselves stymied by fiscal constraints. Second, the employment maximisation strategy, even for mothers, may not enjoy widespread partisan support, especially among christian democrats. Finally, the multi-pillar pension approach sketched here depends on robust collective bargaining institutions and strong state regulation of occupational pensions. These preconditions may be difficult to reproduce elsewhere.

Despite the effectiveness of the employment-maximising, multi-pillar strategy, the last decade has witnessed a modest retreat from some of its central elements, especially in Sweden and the Netherlands, signalling the extent of the political challenge involved. Both countries' commitment to active labour market policy has waned, largely because of the political decline of social democracy. Both countries have reduced income support for the unemployed, and job-seekers face much tougher incentives to take up employment. This does not augur well for the political support necessary to sustain a commitment to both labour flexibility and income security in old age.

Notes

1. On labour markets, see Bruno Palier and Kathleen Thelen, 'Institutionalizing dualism: complementarities and change in France and Germany', *Politics and Society* 38/1 (2010), pp. 119–48.
2. On pensions, see Traute Meyer, Paul Bridgen, and Barbara Riedmüller (eds), *Private Pensions Versus Social Inclusion? Non-state Arrangements for Citizens at Risk in Europe* (Cheltenham: Edward Elgar, 2007).
3. Jonah D. Levy, 'Vice into virtue? Progressive politics and welfare reform in continental Europe', *Politics and Society* 27/2 (1997), pp. 239–73.

4. Eurostat, *Population Statistics* (Luxembourg: Office for Official Publications of the European Communities, 2004).
5. Eurostat, http://www.eurostat.eu (accessed 15 May 2015).
6. *Ibid.*
7. Karl Hinrichs and Matteo Jessoula (eds), *Labour Market Flexibility and Pension Reforms* (Basingstoke: Palgrave Macmillan, 2012).
8. *Ibid.;* Traute Meyer, *Beveridge statt Bismarck!* (Berlin: Friedrich Ebert Stiftung, 2013).
9. Herman M. Schwartz, 'The Danish 'miracle': luck, pluck or stuck?' *Comparative Political Studies* 34/2 (2001), pp. 131–55.
10. For information on policy trajectories, see Ellen M. Immergut, Karen M. Anderson, and Isabelle Schulze (eds), *The Handbook of West European Pension Politics* (Oxford: Oxford University Press, 2007).
11. On Denmark, see Erik Albaek, Leslie C. Eliason, Asbjørn Sonne Norgaard, and Herman M. Schwartz, *Crisis, Miracles and Beyond. Negotiated Adaptation of the Danish Welfare State* (Aarhus: Aarhus University Press, 2008). On the Netherlands, see Jelle Visser and Anton Hemerijck, *A Dutch Miracle* (Amsterdam: Amsterdam University Press, 1997).
12. On the Netherlands, see Patricia Van Echtelt and Edith Josten, 'Werken voor je geld' in Vic Veldeer, Jedid-Jah Jonker, Lonneke Van Noije, and Cok Vrooman (eds) *Een beroep op de burger. Minder verzorgingsstaat, meer eigen verantwoordelijkheid? Sociaal en Cultureel Rapport 2012* (Den Haag: Sociaal en Cultureel Planbureau, 2012), pp. 95–139.
13. There are important differences in the design of the basic pension in the three countries: it is fairly high in the Netherlands and Denmark (about 1,000 euros per month for a single pensioner) but lower in Sweden. The size of the basic pension is partly dependent on other pension income in Denmark and Sweden (see the chapters in Immergut, Anderson, and Schulze, 2007).
14. Kimberly Morgan, *Working Mothers and the State* (Palo Alto: Stanford University Press, 2007).
15. Paul Bridgen and Traute Meyer, 'The liberalisation of the German social model: public-private pension reform in Germany since 2001', *Journal of Social Policy* 43/1 (2014), pp. 37–68; Meyer, *Beveridge statt Bismarck!*.
16. Meyer, *Beveridge statt Bismarck!*; Karl Hinrichs, 'Germany: a flexible labour market plus pension reforms means poverty in old age', in Karl Hinrichs and Matteo Jessoula (eds), *Labour Market Flexibility and Pension Reforms* (Basingstoke: Palgrave Macmillan, 2012), pp. 29–61.
17. Karen M. Anderson and Mona Backhans, 'Sweden: Pensions, health and long-term care', Analyatical Support on Social Protection Reforms and their Socio-Economic Impact, European Commission (2013). Available at http://ec.europa.eu/social/BlobServlet?docId=12982&langId=en (accessed 21 March 2015).

CHAPTER 7

Technology, the Labour Market and Inequality

Ensuring the Benefits of New Technology are Widely Shared

Alan Manning

There is currently a high level of angst about the likely impact of changes in technology on our labour markets and the implications those changes will have for the wider society. It is not hard to identify the source of the concern. The years since the financial crisis have seen a remarkable squeeze on living standards with falls in many countries that have not been experienced for a generation or more. In the UK, real hourly earnings at the median are now no higher than they were in 2000; the real earnings of those at the top of the distribution have continued to rise. This might be just a short-run phenomenon reflecting the lingering impact of the financial crisis, but the fear is that it is caused by something longer-term, something more structural. And it is the nature of new technology that is often fingered as the prime suspect for the source of structural problems. In this chapter, I will discuss the way in which technology is changing the labour market, the implications of these changes and the policy responses that are needed. The conclusion is that sizeable changes are happening, that we can do little to stop them (even if we wanted to) but there is no inevitable link to rising inequality. With appropriate progressive policies, we can make sure that growth is inclusive, that it delivers benefits for all.

Job Polarisation

One of the difficulties facing middling workers in the UK is the way in which the occupational structure of employment has been polarising for at least the last 20 years, and perhaps longer. There has been very rapid growth in the employment share of high-wage occupations (managers and professionals), more modest but still positive growth in the employment share of low-wage occupations (shop assistants and care assistants) and falls in the employment share of jobs in the middle of the distribution (clerical jobs and many manufacturing jobs). This phenomenon seems to be occurring in most, if not all, of the richest economies.[1] And, in the UK, there seems to be no sign that polarisation is coming to an end. Figure 7.1 shows how the employment share of different deciles of the occupational wage distribution has changed over the period 2002 to 2010 in the UK.

The most compelling explanation for job polarisation is to be found in the nature of technical progress, what is known as the routinisation hypothesis. As pointed out by David Autor, Frank Levy, and Richard Murnane, machines come to replace people on tasks that are easily routinised, for which a programme of manageable length can be written to perform the task well.[2] The job of a skilled craft worker in manufacturing often involves precise but repetitive work and it is relatively easy to design a machine to do this job. Similarly, being a bank clerk used to require the ability to do arithmetic quickly and accurately (so these were not low-skilled jobs), but computers can do the sums both faster and without error. The demand for both of these types of jobs has been falling. But it is not – as yet – easy to

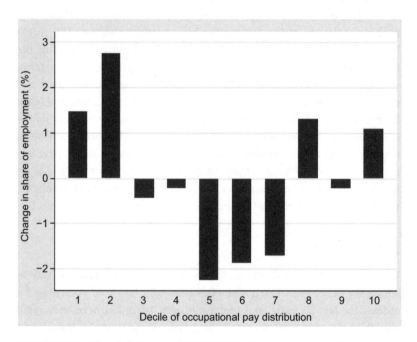

FIGURE 7.1   Job polarisation in the UK, 2002–10.
Source: Labour Force Survey (2010).

design a computer that will manage people, telling them what to do and motivating them. So management remains something in which people have a comparative advantage over machines. And, a job like cleaning that we think of as being unskilled because the ability to do it requires no special aptitude is currently quite beyond the capability of computers. Humans have evolved to be able to do tasks like cleaning without any seeming effort but the amount of information processing going on is actually huge.

The link between Figure 7.1 and the 'squeezed middle' should be clear – it is competition for workers that props up wages and if the demand for the types of jobs done by workers in the middle of the distribution is falling, then it is perhaps not surprising that their living standards are being squeezed. All of this is about the past – what about the future? If routinisation is the primary cause of job polarisation then it is quite likely that it will continue. Computers have become ever more powerful. There was once a time when the best human chess player would beat any computer with ease. Today that is no longer the case.

There is a tendency among some to extrapolate current trends in job polarisation into the indefinite future and to see a society in which larger and larger swathes of human labour are replaced by machines and the only human labour required are the services of a small elite who are needed to design these machines (and perhaps eventually even these are unnecessary). In this dystopian vision most humans will go the way of horses who were once literally the workhorses of the economy but whose costs to rear and feed rose above those of machines that did the same work so ended up surplus to requirements. There are other more considered analyses. Carl Frey and Michael Osborne have drawn on the expertise of robotics researchers to try to predict the types of jobs that will be replaced by machines by 2030 – their estimates suggest that it is low-skilled jobs that are likely to be the most vulnerable.[3]

I do not pretend to have any expertise in predicting the future course of technology. But I do think that while technology will undoubtedly continue to displace humans in some tasks, there is no particular reason to think that the tasks so affected will always be in the middle of the pay distribution. If computers end up being able to diagnose illness and prescribe treatment in a way that is more effective than doctors (and this is an area of active research, including IBM's Watson computer),[4] then it is the demand for doctors that will fall, and they are amongst the highest paid of occupations. Not all middling occupations are currently being displaced – nurses earn about the average salary, the most important part of their work is not being done by computers and the ageing population will lead to an increasing demand for healthcare workers. But, whatever form technological change takes, there is no escaping from it. One cannot build a wall to keep this wave out – there is no alternative but to try to ride it. Fortunately, there are good reasons to think we can do that while keeping the balance in our society.

Opportunities

Technological change – almost by definition – allows us to do everything we could in the past and more, so should make us better off. We can use these new-found abilities to harm people (think of ever-more destructive weapons) to engage in metaphorical arms races for control over limited resources (think of the tiny advantage some new trading algorithm based on a super-fast computer might give a trader) or we can use them to make us all better off. We need to make sure the latter is the course we follow.

Job polarisation is simply the most recent incarnation of a phenomenon that has been with us since at least the start of the industrial revolution – machines have been displacing human labour for a very long time. But, although there have always been some losers (those workers with specific skills undercut by mechanisation), this has not been a bad thing – it has been *the* source of the increase in our material living standards and the general quality of our lives. It has enabled us to produce more while doing less. In spite of this, there have always been some commentators who argue that technical change has been bad for workers as a whole and it is important to be aware of this bias in evaluating claims about the impact of technology in the future. I think the reason for this bias is that often the losers from technical change are very visible – workers whose skills are made worthless by mechanisation and have sometimes been reduced to destitution. And the visible beneficiaries – those working with the new machines – seem to be much fewer in number. But this analysis misses the most important positive impact of technology. New technology results in prices falling so that consumers can buy what they did before and have money left over to spend on other things. As they buy more haircuts, to give one example, the employment of hairdressers will rise and, absurd though it sounds, these newly-employed hairdressers owe their jobs to new technology in some distant part of the economy. Many accounts of the impact of technology completely overlook these effects but they are the most important.

One way of thinking about whether new technology is the source of problems or opportunities is to consider whether we would like more or less investment. In fact, rather than too much capital investment in robots, it seems more likely that the crisis in living standards is caused by too little capital investment. Rises in wages have traditionally been associated with giving workers more capital with which to work and new capital tends to embody the latest technology. But the current levels of capital investment in the UK economy – never its strongest point – have become embarrassingly low in recent years. The CIA World Factbook provides data on the share of investment in GDP and the UK's position is currently 139th out of 153 countries, listed just behind El Salvador (though the US is even worse).

Some ask 'what will we do with ourselves when there are no jobs because the machines are so much better and cheaper than people?' This is a bit like asking 'what do British aristocrats do when all the jobs on the estate are done by servants?' The answer is that they do what they want. But, of course, the gentry have the economic resources to pay servants to do the work so the important question is 'who owns the machines?' As Thomas Piketty's book shows,[5] we cannot rely on the economics of the market interacting with technological progress to deliver inclusive growth and a fair distribution of wealth; there is no reason to believe in any automatic mechanism to make sure that it does. Making sure that growth is inclusive is the job of the political process, and progressive politics in particular, as it is motivated primarily by the underlying belief that the distribution of rewards is unfair.

So, what are the policies that are needed to deliver inclusive growth?

Policies for Inclusive Growth

Financial Market Regulation and Trust-Busting

It is imperative that new technology is used to genuinely improve the output of the economy, and that it is not used to gain rents for one group at the expense of others. Perhaps the best example of this happening is the high-speed traders vividly portrayed in Michael Lewis' book *Flash Boys*.[6] They used new technology to make fortunes for themselves, primarily at the expense of the rest of us. The financial sector is the main source of this problem at the moment; prudent and fair regulation of that sector remains critical, but unfinished business. Other examples are the 'tech giants' that have invented brilliant products that have benefitted society as a whole but have, in the process, acquired significant market power and enormous financial reserves that they understandably want to use to continue that market power. But, just like the conglomerates at the end of the nineteenth century, a bit of trust-busting would probably not go amiss.

It will also be necessary to tackle vested interests, such as in the professions that have done so well in recent years. Technology may well undermine the mystique of expertise that surrounds so many workers in the professions, whether medical, legal, educational, and financial. As their positions will be threatened by computerisation, there will be a big fight to protect entrenched privileges; the professions are probably the best-organised workers in today's labour market.

Education

In large part, job polarisation matters because it raises inequality as the labour market splits into high- and low-wage jobs. But, the wages of different occupations are influenced by both the demand for the skills required to do the job and the supply of workers with the necessary skills. The simplest way to convince oneself that the supply of skills is important is to imagine an economy where everyone had the same skills but someone still has to clean the toilets. In such an economy, the toilet cleaner will have to be paid more than everyone else because it is the most unpleasant job and professional footballers and chief executives and pop stars would all be paid less. If this world sounds unbelievable it is because our world is one where not everyone has the same level of skills and the skills required to clean toilets are not in short supply.

It is sometimes argued that the hollowing-out that comes from job polarisation means that a general increase in education and skills for all is a mistaken policy, that what is needed is a very high-quality education for the segment of the population that are destined for the high-paid jobs and only basic education for those who will be working in the low-paid jobs. However, while it is true that there is little point in equipping workers with skills for which there is going to be no demand in the future, it is not true that increasing the level of education across the board is irrelevant. Imagine a situation where all the middling jobs disappear, leaving only high and low-skill jobs. The pay of the high-skill jobs relative to the low-skill jobs will be influenced by the fraction of the population who can do high-skill jobs and inequality will be lower the higher this fraction will be. Aiming for equality in the distribution of human capital will be as important as it ever has been.

It is necessary to do more to remedy inequalities in our education system to ensure that it is a fair opportunity for all and that parental wealth and privilege cannot buy advantage. We should proactively address areas of failure in education as many inner London schools have done over the past decade, through a combination of more and better-targeted resources, and greater but fairer competition. And we need to make sure that people have the skills to take advantage of change and make good decisions in their lives.

It is sometimes argued that human capital will be increasingly irrelevant in the future as innovation is biased in favour of capital and the return to capital will be rising relative to the wages of labour. Paul Krugman argued as much in the *New York Times* in an op-ed piece entitled 'Rise of the Robots' in December 2012. According to this view, wage growth no longer closely tracks productivity and the share of labour in national income – more or less stable for a long time – is in decline. However, John Van Reenen and Joao Pessao have shown that this view does not stand up well to close scrutiny.[7] Any decoupling between the wage growth of the median worker and labour productivity can be adequately accounted for by the rise in wage inequality and the growing gap between income received by workers and the labour costs paid by employers because of factors like rising healthcare costs, payroll taxes and employer pension contributions. If the share of income going to capital is rising, that makes a focus on wealth inequality all the more important.

Minimum Wages, Executive Pay and Collective Bargaining

Policies to improve access to education take a long time to take effect, powerful though they are. But in the short-run, one can do things to alter the pre-tax distribution of earnings. In coining the phrase 'lovely and lousy' jobs, I do regret allowing my love of alliteration getting the better of my judgment (in my defence, I would add that I never expected it to be used as widely as it has become). It is not a well-chosen phrase because it implies that jobs are inevitably lovely or lousy, but this is linked to the earnings of those who do them. And the earnings in particular occupations are something we can influence.

At the bottom end, recent UK experience has shown that the minimum wage is an effective tool for raising incomes at the bottom – countries like Australia and New Zealand already have minimum wages of around 60 per cent of median earnings without their labour markets suffering a meltdown. In recent years, the Low Pay Commission has become too cautious and needs to be re-invented as a body that takes a more holistic and aggressive approach to low pay.[8]

At the top end of the earnings distribution, we need to regulate finance more effectively: a tricky but essential project. But we also need to find some countervailing power to senior managers who have done very well in recent years. Attempts to rein in their pay by publicising their earnings have not worked and may even have been counterproductive. The people who learned the most from it were other senior executives who then used the knowledge as ammunition to raise their own salaries (the ones who were overpaid tended to keep quiet).

Furthermore, policies that benefit the middling worker are harder to advocate politically. In the UK, the living standards agenda has been more about prices than earnings (probably for the lack of any other ideas), but there are limits to how much can be extracted by curbing monopoly power among utility companies and their ilk. There are also constraints to what can be expected from strengthening workers' individual rights vis-à-vis their employers. Here, some revival of trade union power might be helpful as collective bargaining can be better targeted than legislation ever can. Trade unions have their membership in the middle of the pay distribution, as Figure 7.2 indicates, so they

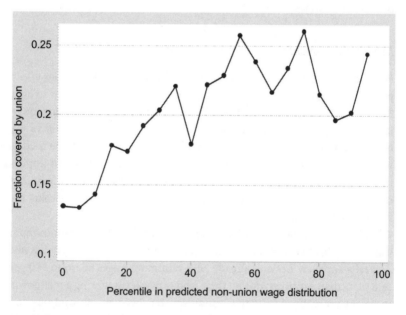

FIGURE 7.2   Trade union membership and pay distribution in the UK.
Source: Labour Force Survey (2010).

are well-placed to deliver benefits for the median worker if they had more power.

However, the problem is that in the UK, union power is weak and does not look set for a revival – as Figure 7.3 shows, under 5 per cent of young workers have ever been a member of a trade union. More fundamentally, they do not see them as a solution to their problems; they have no role model of successful unions to look towards.

Redistribution

The policies I have outlined here are predistributive – better regulation of finance, monopoly-busting, better and more equal education, minimum wages, restraints on executive pay, more collective bargaining. But we should also not be too afraid of old-fashioned redistribution. We need it because this is the backstop policy to deal with the consequences if other policies do not work.

We will need to tax the largest incomes more heavily than we do now. So large has been the increase in the share of income going to the top

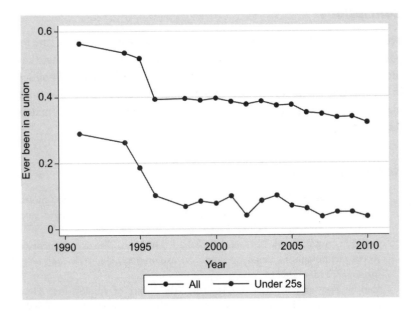

FIGURE 7.3   Union membership rates in the UK, 1990–2010.
Source: British Social Attitudes Survey (2013).

1 per cent that taxing them more heavily only takes them back to the level of earnings they had a few short years ago – it is simply not credible that slightly higher taxes will drastically reduce work effort among high-earners as is being claimed. Thomas Piketty's blockbuster, *Capital in the Twenty-First Century*, has shown not just that the market cannot be relied upon to deliver fair outcomes, but that there is also no guarantee that it can be relied upon to reverse the rise in inequality. More wealth taxation is needed to break down concentrations of wealth. New technology can be an ally here – it can be used to record ownership of wealth and to fight tax evasion.

As Lucy Barnes' contribution to this volume makes clear, a large proportion of British people think the gap between rich and poor is too big. But, one problem with the redistribution agenda is that declining faith and trust in government means that even where inequality is widely seen as a problem, governments are not trusted to deal with it. The UK British Social Attitudes survey shows that fewer people in the UK now want the government to redistribute income.[9] So policies to renew trust in government are needed too.

Conclusions

Technology cannot and should not be resisted. But we need to make sure its potential to be a force for good becomes a reality. There is no guarantee that the benefits of new technology will be widely shared – it is the job of politics in general and progressive politics in particular to make sure it is. Far from making progressive policies more difficult, the advance of technology makes it more essential.

Notes

1. See, for example, Maarten Goos, Alan Manning, and Anna Salomons, 'Explaining job polarization: routine-biased technological change and offshoring', *American Economic Review* 104/8 (2014), pp. 2509–26.
2. David H. Autor, Frank Levy, and Richard J. Murnane, 'The skill content of recent technological change: an empirical exploration', *Quarterly Journal of Economics* 118/4 (2003).
3. Carl B. Frey and Michael A. Osborne, 'The future of employment: How susceptible are jobs to computerisation?', Working Paper, Oxford Martin School (2013). Available at http://www.oxfordmartin.ox.ac.uk/downloads/academic/The_Future_of_Employment.pdf (accessed 15 March 2015).

4. For more information, see http://www.ibm.com/smarterplanet/us/en/ibm watson/ (accessed 18 May 2015).

5. Thomas Piketty, *Capital in the Twenty-First Century* (Cambridge: Harvard University Press, 2014).

6. Michael Lewis, *Flash Boys: Cracking the Money Code* (London: W.W. Norton and Company Ltd., 2014).

7. John Van Reenen and Joao P. Pessao, 'The UK productivity and jobs puzzle: Does the answer lie in labour market flexibility?', Special Paper No. 31 (London: Centre for Economic Performance, 2013). Available at: http://cep.lse.ac.uk/ pubs/download/special/cepsp31.pdf (accessed 15 March 2015).

8. As, for example, suggested in James Plunkett, Alex Hurrell, and Conor D'Arcy, 'More than a minimum: The review of the minimum wage', Resolution Foundation (2014).

9. British Social Attitudes, Series REDISTRB (2013), available at http://www. britsocat.com (accessed 18 May 2015).

CHAPTER 8

Labour Market Institutions as Pillars of Predistribution

Focusing on Pre-tax Income Distribution to Tackle Inequality

Rémi Bazillier[1]

I n previous research papers, I have argued that inequalities and efficiency are not necessarily antagonistic and that, in numerous cases, more equality can be a condition of efficiency.[2] Fiscal redistribution cannot be the only tool to achieve more equality. There also needs to be a closer look at the *ex ante* distribution of income. The goal for progressives cannot only be to let the market generate a certain level of inequality and then to allow the state to correct *ex post* the distribution of income. It is then necessary to propose different policies aiming at directly reducing inequalities in the production process. The role of institutions and economic incentives are therefore crucial. It echoes the recent debate on predistribution in the UK,[3] but also the emphasis on the 'égalité réelle' (the 'equality for real') in France and the definition of a socialism of redistribution and a socialism of production.

In this chapter, I will argue that strengthening labour market institutions should be seen as a major pillar of predistribution policies. By reviewing the academic literature on the economic effects of these institutions, I will show that:

1. they are positively correlated with the level of income equality,
2. they can be a factor of productivity enhancement, and
3. they do not necessarily contribute to the insider/outsider divide within the labour market.

This chapter argues for a fresh vision of such institutions, challenging the 'common wisdom' assuming that more flexibility and less job security are systematically good for economic efficiency. By doing so, progressives should be able to propose an alternative vision of labour market policies, combining both equality and economic efficiency. I provide theoretical and empirical arguments showing that the TINA ('There Is No Alternative') message on labour market reforms and deregulation is not inescapable. The goal is not to come back to a traditional vision of socialism only based on worker protection, but to combine this traditional goal with the quest for a more productive economy.

Booming Innovations in the Productive Sector

Carlin[4] argues that predistribution policies should focus on booming innovations and productivity in the 'competitive' sector (the industrial sector or the tradable goods sector depending on the economic specialisation of the country) in order to be able to increase the size of the 'labour demanding service sector'. The productivity in this sector is lower and cannot increase as much as the productivity in the other. Furthermore, most of these 'stagnant services' are financed by the state through taxation. But the benefits from productivity growth in the dynamic sectors increase the tax base. A higher level of taxation is therefore an outcome of a productive economy. As the consumption of such services is welfare enhancing, this move is positive for the whole of society. Consequently, as these sectors are also labour-demanding and not necessarily skilled-biased, their development can ensure lower levels of unemployment and of inequalities.

The question is, therefore, how to ensure high productivity growth in the 'competitive sectors'. Carlin[5] focuses on the role of competition policy: 'reducing monopoly profits by promoting new entry of business has the potential to reduce prices (boosting real incomes and reducing market inequality) and stimulate innovations'. This is, of course, not the only way to foster productivity. We can instead insist on industrial policies,[6] for instance. By investing in sectors or activities generating positive spillovers for the whole economy, the state can also contribute to increasing productivity.

But one underestimated aspect is the potential role of labour market institutions in fostering productivity. Labour market institutions can be one tool to 'boom innovation in the productive sector', to use Carlin's words. But the argument in favour of the labour market is twofold. It can play the role of fostering productivity in the 'competitive sector'. But it also contributes to a more equal distribution of income throughout the economy.

Labour Market Institutions and Equality

Wage inequality dynamics are influenced by the institutional context, and therefore by labour market institutions. Figure 8.1 shows the relationship between employment protection (respectively for temporary contracts and permanent workers) and inequalities (measured by the Gini coefficient) in some OECD countries. There is a negative correlation between inequalities and employment protection – a major pillar of labour market institutions. Results are similar for other types of labour market institutions such as unemployment benefits, minimum wages or wage-setting mechanisms. Although these figures highlight only a correlational relationship, the relation of causality has been confirmed by several empirical studies.[7] A higher level of employment protection explains a lower level of income inequality. The underlying mechanism is quite simple and rather intuitive.

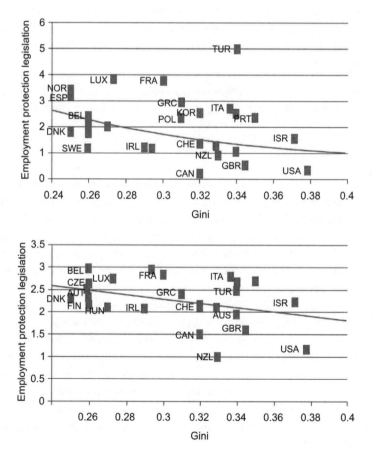

FIGURE 8.1   Employment Protection and Inequalities – Temporary Work.
Source: OECD (Employment protection legislation (EPL) and Gini).

Strengthening labour market institutions reinforces the bargaining power of workers.

Employment protection reduces the probability of being fired and therefore increases workers' bargaining capacity. Unemployment insurance increases what is known in game theory as the 'outside option', that is, a payoff the worker can receive if bargaining fails. A better outside option increases the worker's capacity to get a bigger pay-off. The minimum wage sets a bottom line in wage bargaining and reinforces the position of employed low-wage workers. Finally, centralised wage-setting mechanisms reinforce the role of trade unions and increases the probability of obtaining a higher wage. Also, more centralised wage-setting mechanisms tend to minimise wage differentials between sectors in order to maintain worker mobility between sectors. Koeniger et al. show empirically that changes in labour market institutions can account for much of the change in wage inequality:

> Over the 26-year period, institutional changes were associated with a 23 per cent reduction in male wage inequality in France, where minimum wages increased and employment protection became stricter, but with an increase of up to 11 per cent in the USA and UK, where unions became less powerful and (in the USA) minimum wages fell'[8].

However, increasing wage compression (or reducing wage inequality) is not a sufficient condition for reducing overall income inequality. Additionally, strengthening trade unions' power tends, all things being equal, to increase the labour share. If both phenomenon are associated (increase of the labour share and wage compression), the effect on income inequality is straightforward. The problem is that stronger labour market institutions may have adverse effects on unemployment (even if these negative effects are highly questionable). That is why Checchi and García-Peñalosa[9] first argue that the effect of labour market institutions on inequality should be ambiguous. As seen above, labour market institutions have a non-ambiguous negative impact on wage compression. But the impact on the overall distribution of income may be unclear due to the increase in the number of individuals with low income (and the unemployed). Nevertheless, increasing unemployment benefits should reduce income inequality in any case by increasing their income. The question is open for other labour market institutions.

Checchi and García-Peñalosa[10] therefore propose to test the final effect on income inequality by using econometric techniques. In short, they find:

1. Unemployment benefit reduces inequality both directly and by increasing the wage share.
2. Employment protection reduces unemployment and income inequality.

However, they found no effect of union density, wage bargaining coordination and minimum wage. A 10 per cent increase in unemployment benefits or employment protection would decrease inequality (measured by the Gini coefficient) by more than 1 per cent. They also try to estimate what would be the level of inequality in different countries if they adopt labour market institutions of another country or region. Figure 8.2 shows what would be the level of inequality in Norway and Sweden if they reduced their level of employment protection in order to reach the much lower level of employment protection observed in the US. Results are striking. In the 1980s, it would have led to an increase of inequality by almost one-third. The gap is lower after the year 2000 (around 15 per cent) due to the increase of flexibility in the Nordic labour markets and the large increase of inequalities observed in these countries. All in all, labour market institutions are associated with more wage compression within firms but also with lower total earning inequalities at the macroeconomic level.

Advocates of predistribution argue that it is necessary to tackle inequality before redistribution from the state. Surprisingly, the role of such institutions

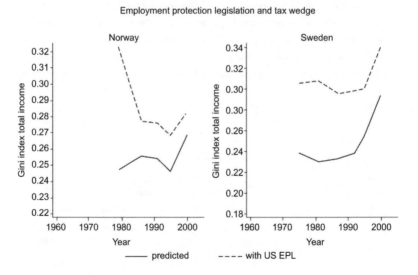

FIGURE 8.2 Counterfactual with US labour market institutions.
Source: Checchi and García-Peñalosa (2008).

is often underestimated: perhaps due to the fear that stronger labour market institutions have a cost in terms of efficiency, or increase the gap between insiders and outsiders. As already mentioned, it is not necessarily the case. First, I will review the arguments related to the insider/outsider debate and then introduce new evidence that indicates efficiencies in strong labour market institutions if the design of such an institutional framework is appropriate.

Labour Market Institutions and the Insider/Outsider Debate

One of the traditional criticisms of labour market institutions is they create a gap between protected workers with high wages and long-term prospects (the insiders) and the outsiders, who have to survive on short time contracts, temporary work and periods of unemployment. These workers suffer from low wages, low levels of job security and low social security. The fear of a growing two-tier system has often been a major obstacle of an improvement in labour market institutions. But, a first look at the data puts things into perspective. As we can see in Figure 8.3, the correlation between employment protection and the percentage of permanent contract is slightly negative but very low (around 5 per cent).

The level of employment protection per se cannot explain, as such, the development of a two-tier system. Outsiders can either be unemployed or precarious. If employment protection explains a higher level of unemployment, the argument may be understandable. But as it is shown in most studies focusing on the effect of EPL on unemployment, empirical evidence is very mixed. For instance, Checchi and García-Peñalosa[11] found

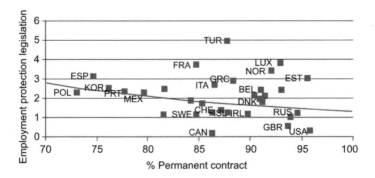

FIGURE 8.3 Employment protection and percentage of permanent contract.
Source: OECD EPL Index and OECD Employment Statistics Database.

that a 10 per cent increase in job security is associated with a 6.6 per cent decrease of unemployment.

But if outsiders are mainly precarious workers with short-term contracts, part-time jobs and low levels of social security, the gap between employment protection regulations for permanent and transitory workers may be the main cause of such divides within the labour market. In other words, strong employment protection for permanent workers associated with a very low level of protection for short-term contracts is probably less than optimal as it widens the gap between protected workers and the others.

However, lowering employment protection for permanent workers is not the appropriate answer. In most countries where such a gap exists, it is mainly explained by the existence of an unregulated labour market regarding short-term contracts. These types of contracts create negative externalities at the macroeconomic level: they cost for society as a whole. At the individual level, they create worker instability. With a short-term contract, the feasibility of getting a loan is reduced, impacting on the capacity to invest. Housing becomes a problem, even for tenants because of the strong guarantees given by the owners. It has also negative consequences for consumption. Because of uncertainty, the incentive to save is much higher. At the collective level, the high probability of becoming unemployed at the end of a contract term increases demand for financing unemployment insurance. All of these costs are not internalised by firms. On the contrary, if there is less regulation for this type of contract, it is less costly to implement. Labour market policies aimed at reducing the gap between insiders and outsiders by lowering permanent worker protection is likely to have adverse effects. On the other hand, increasing the cost associated with the hiring of transitory workers may contribute to internalisation (by firms) of the negative externality created by the use of such contracts. And it also indirectly increases the incentive to hire permanent workers by lowering the gap between regulations of short-term and long-term contracts.

In other words, a more equal labour market can be compatible with strong labour market institutions while taking into account the insider/outsider debate. A good example is the difference of labour market institutions between France and Spain. Both countries have almost the same level of employment protection, *overall*. But Spain has much larger discrepancies between employment protection for short-term and permanent contracts. According to Bentolila et al.,[12] during the great recession, 'Spain could have avoided about 45 per cent of its unemployment surge had it adopted the French employment protection legislation'. Here, it is not the level of employment protection which is problematic, but the low level of protection for short-term contracts.

One should be sceptical about two-tier labour market reforms, as it may contribute to an increase of this gap. A global approach to employment protection taking into account short-term and long-term contracts is needed. The challenge for policy-makers is to find the appropriate balance between both types of protection. The use of short-term contracts is unavoidable in some very specific situations. Firms should have this flexibility to use them. But what should be avoided is a situation where short-term and long-term contracts become substitutable. Here, institutions should clearly provide firms with incentives to use long-term contracts by increasing the costs of using short-term contracts.

Labour Market Institutions and Economic Performance

The other key argument in favour of labour market institutions as a pillar of predistribution is that these institutions can be a factor of efficiency in the productive sector. This argument may be counterintuitive, but it can be summarised as follows. Stronger labour market institutions are most often associated with higher costs for firms. This may reduce the average level of competitiveness at the international level, but at the same time, it strengthens the position of the most productive firms. Imagine a market where you have two types of firms using very different technologies and management. If you increase the cost for all firms (by strengthening labour market institutions), only the most productive firms may be able to bear this cost. Less productive firms may be pushed to exit some markets, letting the most productive ones compete with each other. What would be the outcome? The average level of productivity will increase due to the exit of unproductive firms. Most productive firms can hire more workers (formerly employed in low-productivity firms). It increases the tax base, allowing a stronger capacity to finance welfare-enhancing services by the state. It can be called a selection effect.

Beyond this selection effect, changing the regulatory environment has heterogeneous effects on firms. Basically, companies have two options if costs increase: adapting labour costs by firing workers or reducing wages in order to maintain profitability, or try to compensate for the additional costs of such regulations by being more innovative and more productive. This effect is well-known in environmental economics since Porter and van der Linde[13] have shown how tight environmental regulations can be efficient because they foster innovations within firms and thus productivity. In other words, a more stringent regulatory environment increases the incentive for firms to innovate, and therefore to become more productive. The effect is therefore not only a selection effect. There is also an innovation effect. This latter effect has been confirmed by Acharya, Baghai, and Subramanian[14] who investigate the extent to which labour laws foster innovation. They show that 'more stringent labour laws can provide firms a commitment device to not punish short-run failures and thereby spur their employees to pursue value-enhancing innovative activities'. Based on an index of labour laws available for the US, the UK, France, Germany and India over the period 1970–2006, they show that a one standard deviation increase in the dismissal law index explains a rise in the annual number of patents, number of patenting firms, and citations by 6.1 per cent, 7 per cent and 9.2 per cent respectively. The effect is stronger in innovation-intensive sectors. The argument is that stronger employment protection gives an *ex ante* incentive for firms to innovate.

However, they find that dismissal laws are the only type of labour laws that exhibit this positive effect on innovation. The other dimensions which have no effect on innovation are alternative employment contracts, regulation of working time, industrial action and employee representation. Concerning the latter, the effect is positively significant only when considering the impact on the number of patents and the number of patenting firms. They also find that these dismissal laws have a positive and significant effect on economic growth. As innovation is an important factor of growth, this result is not surprising. The effect is quite large, a one standard deviation increase in the dismissal law index results in a 2.2 per cent increase in the growth in value-added.

For all these reasons, labour market institutions can be associated with higher productivity. More generally, the linkage between wage policy and productivity has been confirmed by an OECD study.[15] An increase in the minimum to median wages ratio by 10 percentage points is found to increase labour productivity by almost two percentage points. It may be explained by improved incentives for investing in training and a result of substitution of skilled labour for unskilled labour. But it can also be explained by the exit of low-productivity firms to the benefit of firms having better access to technology and therefore to productivity.

No Clear Impact on Employment and Unemployment

If labour market institutions are associated with higher than average levels of productivity, it should be positive for the economic outcome in the long run (as the long run growth potential depends on the evolution of productivity). However, in the short run, an increase in productivity can be associated with a rise in unemployment.

Opponents of employment protection are also claiming that these institutions are lowering the incentive for firms to hire. Knowing that it will be difficult or costly to fire workers, firms may be tempted to reduce their recruitment. By reducing employment protection, firms could find it less risky to hire, which would have a positive impact on employment. On the other side, if it is more difficult or costly to fire workers, the probability for employed workers to lose their job is also lower. This effect is potentially important in times of economic downturn. In other words, the effects of employment protection are more likely to be ambiguous.

There is a large literature studying the effects of labour market institutions on various economic outcomes such as employment and unemployment level, alongside economic growth. Table 8.1 shows the main empirical results

TABLE 8.1   The effect of employment protection on labour markets.

	Stocks		Flows	
Author(s)	Employ-ment	Unemploy-ment	Employ-ment	Unemploy-ment
Emerson (1998)	?	?	–	–
Lazear (1990)	–	+		
Bertola·(1990)	?	?	?	–
Grubb and Wells (1993)	–			
Garibaldi et al. (1997)	?	?	?	–
Addison and Grosso (1996)	?	?		
Jackman et al. (1996)	?	?	–	–
Gregg and Maning (1997)	?	?		–
Boeri (1999)	?	?	+	–
Di tella and MacCulloch (2005)	–	+		
OECD (1998)	?	?	+	–
Kugler and Sait Paul (2000)			+	–
Belot and van Ours (2001)		–		
Nickell et al. (2005)	?	?		
Garibaldi and Violante (2005)	+	≠		

Source: Boeri (2011).

obtained that concern the effects on employment and unemployment. It confirms the ambiguous theoretical relation that may exist between employment protection and unemployment. The number of studies that find a negative impact on employment is more or less equal to the number that shows a positive impact. Employment protection cannot be defined as the 'adversary of employment' as much neoliberal politicians often claim.

Those skeptical of employment protection therefore focus their arguments on the negative impact on employment flows rather than on employment levels (or stocks). Their argument is the following: employment protection decreases the probability to get fired, but also decreases the probability for an unemployed individual to exit from unemployment. By decreasing employment flows, employment protection would impede not only the adjustment of the economy in the short run but also structural change in the longer run. The problem, once again, is that this argument is not validated by the data. As shown in Table 8.1, most papers that study the impact on employment flows indeed find a negative impact on the probability to lose a job. But when it comes to the probability of getting a job, the impact is much more mixed, with half of the studies also showing a positive effect.

Internal Flexibility rather than Deregulated Labour Markets

Firms are facing two types of shocks – long-term and short-term. The latter has adverse effects on demand addressed to a specific firm, sector or even country. The former is the consequence of long-term dynamics, technical progress and innovation. Promoting strong labour market institutions does not mean neglecting the capacity of firms to face such shocks. Both in the short and the long run, a reallocation of labour may be necessary to ensure high productivity levels in the long term. However, this process can generate social tensions and persistent unemployment if it ignores low-skilled workers (which will have adverse effects on inequalities). This problem should not be underplayed and it calls for different policy responses.

First, it emphasises the importance of *active labour market policies* (*ALMP*) and *life-long training*.[16] Firms should anticipate such trends and increase workers' capacity to follow in line with technological changes. Such reallocation of labour (towards more innovative activities) can also be done *within* firms.

Second, there is a need to improve *internal flexibility* rather than *external flexibility*. The goal of labour market institutions is to minimise the cost of shocks in terms of unemployment. Employment protection should therefore increase the cost of firing in order to maintain workers in their jobs and, also, to allow some internal arrangements to share the burden of these negative shocks between shareholders and workers. The best example is 'short-time working arrangements' (STWAs) which were particularly successful in Germany to absorb the negative shock induced by the financial crisis.[17] The recent national collective agreements on the labour market in France (*Accord interprofessionnel pour l'emploi, ANI*) also allows more internal flexibility through the 'saving-job agreements' (*accords de maintien dans l'emploi*). The main challenge of such agreements is to find the relevant and fair risk-sharing mechanisms between workers and firms. Capital income is a direct compensation for taking risks. It would be unfair to transfer the entire burden to workers, even if it is done in order to avoid dismissal.

A fundamental point is that internal flexibility must be seen as substitutable and not *complementary* with external flexibility. In other words, labour market reforms should not include more flexibility in the regulation of employment contracts and more freedom to adjust working-time or wages within firms. If you choose the second option, it should go along with stronger employment protection. Arguably, one criticism of the French labour market reform mentioned above is that it increases both internal and external flexibility. A last fundamental aspect is that internal flexibility can only be acceptable where social dialogue is strong and efficient. Short-time working arrangements or other types of internal flexibility agreements should be conditional on an agreement with trade unions and clearly mention safeguards for workers. Labour laws or collective agreements should frame such arrangements.

Conclusion

In this chapter, I have argued that labour market institutions should be seen as one major pillar of predistribution. This concept emphasises the need to focus on pre-tax income distribution in order to efficiently tackle the challenge of growing inequalities. It does not imply any rejection of redistribution policies; a global approach aimed at tackling inequalities should be concerned with both pre-tax and post-tax distribution of income. That is why this concept of predistribution is important for progressives. However, the traditional view is that predistribution policies should be based on efficient economic policies, aimed at boosting innovation and productivity. But there is a need to define what such policies should be from a progressive perspective. In other words, we need to define what is a progressive and efficient economic policy. There are different ways to increase productivity and wealth, and progressives should not be reluctant to define their own political choices. My central argument is that appropriate labour market institutions can be at the core of such policies: first, because they are equalitarian by nature and, secondly, they can be positively correlated with productivity (and therefore with efficiency), both due to a selection effect and an innovation effect. More flexible labour markets are not the answer.

The fear that employment protection creates too much unemployment is clearly overstated, considering the lack of solid empirical evidence. What is often underestimated is the potential positive impact of such institutions on the incentives for firms to innovate and therefore to become more productive. Taking this dimension into consideration, progressives should propose an alternative labour market policy. It should be compatible not only with the traditional goal of socialists and social democrats to protect workers but also with the need to achieve a more productive and efficient economy.

Notes

1. This chapter is an updated version of a book chapter published in Ernst Stetter, Karl Duffek, and Ania Skrzypek (eds), *Next Left: Framing a New Progressive Narrative* (Brussels: FEPS, 2013), pp. 170–83.

2. See Rémi Bazillier, 'The economic meaning of progressive values', in Ernst Stetter, Karl Duffek, and Ania Skrzypek (eds), *Progressive Values for the 21st Century* (Brussels: FEPS/Renner Institut, 2011), pp. 68–96; Rémi Bazillier, 'Equality must be the core of economic policies: 17 propositions for equality and efficiency', in Ernst Stetter, Karl Duffek, and Ania Skrzypek (eds), *For a New Social Deal* (Brussels: FEPS/Renner Institut, 2013), pp. 102–32.

3. Jacob Hacker, 'The institutional foundations of middle-class democracy', (London: Policy Network, 2011). Available at http://www.policy-network. net/pno_detail.aspx?ID=3998&title=The+institutional+foundations+of+m iddle-class+democracy (accessed 16 March 2015); Ed Miliband, Speech on Predistribution, Policy Network conference (2012). Available at http://www. politics.co.uk/comment-analysis/2012/09/06/ed-miliband-s-redistribution-speech-in-full (accessed 18 May 2015).

4. Wendy Carlin, 'A progressive economic strategy' (London: Policy Network, 2012). Available at http://www.policy-network.net/publications_detail. aspx?ID=4269 (accessed 16 March 2015).

5. *Ibid.*

6. Philippe Aghion, Julian Boulanger, and Elie Cohen, *Rethinking Industrial Policy* (Brussels: Bruegel, 2011); Dani Rodrik, 'Industrial policy for the twenty-first

century', UNIDO Paper (2004). Available at http://www.hks.harvard.edu/fs/ drodrik/Research%20papers/UNIDOSep.pdf (accessed 16 March 2015).

7. Winfried Koeniger, Marco Leonardi, and Luca Nunziata, 'Labor market institutions and wage inequality', *Industrial and Labor Relations Review* 60/3 (2007), pp. 340–56; Daniele Checchi and Cecilia García-Peñalosa, 'Labour market institutions and income inequality', *Economic Policy* 23 (2008), pp. 601–49.

8. Winfried Koeniger, Marco Leonardi, and Luca Nunziata, 'Labor market institutions and wage inequality', in *Industrial and Labor Relations Review* 60/3 (2007), pp. 340–56.

9. Daniele Checchi and Cecilia García-Peñalosa, 'Labour market institutions and income inequality', *Economic Policy* 23 (2008), pp. 601–49.

10. *Ibid.*

11. *Ibid.*

12. Samuel Bentolila, Pierre Cahuc, Juan J. Dolado, and Thomas Le Barbanchon, 'Two-tier labour markets in the great recession: France versus Spain', *Economic Journal* 122/562 (2012), pp. F155–F187, 08.

13. Michael E. Porter and Claas van der Linde, 'Toward a new conception of the environment-competitiveness relationship', *Journal of Economic Perspectives* 9/4 (1995), pp. 97–118.

14. Viral V. Acharya, Ramin P. Baghai, Krishnamurthy Subramanian, 'Labor laws and innovation', NBER Working Paper 16484 (2010).

15. OECD, *Employment Outlook* (Paris: OECD, 2007).

16. OECD, 'Activating the Unemployed, What Countries do?' in *Employment Outlook* (Paris: OECD, 2007), pp. 205–42; Jan Boone and Jan C. Van Ours, 'Bringing unemployed back to work: effective active labor market policies', *De Economist* 157/3 (207), pp. 293–313; David Card, Jochen Kluve, and Andrea Weber, 'Active labour market policy evaluations: a meta-analysis', *Economic Journal* 120/548 (2012), pp. F452–F477.

17. Marion Collewet, Jaap de Koning, and Oana Calavrezo, 'The effect of short-time working arrangements on employment: A comparative microeconometric analysis of Germany and France', AFSE Meeting Paper (2013).

CHAPTER 9

Predistribution and Labour Market Actors

Looking at the Trade Union Movement

Dimitris Tsarouhas

O ver the last few decades, and especially in the aftermath of the global financial crisis, the world has fundamentally changed. Old certainties associated with the role of both the state and the market have shattered amidst widespread disillusion with politics; there has been a massive transfer of wealth from the middle- and low-income classes to the very top, especially in the Anglo-Saxon world. Furthermore, there is a technological revolution underway that blurs the boundaries of public and private action, combined with a Schumpeterian type of creative capitalist destruction and the global reallocation of opportunities and aspirations from the West to the developing world is ongoing. Very few of the old constants that shaped society and economy in the industrialised world remain; the global political economy is in flux.

Defined by its originator Jacob Hacker as a set of market reforms that 'encourage a more equal distribution of economic power and rewards even before government collects taxes and pays out benefits',[1] predistribution is at the heart of a vital and necessary debate among progressives as to how to reshape the political economy in the wake of contradictory trends and challenges.

This chapter focuses on predistribution and the trade unions. In particular, I aim to analyse the concept and its implications for trade unions, then discuss the extent to which the concept offers new opportunities for the trade union movement in an unfavourable political and socio-economic climate. The main argument is that trade unions can and ought to take advantage of what the concept has to offer by implementing a series of policy practices at the workplace and beyond. I suggest a range of policy options involving trade unions to create a more equitable and less insecure labour market environment, and place those on a three-level range, starting from the more minimal to more radical policy options. Further, I argue that a stronger trade union role necessitates a varied approach depending on country and context, but the challenge is common regardless of context-specific details. At a time of declining union density and wherever feasible, the trade union movement should go beyond its 'social partner' status and engage actively with NGOs, community organisations and political parties to reshape the contours of political debate. It is only through such a strategy that predictable attacks on the 'selfish' unions will fail to resonate, and the trade union movement will reach out to new constituencies and, potentially, new members. In fact, such a strategy is a *sine qua non* for the survival of organised labour as a countervailing force to business dominance and the permeating logic of labour market deregulation.

The first section below discusses the limits of 'classical' redistribution, and the second highlights the extent to which predistribution offers a genuinely new approach to social democratic revival. In the third section, I discuss the practical ways through which the concept can and ought to apply to trade unions, whilst the concluding section summarises the main argument.

The Limits of a Tax-and-spend Welfare System

The welfare state originates in Bismarckian social security reforms. In itself, it is neither conservative nor progressive, and a 'social market economy' is a mantra often used by left- as well as right-of-centre politicians in continental Europe. Nevertheless, the gradual expansion and consolidation of the welfare state in western Europe has played a vital role in offering social security to vulnerable groups, whilst allowing for the redistribution of income and opportunities to create less unequal societies.[2] The centre-left has pioneered most welfare state programmes, and used the welfare state for decades to form cross-class alliances that turned it into a dominant political force. It is rightly proud of its achievements; defending them in the face of vociferous neoliberal attacks is a right as well as a responsibility of progressives.

All is not well with the current shape of the welfare state, however, not least regarding its distributive effects on vulnerable groups.[3] One of its proud achievements is its success in tackling old-age poverty, but the flip side is that it invests too little (and too late) in the young. At a time of record-high youth unemployment in many states, and as numbers clearly show that the young have replaced the old as the demographic category most likely to experience income poverty,[4] this is an unsustainable and ultimately wasteful use of valuable resources. Shifting resources to the young and very young (0–2 ages) reaps benefits over the long run,[5] and fulfils the promise of welfare for all. Adopting a new spending strategy on welfare is politically difficult; older generations are much more likely to vote than the young, leading to a vicious circle of misguided spending and disgruntled abstinence from party politics by the young.[6] In the long run, progressives cannot accept that. Secondly, tax-and-spend on welfare programmes, tax credits and the rest are vulnerable to well-rehearsed attacks as a manifestation of 'rewarding the lazy'.

Particularly in residual welfare states, the income and wealth disparity between the well-off and the rest makes the former resentful to the idea of sharing *their* earned income with those who are left behind but who are portrayed as lazy, undeserving, ill-motivated or a combination thereof.[7] The global financial crisis and its aftermath has made things worse still, as public finances come under intense pressure and the political room to manoeuvre by use of tax-and-spend gets ever more limited. This is particularly relevant from a trade union perspective: the old cross-class alliance that underpinned the welfare state has loosened, as the politics of identity has taken hold and neoliberalism has permeated ever more spheres of public life;[8] the constituency to defend the welfare state as we know it has fragmented and is, more often than not, fighting a losing battle.

None of this is to suggest that redistribution and the welfare state should simply be abandoned: it merely suggests that a credible progressive alternative has to go beyond the current paradigm and work out a programme that tackles contemporary problems at source. Predistribution can be one of them.

Why Predistribution?

Predistribution is a powerful concept for various reasons. First, at an intellectual level, it resonates well with those hungry for an original policy idea from the centre-left, a rare phenomenon over recent decades. While right-wing ideas enjoy a hegemonic status and are often treated as an unquestioned orthodoxy, not least through their skilful use of metaphors to convince the public of their righteousness,[9] the left has failed to counter-attack at an ideational level.[10] The debate surrounding predistribution has placed the centre-left on sound footing in this regard, opening up space for creative ideas to flourish.

Secondly, predistribution has a radical potential in that it asks not for better management of the existing game, but for changing some of its rules altogether.[11] The goal is to empower people and offer them a direct stake in the way capitalism works. This is not only good in itself, it also matches the aspirations of citizens who demand a say in how their lives are governed, and who mistrust traditional institutions to do the job for them. Finally, predistribution is a perfect fit for social democratic reformism in that it combines programmatic radicalism with fiscal prudence. Rewriting capitalist rules to reduce inequality and restore middle class faith in the system's ability to deliver goes through measures such as tighter regulation of the finance industry, the creation of savings schemes to offer people options in managing their income[12] or bold education reform to upgrade skills and offer genuine equality of opportunity to people of all backgrounds.[13] Such proposals are innocuous enough to escape the labelling and prejudiced analysis that more radical proposals often face. They can, however, contribute to the long-term transformation of the manner and principles on which capitalism functions – so long as they are combined with more radical action in areas such as the labour market and trade union reform.

Why, and How, Trade Unions Matter

Trade unions are on the defensive everywhere, and have been in that position for decades. When the 'social democratic image of society'[14] began to crumble and as neoliberalism took hold, trade unions were among the primary losers of the new political economy settlement. This resulted both from social and economic change. At a social level, the breakdown of traditional forms of community and the rise in identity politics split union members along generational lines, and the communitarianism/ cosmopolitanism split distanced trade unions from society at large. Large waves of migration into the developed world compounded the problem and ossified the debate in the context of loose employment law regulation and rising numbers of undocumented workers striving to earn a living in below-par working conditions.[15] In economic terms, globalisation and the flexible reallocation of capital in search of more profitable investment undermined centralised collective bargaining and contributed to the decline in union density.[16] In the EU, trade union density fell from 28 to 23 per cent between 2000 and 2008, and the drop has been almost universal across states. Enlargement to central and eastern Europe has boosted the numbers of non-unionised workers across the EU, while membership has hardly increased.[17] In the Anglo-Saxon world, the drop in union membership has been sharper, has lasted longer and has been the result of a sustained anti-labour campaign launched more than 30 years ago.

It is therefore important to underline that even in such a context, trade unions matter greatly. They do so not only with regard to political economy but our democratic political system more generally. First and most obviously, trade unions affect the distribution of income through collective bargaining and the agreements they reach with employers. It is precisely the documented rise in income inequality that has sparked the debate, particularly in the USA, as to the decline of the middle class and what this entails for social and political stability. Although the middle class is understood somewhat differently across the Atlantic and despite the less exorbitant rise in inequality in Europe, the same thesis holds true there as well. Reactivating the trade unions in terms of their 'core business' is thus of utmost importance.

Secondly, trade unions affect the distribution of political power through their links with organised civil society as well as social democratic and labour parties.[18] Again, differences in the USA and Europe are significant, and the party–union link has traditionally been much stronger in Europe. But the decline in the party–union link has offered yet another avenue for neoliberal ideas to take hold in society, and has diminished the prospects of social democratic renewal. The latter has to be based on groundwork operations by activists in communities and workplaces, as well as party political strategies that maximise the centre-left's electoral prospects. Organised labour remains central to the successful execution of such a strategy.

Finally, trade unions provide a necessary counterweight to the lobbying power of corporate interests, whose outlets of communicating their ideas are vast and their ability to skew resources away from the low and middle and towards the top is well-documented.[19] Given that corporate lobbying often leads to the rewriting of the rules to favour the rich and very rich, a strong trade union voice that challenges taken-for-granted assumptions on 'what is good for business is good for the nation' is an invaluable resource for progressives. In fact, social democratic renewal is predicated on an ability to change not just rules, but also the way those rules are *perceived* by the broader public.

Putting Predistribution to Labour Market Practice: Three Levels

If trade unions remain important, what are the precise schemes or policies through which organised labour can contribute to progressive change? To start with, there exists no uniform blueprint for trade union action. Legal rules, political resources and grassroots mobilisation opportunities differ vastly between different countries' trade unions, and very often within states too. What is therefore needed is a multi-faceted programme of action that involves different trade unions in different ways and at different times. The totality of such action corresponds to an efficient use of the predistribution idea to alter workplace dynamics in favour of working people, bestow the unions with a renewed sense of confidence and reactivate their often moribund connection to the community and civil society organisations.

I make a three-fold distinction between different policy measures that form part of an agenda of renewal in the labour market and link those to trade union options and strategies. The first and most basic step centres on legislative measures such as a minimum wage, the rigorous enforcement of current labour law and the upgrading of employee skills by investing in human capital. None of those measures does, in itself, go to the heart of the current trade union malaise, nor does it alter the rules of the game in a fundamental way. These measures provide a floor, however, and they are needed particularly in residual welfare states with weak social protection, weak trade unions and decades of neoliberal economics practised across the board.

A second and more ambitious level that speaks directly to the more radical potential of predistribution concerns the institutional structure of industrial relations and the role of the unions in it. Building on schemes and models such as co-determination and the Ghent system of unemployment insurance serves the purpose of strengthening the *structural* resources of trade unions, and their bargaining power in the workplace as a collective force. Such a level of ambition goes beyond an individualistic, case by case approach to labour market woes and offers a more comprehensive and long-term remedy to issues arising from the built-in inequality between capital and labour.

Finally, a third level of action speaks directly to the decline of trade unionism in recent decades and assigns a primary role to the restoration of trade unions as agents of emancipation, in line with predistribution's more radical potential. I suggest that the trade union movement ought to intensify steps taken towards forming new alliances with civil society, NGOs and other organisations on a common platform of radical change. Institutional reform makes trade unions more powerful at the workplace and offers added security to employees, but does not relieve the unions from the rather passive role of 'social partners' in the labour market, and alienates core constituencies eager to work towards more fundamental transformation both in and outside the labour market. In this third level, therefore, the trade union movement comes together with social movements and articulates a political as well as an economic agenda of change, rediscovering its civic role as an agent of public education and acts both as a stakeholder in the labour market and an emancipatory force outside it.

Level One: Employment Law and Short-Term Measures

The starting point in labour market intervention according to the predistribution principle is the enforcement and expansion of labour market regulation, and in particular employee rights. Conditions differ greatly between states: in the USA, the absence of a constitutionally guaranteed right to collective bargaining has enticed anti-labour laws in states as varied as Milwaukee, California, and Chicago.[20] The reform of trade union law to facilitate collective bargaining has to be a starting point of deeper change at local, state and federal level. In Europe, conditions differ and the rights afforded to organised labour are generally enshrined in legally binding agreements at national and/or EU level. Yet malpractice is rife, particularly in those countries (the UK, eastern and southern Europe) with weak industrial relations systems. Moreover, the economic crisis has led to a wave of new legislation hampering collective bargaining practices and the ability of trade unions to pursue workers' rights. In fact, the employment deregulation agenda today includes the EU as a whole.[21] Raising awareness on the issue and reclaiming the legal and institutional space necessary for effective trade union action in wage bargaining is a necessary step and needs to complement measures designed to address pressing issues of wage inequality.

Primary among them is the minimum wage, a policy option already practised in many countries across the world. Its recent introduction in Germany has further boosted the debate as to the desirability of a minimum wage at European level.[22] The intensity of the debate and the wide embrace of a minimum wage policy is a sign of the desperate state in which millions of workers find themselves, as the minimum wage provides relief from extreme forms of exploitation. There is also some evidence that it can contribute to poverty reduction.[23] It is a sound policy, but not without complications or problems. First, countries where union density remains high and social partnership is embedded in wage setting resist a statutory minimum age, as it will diminish trade union power and their relevance to members. Secondly, a minimum wage provides a minimum floor of workers' protection, yet does little to address the more structural problem of wage inequality, exposing employees to the whims of the market strictly on an individual basis. It also offers little by way of enhancing the collective bargaining power of the workforce.[24]

In order to address such problems, trade unions, in partnership with employers and the state, ought to play a role in investing in skills, especially for those excluded from the labour market, the young, and other vulnerable groups.[25] Tackling wage inequality goes through upgrading the skills of those lower down the pay scale, not least those who have been on the losing end of the technological and economic change of the last two decades. It is only through such measures that the need for minimum wages will be reduced, a high-quality high-value type of political economy can be created and employees will feel less insecure about their future job prospects.

Level Two: The Salience of Institutions

Employment law protection, the recognition of trade union and employee rights, minimum wage policies and skills upgrades form the first part of an overall strategy to put predistributive policies into practice. A second, bolder step is to proceed with long-term institutional changes that will strengthen the collective power of organised labour to negotiate from a positon of strength. Data exists, and has been published by the OECD, clearly demonstrating that enhancing the bargaining power of wage earners in the labour market can go a long way towards reducing pre-tax inequalities. This includes increasing the union density rate by 10 points.[26]

One concrete example of an institutional structure that offers employees a voice and allows for consensus-based decision-making in the workplace is the co-determination system pioneered by Germany. Institutional design matters greatly in industrial relations: on the peak of the economic crisis in the late 2000s, Germany and Austria established joint decision-making forums between employees and employers to avoid massive layoffs by offering work reorganisation schemes centred on working time reduction. Given the plurality of industrial relations regimes and their diverse historical and political origins,[27] institutional reorganisation would involve trade unions working alongside employee representatives to enhance employee say in how the workplace reacts to changing economic circumstances by taking employee rights into account and seeking to facilitate their commitment to high-quality production. The extent to which trade unions would be involved in decision-making should be subject to negotiations and dependent on contextual, local and national factors.

Co-determination would be one step; the more radical redesign of institutions that involve trade unions directly is endorsing the Ghent system of unemployment insurance and trade union organisation. The practical implementation of the Ghent system differs from country to country, but all of those who implement it assign a strong role to trade unions in administering their country's unemployment insurance system.[28] The logic here is different to the co-determination system, in that trade unions assume administrative responsibilities for a central aspect of the labour market and welfare system. In this way, they become active agents in the labour market, therefore assuming an encompassing role that forces them to consider issues beyond their core constituency. At the same time, the Ghent system can form a virtuous circle: an insurance system designed according to the Ghent structure offers cues to non-unionised workers as to the benefits that union membership can offer.[29] This changes the incentive structure for joining a union and offers organised labour additional members, resources and opportunities to claim employee rights in the workplace. As a consequence, 'Ghent' can become a focal point for union recruitment among those employees least represented by unions today: temporary workers, immigrant workers and those employed under precarious work conditions, such as zero-hour contracts.

Moving to this second level of change will undoubtedly be a difficult process, not least for countries whose industrial relations culture shies away from policy cooperation and where social pacts are weak. Trade unions, too, develop their own identities over time that result from ideological, political and institutional patterns shaped in their particular context.[30] They can thus be resistant to changing established forms of operation and adopt new techniques to cope with a rapidly changing external environment.

Level Three: Trade Union Renewal and Change

Although change is difficult, there are circumstances in which it is necessary. Predistribution's goal of emancipation and a stronger collective voice for working people materialises through levels one and two outlined above, in different ways and to different degrees. Its most radical version, however, finds concrete expression when trade unions act not only as channels of communication with firms and/or the state, but when they renew their operation to create common cause with other organisations and social movements. This can lead to a degree of empowerment much higher than Level two practices; it makes trade unions part of a progressive civil society movement with the ultimate aim of addressing some of the root causes of increasing inequality and persistent exclusion by vulnerable groups from the democratic process.

The process of trade union renewal is not merely integral to their own success, it is also important in overcoming some of the limitations arising from the current system of employee representation, and the resulting complications at trade union level. To illustrate, the creation of European Works Councils (EWCs) through a 1994 Directive (revised in 2009) was meant to herald a new era in employee information and consultation for firms employing more than 1,000 staff in two or more EU member states.[31] The literature, however, suggests that the EWCs have hardly served an emancipatory purpose for trade unions, even where EWCs have been put into practice. Frequently, EWCs have been used by management to intensify competition between different plants. Further, trade unions have made use of information and consultation mechanisms to engage in intra-union competition regarding production capacity, thus undermining a more encompassing role they are meant to play.[32] The case is instructive as to the malaise of trade unions today: sticking to a social partnership role, even if that would herald an upgrade of trade union capacity at workplace level, hardly serves the purpose of employee empowerment and can even lead to intra-union competition. This then undermines their role both at the workplace and in society more generally.

An alternative strategy that places trade unions at the heart of modern progressive politics, and genuinely facilitates their ability to influence the prevailing political economy paradigm, involves alliance-building with progressively minded organisations, NGOs and other civil society movements. Establishing a larger membership base and building on existing resources is certainly facilitated by institutional innovation. Nevertheless, opening up to society at large is a precondition for sustainable growth and society-wide influence. More often than not, trade unions tend to operate in an overtly bureaucratic, top-down fashion that alienates their rank and file, among young members in particular. Trade union officials appear absorbed either in business unionism or the maintenance of benefits that increasingly strike society as unfair privileges, all the while maintaining friendly relations with employers at elite level.[33] The result is alienation from society, cynicism and apathy among members, and an inability to make a real difference in working peoples' lives.

The process of renewal begins from a democratisation drive inside the trade union movement to enhance leadership accountability and make intra-union operations fully transparent to members and the public alike.[34] Once internal legitimacy is assured and the democratic process is fully respected, trade unions can engage with society from a different starting point. Many European trade union movements stem from or used to be intrinsically linked to wider popular movements, cooperatives and communes. They played an educational role in enhancing workers' and peoples' knowledge on current affairs, informing and consulting people on political and economic developments.[35] Re-establishing such a role by use of modern technology, social media and communication campaigns in partnership with progressive NGOs and voluntary groups goes a long way in making trade unions a vital part of a new, progressive socio-economic settlement. From a position of strength, trade unions would then be able to add a credible voice to the debate on run-away inequality and the inherent injustices that turbo-capitalism has bequeathed on younger generations. Forming part of the progressive alliance, trade unions would benefit in two ways: their internal organisation would receive a much-needed dosage of democratic renewal, while their external operation would become more effective and tied to peoples' everyday concerns.

All of the above then amounts to a strategy of social movement unionism that articulates a broader message than labour market reform, skills improvement or a living wage. All of these are necessary, and depending on context can prove crucial for predistribution to have an impact. But relying solely on them invites the danger of sidestepping the structural causes of inequality, and the lack of workers' voice both as employees and as concerned citizens.

Conclusion

This chapter has argued that trade unions are at the heart of the predistribution agenda, aiming at less inequality and sustainable growth. Organised labour faces very different conditions in different countries, and an all-sweeping recipe for reform hardly corresponds to diverse conditions on the ground. However, predistribution has much to offer to trade unions everywhere, and the chapter has identified three levels of action and change. From the more moderate need to enforce employment law, assure worker safety and skills, and fight for minimum pay that maintains human dignity, to the more radical vision of trade union renewal to match the aspirations of progressives organised in different civil society groups and associations, predistribution has the potential to usher in genuine reform and long-term structural change.

By way of conclusion, a word of caution: predistribution has many dimensions, from the innocuous to the radical. Implementing a public policy programme based on its core aims and objectives presupposes a willingness to be far-reaching in public policy reform, and being ready to engage in ideological combat.[36] This need of bold action is evident in the labour market and the role of trade unions. Enhancing the role and influence of the latter can go a long way towards more egalitarian pay and democratic decision-making in the workplace and beyond. Given the current state of trade unionism, however, it will be neither easy nor uncontroversial to address such issues and succeed in implementing reform. The time is ripe for an ambitious agenda matched by bold action.

Notes

1. Jacob Hacker, 'The foundations of middle class democracy', in *Priorities for a New Political Economy: Memos to the Left* (London: Policy Network, 2011), p. 35.
2. Evelyne Huber and John D. Stephens, *Development and Crisis of the Welfare State* (Chicago: University of Chicago Press, 2001).
3. Anton Hemerijck, *Changing Welfare States* (Oxford: Oxford University Press, 2013).
4. OECD, *Rising Inequality: Youth and Poor Fall Further Behind*, (Paris: OECD, 2012), p. 6.
5. European Commission, 'The provision of childcare services: a comparative review of 30 European countries', European Commission (2009).
6. David Miliband, 'Decade of Disorder', *New Statesman*, 9–15 August 2013, pp. 34–6.
7. Martin O'Neill, 'Beyond the welfare state: Rawls' radical vision for a better America', *Boston Review,* October (2012).
8. Briggid Lafan, 'The politics of identity and political order in Europe', *Journal of Common Market Studies* 34/1, (1996), pp. 81–102.
9. Andrew Gamble, *The Spectre at the Feast: Capitalist Crisis and the Politics of Recession* (London: Palgrave Macmillan, 2009); Mark Blyth, *Austerity: the History of a Dangerous Idea* (New York: Oxford University Press, 2013).
10. Francis Fukuyama, 'The future of history: can liberal democracy survive the decline of the middle class?', *Foreign Affairs* 6 (2014).
11. Jacob Hacker, 'The foundations of middle class democracy'; Peter Taylor-Gooby, 'Why do people stigmatise the poor at a time of rapidly increasing inequality, and what can be done about it?', *Political Quarterly* 84/1 (2013), pp. 31–42.
12. Kitty Ussher, 'What is Predistribution?' (London: Policy Network, 2012). Available at http://www.policy-network.net/pno_detail.aspx?ID=4272&title=What+is+pre-distribution%3F (accessed 16 March 2015).
13. Patrick Diamond, 'How Labour can give real meaning to predistribution', *New Statesman*, 12 June 2013. Available at http://www.newstatesman.com/

politics/2013/06/how-labour-can-give-real-meaning-predistribution (accessed 18 May 2015).

14. Francis Castles, *The Social Democratic Image of Society* (London: Routledge and Kegan, 1976).

15. ILO, 'Organizing for Social Justice', ILO (2004). Available at http://www.ilo.org/public/portugue/region/eurpro/lisbon/pdf/rep-i-b.pdf (accessed 16 March 2015).

16. Duane Swank, *Global Capital, Political Institutions, and Policy Change in Developed Welfare States* (Cambridge: Cambridge University Press, 2002).

17. Jelle Visser, 'Database on institutional characteristics of trade unions, wage setting, state intervention and social pacts in 34 countries between 1960 and 2008', ICTWSS Database, (Amsterdam: AIAS, 2010).

18. Dimitris Tsarouhas, 'Social democracy and trade unions', in H. Meyer and J. Rutherford (eds), *The Future of European Social Democracy: Building the Good Society* (London: Routledge, 2012), pp. 107–19.

19. Robert Wade, 'How high inequality plus neoliberal governance weakens democracy', *Challenge* 56/6 (2013), pp. 5–37.

20. Katrina Van den Heuvel, 'Predistribution: a big new idea', *The Nation* 295/15 (2012), p. 5.

21. Isabelle Schömann, 'Labour law reforms in Europe: adjusting employment protection legislation for the worse?', ETUI Working Paper (Brussels: ETUI, 2014).

22. Thorsten Schulten, 'Contours of a European minimum wage policy', Berlin: Friedrich Ebert Foundation (2014). Available at http://library.fes.de/pdf-files/id-moe/11008.pdf (accessed 16 March 2015).

23. John T. Addison and McKinley L. Blackburn, 'Minimum wages and poverty', *Industrial and Labor Relations Review* 52/3 (1999), pp. 393–409.

24. David Coats, *Labour and the Unions: Towards a New Settlement* (London: Policy Network, 2013).

25. ILO, 'A skilled workforce for strong, sustainable and balanced growth', Geneva: ILO (2010). Available at http://www.oecd.org/g20/meetings/toronto/G20-Skills-Strategy.pdf (accessed 16 March 2015).

26. OECD, *Economic Policy Reforms 2012: Going for Growth* (Paris: OECD, 2012).

27. Adrian Wilkinson, Geoffrey Wood, and Richard Deeg (eds) *The Oxford Handbook of Employment Relations* (Oxford: Oxford University Press, 2014).

28. Alex Bryson, Bernhard Ebbinghaus, and Jelle Visser, 'Introduction: causes, consequences and cures of union decline', *European Journal of Industrial Relations* 17/2 (2011), pp. 97–105.

29. Bo Rothstein, 'Labor market institutions and working class strength', in Kathleen Thelen and Sven Steinmo (eds), *Structuring Politics: Historical Institutionalism in Comparative Analysis* (New York: Cambridge University Press, 1992), pp. 33–56; Zoltan Fazekas, 'Institutional effects on the presence of trade unions at the workplace: moderation in a multilevel setting', *European Journal of Industrial Relations* 17/2 (2011), pp. 153–69.

30. Richard Hyman, 'Trade union research and cross-national comparison', *European Journal of Industrial Relations* 7/2 (2001), pp. 203–32.

31. 'Directive 2009/28/EC of the European Parliament and of the Council on the establishment of a European Works Council or a procedure in community-scale undertakings and community-scale groups of undertakings for the purposes of informing and consulting employees' (Luxembourg: Official Journal of the European Union, 2009).

32. Bob Hancké, 'European works councils and industrial restructuring in the European motor industry', *European Journal of Industrial Relations* 6/1 (2000), pp. 35–59.

33. See Peter Fairbrother and Charlotte A. B. Yates, 'Unions in crisis, unions in renewal?', in Peter Fairbrother and Charlotte A. B. Yates (eds), *Trade Unions Renewal: A Comparative Study* (London: Routledge, 2003), pp. 1–31.

34. Kim Moody, 'American labor: a movement again?', *Monthly Review* 49/3 (1997), pp. 46–62.

35. Gerassimos Moschonas, *In the Name of Social Democracy* (London: Verso, 2001).

36. Martin O'Neill and Thad Williamson, 'The Promise of Predistribution' (London: Policy Network, 2012). Available at http://www.policy-network.net/pno_detail.aspx?ID=4262&title=The-promise-of-pre-distribution (accessed 16 March 2015).

Part IV

Predistribution and the Social Investment State

CHAPTER 10

Social Investment, Skills and Inequality[1]
The Importance of Institutional Design

Marius R. Busemeyer

The welfare state at the beginning of the twenty-first century faces a set of formidable challenges. Population ageing is predicted to lead to a huge increase in spending on age-related social policies for pensions, health and care policies. Traditional family structures are changing, indicated by the increase of single-parent households and enhanced female labour force participation, creating new demands for early childhood education and family policies. These changes are related to and reinforced by socio-economic structural changes from the industrial to the service and knowledge economy, which leads to new social risks for those without the set of skills necessary to be able to compete in the highly flexible and demanding labour markets of the post-industrial digital age. As a consequence, we have seen a general trend towards increasing inequality in wages, incomes and wealth in almost all OECD countries and in particular in those countries which had been relatively egalitarian before, such as Germany and Sweden.

In times of economic globalisation and continued economic and fiscal crisis, policy-makers are increasingly constrained in their response to these new and old demands vis-à-vis the welfare state. There may be a growing mismatch between what the public expects and demands of the welfare state and the policy-makers' ability to deliver. On this background, the paradigm of the social investment state as a normative reference point has gained in popularity both among academics as well as in political debates.[2,3] Proponents of the social investment paradigm[4] argue in favour of shifting the focus of the welfare state from passive compensation of social risks via social transfers to activating types of social policies, in particular investments in human capital. Instead of compensating for loss of income after a particular social risk (unemployment, illness, etc.) has occurred, the social investment state is supposed to prevent the emergence of social risks in the first place by intervening as early as possible in the life course. This is why investments in early childhood education have become a focal point for discussions on the social investment paradigm. For example, drawing on social science research on the crucial period of early childhood with regard to the later development of intelligence and skills, Esping-Andersen[5] calls for a 'child-centred social investment strategy'. Despite the recent focus on childcare, the social investment logic was also influential in the field of active labour market policy,[6] in particular efforts to promote lifelong learning and the activation of the long-term unemployed.

In the following, I want to approach the link between skills and inequality from a slightly different angle. While the bulk of research on the social investment state has either focused on the very early stages of the life course (early childhood) or the later stages of typical educational careers (active labour market policies), I want to highlight the importance of the institutional set-up of education and training systems at the upper- and post-secondary level as a tremendously important factor shaping patterns of inequality. Post-secondary and tertiary education are the parts of the education system which are most closely linked to labour markets. Therefore, the study of the association between educational institutions and socio-economic inequality is critical in order to understand how educational opportunities are linked to labour market success.[7]

Education in the Social Investment State

There are many definitions of the 'social investment state' as is common in the case of social science concepts. Despite the variety of meanings of social investment, investing in education at different stages of the life course is the crucial element that different definitions have in common.[8] Somewhat simplifying the debate, the common expectation here is that the more the state invests in education and skills, the better. On the individual level, more education implies higher wages and a lower risk of unemployment, so that investing in education could in the long term contribute to a compression of the distribution of skills and wages, that is, lower levels of inequality. If access to education is the crucial factor that determines labour market success, questions about inequality in access to education and the distribution of educational opportunities are central to solving the problem of rising inequality.

I am going to argue that this very general claim needs to be differentiated further. Figure 10.1 displays the simple association between social inequality (measured by the Gini index of the distribution of household income after taxes)[9] and educational inequality. The latter is defined as the strength of the association between socio-economic family background and educational attainment as measured in the OECD's Programme for International Student Assessment (PISA) studies.[10] Higher values imply a stronger impact of social background on educational attainment, that is, higher levels of educational inequality, whereas lower values indicate a weaker association between family background and educational performance, implying smaller class-related differences between children from rich and poor families.

The surprising take-away from this figure is a *non-finding*: Although the fitted line indicates a slightly negative association between the two variables, this relationship is not significant in statistical terms. In other words, there is no simple linear relationship between educational and social inequality. Instead, countries are spread across the whole range of values, forming clusters that are reminiscent of the well-known worlds of welfare capitalism.

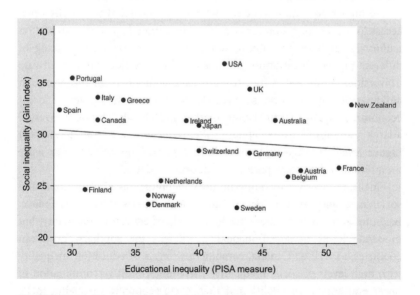

FIGURE 10.1   Educational and social inequality.
Source: Social inequality measure from Solt 2009 (average 1998–2008); measure of educational inequality from OECD 2010: 34 (based on 2009 PISA data). See notes 8 and 9 for further details.

Some countries – in particular the Scandinavian family of nations, that is, Finland, Norway and Denmark – combine low levels of educational inequality with low levels of income inequality. This is not surprising since the Nordic model of education is based on the principles of comprehensive education, aimed at promoting both social as well as educational mobility. In the universal welfare state model, education is a crucial policy instrument to support children from low-income families in getting access to higher levels of education:[11] vocational education and training (VET) is fully integrated into the comprehensive secondary educations, which increases the permeability between VET and higher education.

The liberal countries (notably the USA, New Zealand, Australia, and the UK) show the opposite pattern. They combine above-average levels of social inequality with relatively high levels of educational inequality. Even though secondary education usually follows the comprehensive model as in the Scandinavian countries, effective levels of educational inequality, measured in the sense outlined above, are higher in the liberal country cluster. Seen from a different perspective, liberal countries resemble the Nordic regime. However, the Nordic countries exhibit lower levels of institutional stratification, implying a relatively high degree of openness in the higher education system. In liberal countries, the formally open access to higher education is partly offset by a high degree of stratification *within* the higher education system, that is, a hierarchical ranking of different higher education institutions based on prestige with elite private universities at the top.[12] The strong private component in the provision and financing of education (see below) corresponds to high levels of socio-economic inequality in the labour market. Individuals who have invested a large amount of private capital in their education are likely to support higher levels of wage inequality, since they depend on a higher wage premium in order to pay pack their educational debts.

Finally, there are also counterintuitive combinations of educational and social inequality. In continental European countries (Germany, France, Belgium, and Austria), there are high levels of education inequality, but moderate levels of social inequality, whereas the southern European countries, as well as Canada, combine low levels of education inequality with high levels of social inequality. The counterintuitive combination of lower educational inequality and high socio-economic inequality to be found in southern Europe likely results from the fact that average levels of educational attainment, in terms of both actual performance and the distribution of educational certificates, are comparatively low. In a situation where a large share of the population is equally low-skilled, family background factors are likely to matter less. Still, it is well-known that the labour market institutions to be found in southern Europe often constitute a stark division between 'insiders' and 'outsiders', contributing to high levels of socio-economic inequality.

But what about the continental European countries? How is it possible that above-average levels of educational inequality are associated with below-average levels of social inequality? The answer points to the crucial role of VET in the political economy of social inequality. Countries with a well-developed VET system, for example, Germany, Austria, and Switzerland, usually also display a high degree of institutional stratification in their secondary education systems, exemplified by the early tracking of students onto different vocational or academic tracks with limited opportunities to change between tracks in their later educational careers. It is well-known that class-related differences in access to higher levels of education are particularly pronounced in countries with stratified secondary education systems.[13] However, the existence of a well-developed VET track in secondary education makes employers more likely to invest in skills as well and participate in apprenticeship training schemes. These schemes open up access routes for children from lower-income families to relatively well-paid and secure employment in the industrial, crafts and, increasingly, service occupations.

Of course, this simple graph merely captures a statistical correlation; it does not say anything about causality. However, it hints at an important finding: it is *not* the case that different kinds of educational investments are equally effective in reducing social inequality. The association between education and socio-economic inequality is more complex than could be assumed. In the following, I am going to argue that two factors are important with regard to the contribution of education to lowering inequality: first, the relative importance of vocational versus academic education at the post-secondary level, and second, the division of labour between public and private sources in the funding of education.

Investing in Vocational Education and Training (VET)

Coming back to the first point, it can generally be expected that educational investments are more effective in reducing inequality when they primarily benefit those in the lower half of the initial distribution of skills.[14] When shifting the focus from early childhood education to those sectors of the education system which are closer to the labour market (that is post-secondary education), the distinction between VET on the one hand, and academic higher education in colleges or universities on the other, is central.

The core hypothesis I want to develop in the following is that investing in VET can be a more effective instrument against rising inequality than expanding access to higher education alone. The simple reason is that investments in VET primarily benefit those in the lower half of the academic skills distribution, giving the relatively low-skilled access to high-quality training and skilled employment at a later stage of their employment career.[15] In contrast, expanding access to higher education benefits those who are in the upper strata of the skills distribution. Even if it would be possible politically, expanding access to higher education to such a great extent that as many low-skilled students as possible would get access to this one-sided strategy has natural limitations and can be partially self-defeating if the skill supply in terms of university graduates does not fit with existing labour market structures. For instance, countries such as Greece and Spain with high levels of tertiary enrolment and equally high levels of youth unemployment show that the value of a higher education certificate on the labour market very much depends on the relative distribution of educational certificates and the demand-side structure of the labour market. Furthermore, acquiring human capital creates public as well as private benefits in the form of higher incomes. Publicly subsidising higher education, while neglecting VET, likely reinforces the polarisation of skills and incomes on the labour market because university graduates earn higher wages. In contrast, expanding VET as an alternative to higher education boosts the relative income position of the low skilled, decreasing the relative difference between those with a university degree and those with a VET degree.

In order to substantiate this claim empirically, Figure 10.2 shows the bivariate association between the share of upper secondary students in vocational education relative to all students in upper secondary education, on the one hand, and socio-economic inequality on the other. Again, this figure shows a statistical correlation, not a causal relationship in the strict sense. Nevertheless, I find a rather strong negative association between the VET share and socio-economic inequality, which can also be confirmed in more complex multivariate regression analyses using a large set of control variables.[16] The figure shows that levels of socio-economic inequality tend to be lower in countries with a higher share of upper secondary students in

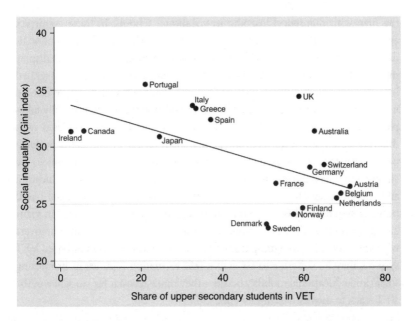

FIGURE 10.2   The share of upper secondary students in VET and socio-economic inequality.
Source: Social inequality measure from Solt 2009; share of upper secondary students from OECD Education Statistics Database, average values ca. 1998–2008.

VET programs. For obvious reasons, this indicator blends over important cross-country differences in terms of the quality of VET, which are hard to measure. This most likely overestimates the real contribution of VET to skill formation in liberal countries such as the UK and Australia, which show high shares of enrolment in VET according to the OECD data. This does not fit with the more qualitative knowledge about these cases, which clearly shows a more limited role of VET in these countries compared to continental Europe. Also, data for the USA is missing, although it is well-known from qualitative case studies that the provision of VET at the post-secondary level is weakly developed.[17] Thus, imaginatively correcting for these factors (by putting the USA in the upper left corner and moving the UK and Australia somewhat to the left on the x-axis) would actually make the association even stronger.

The data on enrolment in VET used in Figure 10.2 also does not distinguish between different *types* of VET, although this distinction has important implications. In countries with *collective skill formation systems*,[18] both unions and employers as well as state actors are involved in the governance of dual apprenticeship-type training schemes that combine practical learning at the firm with theoretical learning in vocational schools. In these countries, employer involvement in initial VET is particularly high. The situation is different in countries such as Belgium, Finland, or Sweden, which also display high VET enrolment levels. As mentioned above, VET is fully integrated into the secondary school systems in these cases, implying a very limited involvement of employers in VET, because vocational education usually takes place in a school setting. These different VET systems are associated with different outcomes in terms of inequality. Firm-based VET systems perform particularly well with regard to youth unemployment. Because apprentices are already employed during their training period, transitions from the education and training phase to employment are much smoother than in school-based training systems.[19] This is also due to the fact that the skills acquired in firm-based apprenticeship training better fit the actual skills needs of employers who are involved in designing training curricula. However, school-based VET systems may be superior to collective skill formation regimes in promoting social and educational mobility because they make it easier for students on the VET track to move on to higher education.

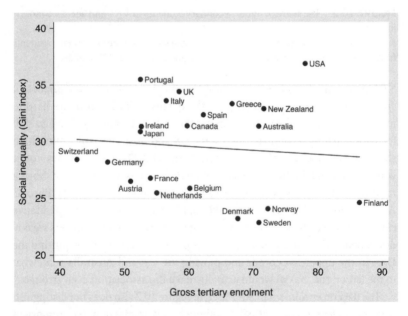

FIGURE 10.3   Tertiary enrolment and socio-economic inequality.
Source: Social inequality measure from Solt 2009; gross tertiary enrolment from UNESCO Institute of Statistics, average values ca. 1998–2008. See note 9 for further details.

Figure 10.3 exhibits the association between gross tertiary enrolment[20] and socio-economic inequality. In contrast to the association between the VET share and inequality, this association is weak, if non-existent. In fact, it is again possible to identify different country clusters. The Scandinavian countries combine high levels of tertiary enrolment with low levels of social inequality. Remembering the fact that the share of upper secondary students in VET is also above average in these countries (cf. Figure 10.2), these findings jointly indicate that the Scandinavian education systems seem to have managed to create educational pathways for low-skilled youths by keeping VET alive as an educational alternative on the secondary level, facilitating educational and social mobility from VET to higher education. In contrast, liberal market economies and southern European countries combine high levels of tertiary enrolment with high levels of socio-economic inequality, which could hint at the role of educational financing (in the case of liberal countries) and labour market structures (in the case of southern European countries) that affect the transition from higher education to the labour market. In any case, the important take-away point from comparing Figure 10.3 with Figure 10.2 is that a well-developed VET system tends to be associated with lower levels of socio-economic inequality, whereas opening up access to higher education as such may be a necessary, but is certainly not a sufficient condition for achieving low levels of social inequality. This is likely related to the way higher education is financed, which is what I discuss next.

Higher Education Financing

In addition to the distribution of students across different types of post-secondary education (vocational versus academic), the division of labour between public and private sources in the financing of education affects the potential contribution of educational investments to lowering inequality.[21] OECD countries differ greatly with regard to the overall level of spending on education as well as the relative distribution between public and private sources of funding.[22] In the Scandinavian countries, the private share in education financing is extremely low. This is true even though educational reforms in countries such as Sweden have increased the role of formally private (independent) schools, which are still financed with public moneys. Anglo-Saxon countries such as the USA, Canada, Australia and increasingly the UK, as well as East Asian countries (Japan, Korea), exhibit the highest levels of private education spending in international comparison. Private spending mostly consists of tuition fees, but also includes donations and contributions to educational institutions from households, businesses or foundations. For that reason, the share of private spending is higher in tertiary (university and college) education compared to other parts of the education system and the cross-national variation is higher in this sector as well. In the liberal and East Asian countries mentioned above, the private spending share in higher education can easily exceed 50 per cent.

There are good reasons to expect that a higher share of private education spending will be associated with higher levels of socio-economic inequality. The most obvious one would be to expect that high tuition fees could deter students from low socio-economic backgrounds from participating in higher education. Even though this deterrence effect may be mitigated through educational loans and scholarships, it is likely to become stronger when tuition fees reach extremely high levels and the relative pay-off of a university degree declines because of credential competition as seems to be happening in some liberal countries, such as the USA at the moment. If low-income students are disadvantaged from getting a university education and no viable alternatives in the form of VET are available, this is likely to reinforce existing educational and social inequalities.

An additional, more indirect, effect runs through public attitudes towards the welfare state and redistribution more generally defined. I find that support for government-induced redistribution is lower in countries with a high level of private education spending, which could be related to the fact that individuals who have spent a significant amount of money on their own education are unlikely to support the government taking away some of the returns on these investments via the welfare state.[23] Hence, the private financing of education also affects public perceptions about the role and scope of the welfare state.

In Figure 10.4, I plot the private share of education financing against the level of socio-economic inequality measured as before. The figure reveals a strong positive association, which is also robust in more complex multivariate regression analysis.[24] Again, it should be interpreted as a correlational relationship, since the direction of causality is likely to run in both directions. Still, the figure confirms commonly-held beliefs about the link between private education financing and inequality: Countries with higher levels of private financing also exhibit higher levels of socio-economic inequality, notably Canada, the USA, the UK, New Zealand and Australia as well as Japan. Vice versa, inequality is lower in countries where higher education is financed from public sources (the Scandinavian

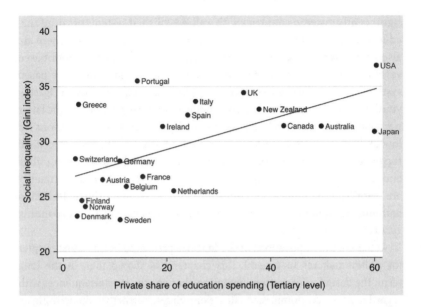

FIGURE 10.4   Private share of education spending and socio-economic inequality. *Source*: Social inequality measure from Solt 2009; private share of education spending from OECD Education Statistics Database, average values ca. 1998–2008. See note 9 for further details.

countries, but also some continental European countries such as Belgium, France, Austria and the Netherlands as well as – to some extent – Germany and Switzerland). Taken together, Figures 10.3 and 10.4 jointly imply that the level of socio-economic inequality is *not* affected by the relative size of the higher education sector, but by the way higher education is *financed*.

Conclusions and Implications for Policy-making

In this chapter, I have argued about how and why education matters with regard to socio-economic inequality. In particular, I argue that the commonly-held view that more education is better under any circumstances needs to be refined. Not all kinds of education are equally effective in mitigating socio-economic inequality, and focusing on the abolition of educational inequalities alone might not be sufficient either if the links between education and the labour market are not taken into account.

The brief presentation of empirical evidence[25] indicates that there are two factors, which are crucial. First, levels of socio-economic inequality are significantly lower in countries with well-established systems of vocational education and training on the upper- and post-secondary level. There are also important differences between different *types* of VET (school-based versus workplace-based). Research clearly shows that workplace-based systems (dual apprenticeship training) is more effective in mitigating youth unemployment than purely school-based forms,[26] whereas the latter perform better in decreasing wage inequality by facilitating transitions for low-skilled students from VET to higher education. The second critical factor identified in this chapter is the division of labour between public and private sources of education funding. Levels of wage inequality are significantly higher in countries with a strong private financing component, potentially counteracting the equalising effects of expanding access to tertiary education.

What are the implications of the findings presented in this short chapter for policy-makers? In general, this chapter has shown that, in the long term, the design of education institutions has enormous consequences with regard to socio-economic inequality. For policy-makers that aim to mitigate the trend towards increasing inequality, this is good news: it indicates that policy changes, although difficult to bring about in the short term, do matter in the long run. It is not the case that changes in socio-economic inequality are driven by anonymous market forces or 'skill-biased technological change'[27] alone. Policies and politics matter.

However, policy reforms that might pay off in the long term are often difficult to implement in the short term. The UK experience shows that establishing or reviving apprenticeship training is particularly difficult in a liberal market economy, because employers continue to be hesitant to get involved and be committed.[28] The case of Ireland, however, shows that establishing institutions of collective skill formation is possible. In this case, attempts to establish a collective skill formation system – albeit on a small scale – were successful because policy-makers tried to get both employers *and* unions involved in governing the system rather than catering to the perceived needs of employers alone. Furthermore, the Scandinavian example suggests that although firm-based training may have many advantages, school-based forms of VET might have beneficial effects with regard to lowering inequality too. Thus, instead of trying to increase employer involvement at any cost, policy-makers in the UK might want to enhance public commitment to VET instead, for example, by promoting and expanding high-quality opportunities in VET in secondary schools.

Enhancing public commitment to the promotion of educational opportunities is also relevant in the case of higher education. The empirical evidence presented above documents a strong association between the private share of education financing and levels of wage and socio-economic inequality. One reason for this might be the fact that very high tuition fees create effective barriers of access for prospective students from lower-income families. The second reason, which might have strong implications not only for education as such but also for the political sustainability of the welfare state, is that high levels of private financing depress public support for government measures that lower inequality. Hence, increasing the public share in the financing of higher education should be a high priority for left-wing governments in liberal countries. Instead of resorting to tuition fees, alternative measures to bolster education finances should be considered.

Notes

1. This chapter partly draws on a talk I gave at the 'Bremer Universitätsgespräche 2013' on November 28, 2013 and published as: 'Soziale Investitionen und Ungleichheit: Erkenntnisse aus dem internationalen Vergleich' [Social investment and inequality: Findings from international comparisons], in Wolfgang-Ritter-Stiftung, Universität Bremen, Gesellschaft der Freunde der Universität Bremen und der Jacobs University Bremen (eds), *Die Zukunft des Sozialstaates* [*The Future of the Welfare State*], Dokumentation der 26. Bremer Universitätsgespräche, Oldburg: Universitätsverlag Isenseé, S. 61–70.

2. Giuliano Bonoli, The Origins of Active Social Policy (Oxford: Oxford University Press, 2013); Anton Hemerijck, 'Two or three waves of welfare state transformation?', in N. Morel, B. Palier, and J. Palme (eds), Towards a Social Investment Welfare State? Ideas, Policies and Challenges (Bristol, UK; Chicago, IL: Policy Press, 2012); Nathalie Morel, Bruno Palier, and Joakim Palme, 'Beyond the welfare state as we knew it?' in N. Morel, B. Palier, and J. Palme (eds), Towards a Social Investment Welfare State? Ideas, Policies and Challenges (Bristol, UK; Chicago, IL: Policy Press, 2012) and Nathalie Morel, Bruno Palier, and Joakim Palme, 'Beyond the welfare state as we knew it?' in N. Morel, B. Palier, and J. Palme (eds), Towards a Social Investment Welfare State? Ideas, Policies and Challenges (Bristol, UK; Chicago, IL: Policy Press, 2012) for a general overview of the debate.

3. See Giuliano Bonoli,*The Origins of Active Social Policy: Labour Market and Childcare Policies in a Comparative Perspective* (Oxford: Oxford University Press, 2013); Hemerijck, 'Two or three waves of welfare state transformation?' pp. 33–60; Morel et al., 'Beyond the welfare state as we knew it?', pp. 1–30.

4. Anthony Giddens, *The Third Way: The Revival of Social Democracy* (Cambridge: Polity Press, 1998); Gøsta Esping-Andersen, 'A child-centred social investment strategy', in G. Esping-Andersen (ed.), *Why We Need a New Welfare State* (Oxford: Oxford University Press, 2002), pp. 26–67.

5. Esping-Andersen, 'A child-centred social investment strategy'.

6. Bonoli, *The Origins of Active Social Policy*.

7. Marius R. Busemeyer, *Skills and Inequality: The Political Economy of Education and Training Reforms in Western Welfare States* (Cambridge: Cambridge University Press, 2015); Heike Solga, 'Education, economic inequality and the promises of the social investment state', *Socio-Economic Review* 12/2 (2014), pp. 269–97.

8. Morel et al., *Towards a Social Investment Welfare State?*, pp. 1–30; Peter, Taylor-Gooby, 'The new welfare state settlement in Europe', *European Societies* 10/1 (2008), pp. 3–24.

9. Frederick Solt, 'Standardizing the world income inequality database', *Social Science Quarterly* 90/2 (2009), pp. 231–42.

10. OECD, 'PISA 2009 Results: Overcoming social background: Equity in learning opportunities and outcomes, volume II' (Paris: OECD, 2010), p. 34. Available at http://www.oecd.org/pisa/pisaproducts/48852584.pdf (accessed 17 March 2015).

11. Bo Rothstein, *The Social Democratic State: The Swedish Model and the Bureaucratic Problem of Social Reforms* (Pittsburgh: University of Pittsburgh Press, 1996).

12. Jutta Allemdinger, 'Educational systems and labour market outcomes', *European Sociological Review* 5/3 (1989), pp. 231–50.

13. Fabian T. Pfeffer, 'Persistent inequality in educational attainment and its institutional context', *European Sociological Review* 24/5 (2008), pp. 545–65.

14. See Esping-Andersen, 'A child-centred social investment strategy', for an application of this argument to the case of early childhood education.

15. Margarita Estévez-Abe, Torben Iversen, and David Soskice, 'Social protection and the formation of skills: a reinterpretation of the welfare state', in P. A. Hall and David Soskice (eds), *Varieties of Liberalization and the New Politics of Social Solidarity* (Oxford: Oxford University Press, 2001), pp. 145–83.

16. Busemeyer, *Skills and Inequality*, Chapter 4.

17. Kathleen Thelen, *Varieties of Liberalization and the New Politics of Social Solidarity* (Cambridge: Cambridge University Press, 2014).

18. Marius R. Busemeyer and Christine Trampusch (eds), *The Political Economy of Collective Skill Formation* (Oxford: Oxford University Press, 2012).

19. Maarten H. J. Wolbers, 'Patterns of labour market entry: A comparative perspective on school-to-work transitions in 11 European countries', *Acta Sociologica* 50/3 (2007), pp. 189–210.

20. Gross tertiary enrolment rates simply calculate the ratio between the number of students in a particular country and the size of a typical age cohort, neglecting differences in the share of foreign students and the age structure of the student

population. It should therefore be treated as a rough indicator of the openness of access to tertiary education.

21. Busemeyer, *Skills and Inequality*; Marius R. Busemeyer and Torben Iversen, 'The politics of opting out: explaining educational financing and popular support for public spending', *Socio-Economic Review* 12/2 (2014), pp. 299–328.

22. Marius R. Busemeyer, 'The determinants of public education spending in 21 OECD democracies, 1980–2001', *Journal of European Public Policy* 14/4 (2007), pp. 582–610; Frieder Wolf, 'The division of labour in education funding: a cross-national comparison of public and private education expenditure in 28 OECD countries', *Acta Politica* 44 (2009), pp. 50–73; Frieder Wolf and Reimut Zohlnhöfer, 'Investing in human capital? The determinants of private education expenditure in 26 OECD countries', *Journal of European Social Policy* 19/3 (2009), pp. 230–44.

23. Marius R. Busemeyer, 'Education funding and individual preferences for redistribution', *European Sociological Review* 29/4 (2013), pp. 707–19.

24. Busemeyer, *Skills and Inequality*, Chapter 4.

25. Backed up by more detailed analyses in Busemeyer, *Skills and Inequality*.

26. Marius R. Busemeyer and Torben Iversen, 'Collective skill systems, wage bargaining, and labor market stratification', in M. R. Busemeyer and C. Trampusch (eds), *The Political Economy of Collective Skill Formation* (Oxford: Oxford University Press, 2012), pp. 205–33; Busemeyer, *Skills and Inequality*.

27. Claudia Goldin and Laurence F. Katz, *The Race between Education and Technology* (Cambridge: Belknap Press, 2008).

28. Alison Fuller and Lorna Unwin, 'Vocational education and training in the spotlight: Back to the future for the UK's Coalition government?', *London Review of Education* 9/2 (2011), pp. 191–204.

CHAPTER 11

Looking to the Nordics?
The Swedish Social Investment Model in View of 2030

Ingrid Esser

Predistributive social policy, that in its logic emphasises 'preparing' rather than 'repairing', has a long history in the Nordic countries, although the terminology for such policy logic has differed over time. While *predistribution* broadly signifies market reforms affecting the distribution of economic power and rewards (that is, before redistribution takes place through taxes and benefits)[1], this chapter focuses on one of its elements, the more specific idea of *social investment*. The main logic of social investment is to strengthen people's skills and capacities for full participation in employment and social life over the entire life course. In Sweden, this agenda carries a legacy from the 1930s. The ageing population and low fertility at this time raised the 'population question', with equal concern for the quantity as well as the quality of the population in terms of the social conditions for human capital formation.[2] To tackle these challenges, an agenda was formulated that would combine policy instruments across several areas, including both direct economic support to families and indirect support to housing. The agenda also included opportunities for female labour force participation through the development of elderly and (child) day care, a development which continued also in the postwar period, when demand for female labour increased in chorus with the expanding public sector.

The broader policy implementation in line with the idea of social investment was formed in the early postwar years by trade union economists Gösta Rehn and Rudolf Meidner (*the Rehn–Meidner model*). The scope of this model included complementary and interrelated policies across the macroeconomy, the labour market and the welfare state in pursuit of strong economic development, as well as encompassing social protection. By the late 1980s, the Nordic welfare states were relatively well developed social investment welfare states. The Swedish model, albeit laden with macroeconomic imbalances (high inflation and repeated devaluations, etc.), was achieving beneficial economic as well as social outcomes; economic growth, full employment, low unemployment, inequality and poverty, high gender equality and provision of equal life chances through a well-developed educational system of high quality for all.[3]

In view of the Nordic model representing an early matured social investment model, the purpose in this chapter is to address some central changes and challenges the model is facing through times of recent crises. Specific focus lies with the Swedish case as a type case of the Nordic model. In broader comparative perspective, the Nordic states still form a distinct institutional family across central policy spheres, although large variation in electoral behaviour has recently been noted.[4] In an attempt to evaluate the challenges posed to the Nordic model in view of 2030, a fruitful approach is to evaluate policy changes and outcomes during the recent time period, as undertaken within the comparative Nordic project 'NordMod 2030'.[5] The account given here is based on some central challenges described in the project's Swedish country report.[6]

Next follows a short account of the social investment approach, the Swedish model and a general background against which institutional changes have occurred since the 1990s crisis. Thereafter, changes in three central areas posing challenges to the Swedish model are described, followed by a concluding discussion.

Spurred by the new socio-economic context and new risks developing in the post-industrial era, new interest and thinking on social investment emerged in the mid-1990s.[7] The idea contains the 'dual ambition to modernise the welfare state and the needs structure of contemporary societies [...] to ensure the financial and political sustainability of the welfare state, and to sustain a different economy – the knowledge-based economy'.[8] Policy focus lies with investing in human capital during the entire life course in order to prepare individuals, families, and societies for labour market transformations, constructive coping with new social risks as well as an ageing society. The logic hinges 'on the number and productivity of future taxpayers and policies that broaden the tax-base (by raising employment levels)', which should 'increase the productivity as well as the quality of work (and therefore increase wages)' – in short – 'investing in human capital should enable the creation of more and better jobs'.[9] A crucial notion is understanding investments in human capital and reproduction as in fact a productive strategy, that is the reproduction of a nation's productive capacity, which is also necessary to maintain the intergenerational redistributive system.[10] In these aspirations, the approach shares a focus both on the demand side with neoliberalism, as well as trust in state intervention with Keynesianism. While terminology has differed across time and context, there is reasonable consensus today on how social investment represents the underlying policy logic of conceptions such as 'social development', 'the developmental welfare state', 'the social investment state', 'the enabling state' as well as 'inclusive liberalism'.[11] At the same time, the flexibility of this concept has been somewhat problematic, as it has in fact represented the Nordic, 'social democratic' approach as well as the 'Third Way' approach based on an 'Anglo-liberal' view of social policy.[12] Certainly, this makes the approach appealing to many policy-makers, but consequently also draws broader critique. Recent discussion has brought attention to how these differences may explain the differential outcomes and success of the model.

The *new risks* to be addressed by the welfare state defined by Bonoli are: (1) reconciling work and family life; (2) single parenthood; (3) having a frail relative; (4) possessing low or obsolete skills; (5) insufficient social security coverage.[13] The public policies emphasised to address these risks are grouped across three areas: (1) the improvement of human capital, addressed by education and training policies, (2) reconciliation between the productive sphere of the economy and the reproductive sphere of the family, addressed by family policies, child and elderly care services, and (3) beneficial employment relations vis-à-vis increasingly differentiated employment patterns, addressed by policies and regulations that effectively facilitate transitions into employment and avoids entrapment in inactivity.[14] However, more traditional types of public policies, such as sick pay or generous unemployment benefits along with adequate rehabilitation programmes and active labour market policies, also play an important part in the protection of individuals' skills. In this way, policy measures often conceived as relating to old risks also play an important role in relation to the new risks. A strong case has recently been made that effective policies in poverty reduction calls for a balanced approach that combines the investment strategy with a protection strategy as 'complementary pillars of an active welfare state',[15] a combination that has been termed the Nordic approach to social investment.[16] Failing to pursue such a balanced approach appears to be an important explanation behind failing to reduce poverty in jobless/workpoor households in some European countries, where one-sided policy focus is even potentially counterproductive.[17]

The following is anchored in an institutional approach, where institutions are regarded as intervening variables between driving forces and outcomes, and as such temporary solutions to ongoing power conflicts.[18] As they constitute constraints as well as opportunities for action, path-dependent institutional development is an essential aspect in understanding institutional change. Early welfare state research also emphasised important interconnectedness between mutually interdependent and symbiotic welfare state and labour market institutions.[19] Such inter-connectedness is also central in the production regime approach, stressing inter-relatedness across broad spheres of production.[20] Arguably, such inter-connectedness and complementarities across policies and institutions, re-appears centre stage in social investment thinking.

The Swedish Model

Characteristics of the Swedish model can be summarised by:
- *Strong parties in industrial relations systems,* who negotiate collective agreements with little involvement of the government/state. Collective agreements regulate most conditions in the labour market and are based on solidaristic wage principles in terms of equal pay for equal work, also with macroeconomic consideration.
- *Full employment priority* (for men and women), both as a value in itself, and as a means of financing an encompassing and extensive welfare state.
- *Encompassing social security* through universal and earnings related social insurances for all against common social risks, designed to sustain individuals' standard of living for a given period of time.
- *Universal social services of high quality available to all citizens* regardless of individuals' resources or geographical location, publicly financed and publicly provided. Fundamental is the educational and training system for lifelong learning, available from early pre-school ages and throughout adulthood.
- *Good outcomes* such as low unemployment, low poverty, gender equality and equality in opportunities and life chances.
- *A political class alliance* between the lower and middle (income) classes, where both groups not only contribute but also benefit from the encompassing social security and social services.

Political, Economic and Social Background 1990–2013

Following a long history of governments dominated by the Social Democratic Party, a centre-right government came to rule between 1991 and 1994, which was replaced by a Social Democrat-Left government until

2006, followed again by a centre-right coalition until 2014. In the recent election, the Social Democrats managed a slim win, forming a minority government together with the Green Party. New to Swedish politics was the far-right Sweden-Democrats that came in third force, doubling their share of the vote to 13 per cent – also holding the balance of power. During this time period, Sweden experienced two deep economic recessions – the crisis in the early 1990s and the financial crisis in late 2008. While the first crisis fundamentally changed Swedish macroeconomic policies, the second did not have the same impact. One could say that several macroeconomic adjusters and priorities were developed in reaction to the first crisis and in place to protect the economy against prolonged and deep recessions, and as such helped guide the way through the second crisis, from which Sweden rebounded relatively quickly. Notably, many of the larger social and labour market policy reforms in the late 2000s were actually instated prior to crisis, following the change of government in 2006, thus not part of the actual crisis management.

The full employment agenda before 1990 meant that unemployment stood at below 3 per cent. However, with the onset of the crisis in 1991, unemployment skyrocketed from 1.8 per cent to 9.9 per cent in 1997, and has never returned to pre-1990 crisis rates. In 2001–2, it inched below 5 per cent, but has thereafter increased and is currently at 8 per cent. Particularly troublesome is high youth unemployment – the latter peaking at 25 per cent in 2009, although substantially lower (9.6 per cent) in NEET-statistics (unemployed persons not in employment, education or training), where Nordic rates are among the lowest in European perspective.[21] In terms of the tax base, Sweden has very high proportions of both female and male labour force participation, but saw a major drop with the first crisis, with quite slow and only partial recovery. Especially high, in comparative perspective, is female full-time employment and the participation of the older workforce, where the average exit age today is at 64 years for both men and women.

Power Balance in Industrial Relations?

The power balance in industrial relations has seen important changes in this time period as well. Union density still remains internationally high, but has dropped from 85 to 70 per cent since the mid-1990s. Largely, this was due to changes to unemployment insurance membership rules in 2006. Coverage of collective bargaining agreements remains high (over

90 per cent), even though the centralised coordinated bargaining system has been extensively renegotiated. The signing of the *Industrial Agreement* (1997) and the creation of the *Swedish National Mediation Office* (2001) seems to have created a new reasonably stable system of wage negotiations, thus withstanding an increasing risk of decentralisation, decreased co-ordination and dissolution of the solidaristic wage norm, which could bring out higher wage dispersion. This has resulted in rather low nominal wage increases (but high real wage increases due to low inflation) and a reasonably peaceful labour market. Still, the system is dependent on strong parties in the labour market and unions face the challenge of attracting employees in jobs that are traditionally less unionised.

In Sweden, minimum wages are not regulated by law, but subject to negotiations between the employers and employees. The role of wage setting and minimum wages must be regarded as central to the social investment strategy, as it seeks to decrease poverty by raising employment. Yet, it cannot be taken for granted that a goal of low poverty is complementary to the goal of high employment.[22] While increased employment requires public resources for lowering the cost of job creation, it is less costly to reduce reservation wages (by reducing the generosity of social protection), which may in fact increase the number of working poor if reservation wages are set below the poverty line. Data on minimum wages and taxation in Sweden do not, however, give evidence to a low-wage strategy being in play. To the contrary, minimum wages have steadily risen since the mid-1990s, notably so in relation to the poverty line. This implies that the work required to reach a net income above the poverty line has decreased over the past decade, although with a levelling out in the most recent years.[23]

Full Employment, Inequality and Poverty

Until the 1990s, full employment has been an effective strategy in Sweden to reduce poverty, a strategy which also echoes within the social investment approach. Yet, we can note that the Swedish policy discussion has historically focused rather on combatting inequalities (rather than poverty), both as a goal in itself and as an instrument in a strategy aimed at creating an open society with high social mobility and fluidity.[24] Also, this strategy has facilitated effective poverty reduction through earnings-related social insurance. This changed with the 1990s crisis. Notably, but not further discussed here, there has been a switch in macroeconomic priorities from low unemployment to low inflation in line with the EU-inflation target, for example through novel budget regulations and the instatement of an independent central bank. Critical voices have argued that Sweden has overperformed in budget control and in meeting the inflation target, and in consequence also suffered unduly high unemployment.[25]

Swedish poverty (proportion of persons with incomes below 60 per cent of the median income) has by international comparison been low. Since the mid-2000s, it has, however, increased to levels found in Sweden in the 1970s and comparable to poverty levels in Denmark and Finland today, although still decidedly lower than in Germany or the UK, for instance. Especially pronounced are elevated levels of poverty among vulnerable groups, such as the elderly and households with single mothers. To the contrary, poverty in households with children does not differ from the general average.

Active and Passive Unemployment Protection Measures

Swedish policies, early on, emphasised active measures through the development of active labour market programs (ALMPs) so as to aid matching and transition between jobs – from less profitable to growing sectors in the economy. Pre-1990, the shares of the public labour market spending were 75 and 25 per cent on active and passive measures, respectively. While unemployment increased from 1.8 to 8.7 per cent between 1990 and 2010, expenditure on active measures decreased by a third. The type and content of ALMP measures also changed entirely; spending on training was greatly reduced while it increased in relation to job search efforts, such as the use of job coaches and strengthened demands on being active.

Turning to passive unemployment protection, it should firstly be noted that this type of protection may also constitute a productive factor by means of rewarding formal labour force attachment that improves matching, caters to macroeconomic stabilisation and promotes economic restructuring.[26] As such, it caters to both the old and new risks discussed here.

The development in this area has drifted away from benefits' traditional universal and earnings-related character, to a focus on control and disciplinary measures. Firstly, although coverage according to specified regulations is well above 90 per cent of the active population, the take-up ratio in terms of share of unemployed persons receiving earnings-related unemployment benefits has dwindled from 1:2 to 1:3 persons. Main explanations are difficulties among new entrants to the labour market (young and immigrants) to qualify for unemployment benefits by fulfilling the work criteria (made more strict in 2007), and increasing numbers of unemployed persons who have exhausted their benefits. Secondly, as a consequence of non-decisions, the income ceiling has not been raised since 2002, even lowered in 2007, resulting in a very small proportion (11 per cent) of recipients actually receiving the stipulated 80 per cent of previous earnings. Further contributing to lower net replacement rates, are the large tax cuts introduced in 2007 on income from paid work but not social insurances. In parallel, the strengthened disciplinary aspects of the insurance include, for example, wider job searches made earlier during unemployment and monthly reporting of job search activities. As such, the form of the earnings-related unemployment insurance scheme appears to be intact but increasingly void of content to the majority of unemployed persons. This implies a shift away from previous ideals of the Swedish model on the mutual responsibility of both individuals and the state to reach the goal of full employment – where the role of the state typically included macroeconomic measures facilitating job creation, provision of appropriate education and retraining possibilities, so that no one should be unemployed against their will.

Sick Pay and Sickness Absence

While the early 1990s were dominated by sharply rising unemployment, the second half faced sharply increasing sickness absence (the highest in the EU-15 in 2003). Predominantly, this was a consequence of increased long-term absence rather than an increased number of sick persons. Absence is higher among women and in care and social service occupations, with a clear increase especially of psycho-social diagnoses. An overall assessment points to how a central driving factor is the increased pressure for change in the workplace and a decreased tolerance for differences in performance on the labour market. Such developments, combined with perceptions of increased demands, but less freedom in working and low labour mobility, increases the risk of stress-related disorders.[27] Some sickness absence may also have been linked to the high unemployment rate, as some persons have remained on sick leave while they rather should have been classified as job seekers in need of job change.[28]

One of the most important policy changes occurred in 2008, relating to escalating sickness absence – the introduction of a limited duration (one year) sick pay, previously unlimited. During this year, work ability was to be continuously assessed against an increasingly broad spectrum of job tasks in the work place and ultimately against jobs in the entire labour market. In this way, as in the unemployment insurance scheme, there has been a switch towards increased control and discipline.

Work and Family

Family policies in Sweden have, crucially, combined generous earnings-related parental leave benefits (introduced in 1974), with universal and extensive child care of high quality and at relatively low cost, and as such represent a dual-earner (and possibly dual-carer) family policy model. The model has proved beneficial to high female labour force participation, high proportions of full-time female employment and relatively high fertility by European comparison.[29] Yet, the utilisation of parental leave still remains heavily skewed. Women utilise 76 per cent of the leave days, despite efforts to increase gender equality, for instance by introducing individualised parental leave months ('daddy months') or a sharing-parental-leave-equality bonus (2008).

Moreover, labour force participation remains gendered. Men's participation remains a few percentage points higher since the 1980s, and women dominate among part-time workers. Wage differentials have decreased slightly over time. In 2011, women's wages were 86 per cent of men's, or 93 per cent once differences in age, education, sector, occupation and working hours are accounted for, leaving 7 per cent of the wage difference unexplained. Arguably, this provides some economic rationale for unequal sharing of parental leave. Yet, research indicates how even in families where the mother has the higher education or a high income, leave is still not shared equally. Hence, income does not appear to be the consistently crucial factor in sharing of parental leave, wherefore opportunities to equalise distribution of parental leave through economic incentives is limited.[30]

As noted above, the risk of poverty is especially high among lone-mother households. This is explained by many of these households being work poor and, as such, also overrepresented among households relying on social assistance.[31] Yet, in comparative perspective, child poverty in lone mother households is still significantly lower in Sweden along with other countries with more generous social transfer income packages. Notably, the Swedish support takes on the distinct character of ensuring that lone mothers are both paid workers and carers, facilitated by full-time child care available at quite low cost. These differences hold true also when accounting for demographic characteristics and employment status of lone parents.[31]

Social Expenditure and Services

In a recent comparison of social expenditure separated by policies addressing old and new risks 1985–2009, the overall trend is one of stability.[32] The distinct increases seen in spending on old risks during the time period were related to decreasing GDP through times of crises rather than increased spending in these policy areas. The expenditure related to new risks has instead increased slightly overall, especially in relation to childcare expenditure, which has increased gradually since the early 1990s, whereas the opposite holds for spending on active labour market policies.[33]

Another fundamental change worth noting, but not further discussed due to space consideration, is the introduction of public choice and increased private provision of still mainly publicly-financed social services. Expected outcomes were increased efficiency, improved quality, flexibility and variability in services. This commenced with reforms of the centre-right government in the early 1990s and gained new momentum with reforms in 2007–8, especially within education, sickness and care services. Remarkably, the outcomes of privatisation have been subject to meagre systematic evaluation, yet heavily debated as outcomes overall appear to be ambiguous.[34] In particular, the dwindling OECD Programme for International Student Assessment (PISA) scores, substantial inflation of grading and some indications of increased segregation, attributed to the new school system has drawn national as well as international attention.

The Political Economy

While universalism is formally intact across social insurances, the actual take-up ratio has plummeted in the case of unemployment insurance. Also, the replacement rate of unemployment benefits and, to some extent, of sick pay has been hollowed out due to lowered and lagging income ceilings. This creates strong incentives for middle- and high-income earners to seek (and pay for) complementary insurances, either through collective agreements or private insurances. Such developments can be expected to eventually undermine the solidarity behind collectively financed universal and encompassing social security for all citizens, whereby broad political support eventually will be at stake. Changes along this line could generate a cleavage between insiders and outsiders in the labour market, where the former are less willing to contribute to social security that primarily cater to the latter. Interestingly, recent attitude surveys lend evidence to widespread support and increasing willingness to contribute to the financing of collective welfare, especially in relation to sickness and care services, as well as support for the elderly.[35]

Lessons Learned from Sweden?

During the time period evaluated, the Swedish model can be said to have moved in the direction of a 'social investment light' model, especially during recent years with the priorities of the centre-right government for massive tax cuts over expansion and investment in human capital, for example in the form of resources directed to retraining, re-education and other traditional forms of active labour market measures. An important aspect is also the erosion of social protection, especially unemployment insurance benefits, particularly during years of solid economic performance. While the Swedish economy recovered quickly after the 2008 financial crisis, unemployment remains historically high, not least with persistent and high rates of youth unemployment. Relative poverty is higher than in several decades, especially among vulnerable groups, and inequality has been rising, especially since the mid-2000s.

In contrast, the new left-green government of 2014 has recently announced a clear shift in priorities towards increased investments in education and training, restorations of social insurances, as well as resources for increased employment in the public sector. These differences – on the one hand, priorities of extensive tax cuts, or on the other hand, increased social investment – indeed indicate the existence of clear political alternatives within the Swedish social investment model. A crucial aspect, calling for further evaluation, is the question of to what extent these developments are effective strategies for poverty reduction and increased employment, and to what extent the chosen strategy depends on a strong complementary pillar of traditional social protection – a question that appears to be highly relevant in a broad European context.

Given the understanding of an effective social investment strategy as one that strikes a good balance between mutually reinforcing social promotion and protection, that is, between several social, economic and labour market policies, one should not expect to be picking single quick-fix policies from an á la carte menu to evade social problems embedded in rather complex and integrated institutional structures. Central is the need to recognise path-dependent policy outcomes of such complementary institutions, whereby virtuous cycles of development may be created. An example is offered by Vandenbroucke and Vleminckx, whereby an educational system designed for increased equality is easier to establish in a more egalitarian rather than inegalitarian welfare state.[36]

In another phrasing, social investment policy choices have been understood as taking a 'high' or 'low' road to full employment. In the scenario where priorities are given to an expansion of employment in the low-skill-low-wage sector, increased income differences and inequality could be expected, while on the other hand, an expansion through investment in human capital might entail a more equal wage dispersion. In the Swedish case, the latter has been argued to increase the preparedness to embrace innovation and the necessary structural change of the economy, while there is little evidence that the emergence of a low-wage sector with a low-skilled workforce fosters innovation and a more dynamic economy.[37] While policy-makers in Sweden have recently had the opportunity to pursue quite different policy roads, the political economy of the welfare state tells us that hollowed-out social protection and fundamentally altered socio-economic patterns may in turn limit policy alternatives by undermining the interest coalition between social groups that, in the past, have supported the Nordic approach to social investment.

Notes

1.   Jacob S. Hacker, 'The institutional foundations of middle-class democracy' (London: Policy Network, 2011). Available at http://www.policy-network.net/ pno_detail.aspx?ID=3998&title=The+institutional+foundations+of+middle-class+democracy (accessed 18 March 2015).

2.   Joakim Palme and Axel Cronert, '"The Enlightened Path" or "the Third Way" for the Lions?', in ImPROVE Workshop, 8–9 April (Antwerp, 2014), p. 1.

3.   Ingrid Esser and Ola Sjöberg, 'Arbetsmarknadsmodeller', in Adel Daoud and Bengt Larsson (eds), Ekonomi & Samhälle (Stockholm: Liber, 2014), pp. 150–70 (kap. 7), pp. 165–6.

4.   Jon Kvist, Johan Fritzell, Bjørn Hvinden and Olli Kangas, Changing Social Equality: The Nordic Welfare Model in the 21st Century (Bristol: Policy Press, 2011); Åsa Bengtsson et al., The Nordic Voter: Myths of Exceptionalism (Colchester: ECPR Press, 2014).

5.   See NordMod2030. Available at http://www.fafo.no/nordmod2030/index.html (accessed 18 May 2015).

6.   Tomas Berglund and Ingrid Esser, 'Modell i Förändring. Landrapport Om Sverige', Fafo-rapport 2014:10 NordMod 2030, Delrapport 8 (Oslo: FAFO, 2014).

7.   For example, Klaus Armingeon and Guilano Bonoli, The Politics of Post-Industrial Welfare States: Adapting Post-War Social Policies to New Social Risks (London: Routledge, 2006); Gøsta Esping-Andersen et al., Why We Need a New Welfare

State (Oxford: Oxford University Press, 2002); Anthony Giddens, *The Third Way: The Renewal of Social Democracy* (Cambridge: Polity Press, 1998); OECD, *Beyond 2000: The New Social Policy Agenda* (Paris: OECD, 1996); M. Rodrigues, *The New Knowledge Economy in Europe. A Strategy for International Competitiveness and Social Cohesion* (Northampton, MA: Edward Elgar, 2003).

8. Nathalie Morel, Bruno Palier, and Joakim Palme, 'Social investment: a paradigm in search of a new economic model and political mobilization', in Nathalie Morel, Bruno Palier, and Joakim Palme (eds), *Towards a Social Investment Welfare State? Ideas, Policies and Challenges* (Bristol: Policy Press, 2012), pp. 353–76, p. 354.

9. *Ibid.*

10. Thomas Lindh, 'Social investment in the ageing populations of Europe', in Nathalie Morel, Bruno Palier, and Joakim Palme (eds), *Towards a Social Investment Welfare State? Ideas, Policies and Challenges* (Bristol: Policy Press, 2012), p. 272; Education was found to be the central driving factor for GDP growth in Europe according to Thomas Lindh and Joakim Palme, 'Sustainable Policies in an Ageing Europe' (Stockholm: Institute for Futures Studies, Research Report Series, Society and the Future No. 3, 2006). In this view the labelling of investment in, for example, education and family support as 'public consumption' in the National Accounts is misrepresentative, following Thomas Lindh, p. 277.

11. Morel, Palier and Palme, 'Social investment', p. 1.

12. Jane Jenson, 'Diffusing ideas for after neoliberalism: the social investment perspective in Europe and Latin America', *Global Social Policy*, 10 (2010).

13. The 'old risks' include unemployment, old age, ill health, sickness and disability, and the financial burden of raising children. Guilano Bonoli, 'New social risks and the politics of post-industrial social policies', in K. Armingeon and G. Boloni (eds), *The Politics of Post-Industrial Welfare States: Adapting Post-War Social Policies to New Social Risks* (London and New York, NY: Routledge, 2006), pp. 3–26.

14. Anton Hemerijck, 'Two or three waves of welfare state transformation?', in Nathalie Morel, Bruno Palier, and Joakim Palme (eds), *Towards a Social Investment Welfare State? Ideas, Policies and Challenges* (Bristol: Policy Press, 2012), pp. 33–60.

15. Frank Vandenbroucke and Koen Vleminckx, 'Disappointing poverty trends: is the social investment state to blame?', *Journal of European Social Policy* 21 (2011), p. 451.

16. Hemerijck, 'Two or three waves of welfare state transformation?'.

17. *Ibid.*; Vandenbroucke and Vleminckx, 'Disappointing poverty trends'.

18. For example, Walter Korpi, 'Power resources approach vs. action and conflict: on causal and intentional explanation in the study of power', *Sociological Theory* 3 (1985).

19. For example, Gøsta Esping-Andersen, *The Three Worlds of Welfare Capitalism* (Cambridge: Polity Press, 1990).

20. For example, Peter A. Hall and D. Soskice, *Varieties of Capitalism: The Institutional Foundations of Comparative Advantage* (Oxford: Oxford University Press, 2001).

21. EUROSTAT, 'European Commission Online Statistics' (European Labour Force Statistics. Statistics Department, http://epp.eurostat.ec.europa.eu/portal/page/portal/statistics/search_database: Statistical Office of the European Communities, EUROSTAT, 2014) (accessed 18 May 2015).

22. Anthony B. Atkinson, 'Poverty and the EU: The new decade', Universita degli Studi di Macerata: Macerata Lectures on European Economic Policy, May. Working Paper No. 24 (2010).

23. Joakim Palme and Axel Cronert, '"The Enlightened Path" or "the Third Way" for the Lions?', in ImPROVE Workshop, 8–9 April (Antwerp, 2014), p. 16.

24. Robert Erikson, 'Politics and class mobility: does politics influence rates of social mobility?', in I. Persson, Generating Inequality in the Welfare State: The Swedish Experience (Oslo: Norwegian University Press, 1990), pp. 247–66.

25. Berglund and Esser, 'Modell i Förändring', p. 186.

26. Joakim Palme et al., 'European Social Models, Protection and Inclusion', Research Report. Institute for Future Studies, Stockholm (2009).

27. For example, Staffan Marklund et al., 'Den Höga Sjukfrånvaron – Problem Och Lösningar', Arbetslivsinstitutet, i samarbete med Statens folkhälsoinstitut, Institutet för Psykosocial Medicin och Riksförsäkringsverket. Stockholm: Arbetslivsinstitutet (2005).

28. Ibid.

29. Walter Korpi, 'Faces of inequality: gender, class, and patterns of inequalities in different types of welfare states', Social Politics 7 (2000).

30. Försäkringskassan, 'De jämställda föräldrarna. Vad ökar sannolikheten för ett jämställt föräldrapenninguttag?' (Socialförsäkringsrapport 2013:8; Stockholm: Försäkringskassan, 2013).

31. Yekaterina Chzhen and York Bradshaw, 'Lone parents, poverty and policy in the European Union', Journal of European Social Policy 22 (2012).

32. Following L. Meeusen and A. Nys, 'Are new social risk expenditures crowding out the old?', CSB Working Paper 12:08. Antwerpen: Centrum voor Sociaal Beleid, Universiteit Antwerpen (2012).

33. Palme and Cronert, pp. 5-6.

34. Laura Hartman, 'Slutsatser' [Conclusion], in Laura Hartman (ed.), Konkurrensens Konsekvenser. Vad händer i svensk välfärd? (Consequences of Competition. What Is Happeining in Swedish Welfare?) (Stockholm: SNS Förlag, 2011), pp. 258–76.

35. Berglund and Esser, 'Modell i Förändring'; Stefan Svallfors, 'A bedrock of support? Trends in welfare state attitudes in Sweden, 1981–2010', Social Policy and Administration 45 (2011).

36. Vandenbroucke and Vleminckx, 'Disappointing poverty trends', p. 451.

37. Gun-Britt Trydegård, 'Från Fattigvård Till Kundval – Den Svenska Äldreomsrogens Framväxt', in Hans Swärd, Per Gunnar Edebalk, and Eskil Wadensjö (eds), Vägar Till Välfärd – Idéer, Inspiratörer, Kontroverser, Perspektiv (Stockholm: Liber, 2013), pp. 139–52.

CHAPTER 12

The Demography of Predistribution
Families, Economic Inequalities and Social Policies

Sophie Moullin

Inequality and ageing are two of the heaviest weights on welfare states. Redistribution through tax and transfers, although increasing overall in the OECD since the 1990s, has not been able to offset the rise in inequality in market incomes and wealth[1] – the 'predistribution' of economic resources. Meanwhile, it is estimated the fiscal impact of the 2008 financial crisis in rich countries over the next 40 years will be but 5 per cent of that of ageing.[2] This chapter considers one point where the policy concerns of inequality and ageing come together: family formation.

Across advanced democracies, reduced fertility rates alongside longer lifespans have meant we are experiencing an era of population ageing.[3] Even small differences in fertility can make a big difference to the economic and social effects of ageing.[4] Low fertility therefore presses questions of the future financing of welfare states,[5] and of intergenerational equity.[6] Ageing has led to a revival of policy interest in increasing fertility, and many make the case for increased public spending on, for example, childcare on this basis.[7] The headline decline in fertility, however, can detract from disparities in the context of fertility, in how people form families.

Disparities in family formation – specifically, the commitment and stability into which children are born and raised – echo socio-economic inequalities. But they also work to amplify and augment such inequalities.[8] Demographic change has, by and large, not led to a neutral diversity of families. It has contributed to 'diverging destinies' in economic experience and well-being, particularly for women and children.[9] An integral tenet of predistribution is therefore to counter this trend, and its adverse effects. The welfare of children and families, intra- as well as intergenerational equity, is at stake.

The Polarisation of Family Demography

In almost all Western countries, trends in family formation and stability are polarising. Those in higher social classes are having fewer children, later, in more stable relationships. But lower classes are still having children relatively young – and in less stable relationships. The rates of non-marital childbearing, lone parenting and parental separation vary across Western countries. What is consistent is their social class gradients.[10]

As on other indicators of social welfare, the USA is an extreme. There, while the proportion of new mothers who were unmarried quadrupled in the bottom 25 per cent of the education distribution, from 11 per cent in 1960 to approaching half by 2000, for the most educated quartile it barely doubled in the same period, to remain under 8 per cent.[11] The data from other English-speaking, 'Anglo-Saxon' countries now tell a similar story,[12] with the UK having some of the starkest educational gaps in the relative risk of having a child unmarried.[13]

Even in more egalitarian and socially liberal countries where it is common for parents to cohabit rather than marry, such as in Norway and France, it is still more common for parents with low levels of education to do so.[14] Moreover, although in these countries cohabitation has similar legal, tax and benefit statuses to marriage, and carries little social stigma, cohabiting partnerships with children are less stable. Even Sweden has seen a widening class gap in having children within cohabiting relationships, and in family stability. For children with more educated parents, the risk of experiencing parental separation before age 15 grew by 16 per cent between those born in the 1970s and those born in the 1990s. For children of less educated parents, however, the risk of experiencing parental separation increased by 50 per cent.[15]

Marriage, in part because it is more socially selective and more egalitarian, predicts relationship stability.[16] Yet the stability of married relationships also varies by class. Overall in the West, divorce rates are reducing. But more educated women have decreased their risk to a greater extent than less educated women. Since the late 1980s, in no major rich country was there a significant increase in the risk of divorce for women with high levels of education.[17] Together, the corollary is widening social class gaps in the experience of parental relationship transitions and time spent in lone parent households, for which parental relationship commitment at a child's birth remains a reasonable, if imperfect, predictor.[18]

Family Demography's Part in Inequality

The form and stability of family relationships is associated with the well-being of adults and children. Men and women's mental and physical health and behaviours are affected.[19] The effect on children's social and emotional development is real and lasting.[20] Family relationships' role in well-being and their inequalities themselves could be a case for policy concern – arguably the strongest case.[21] But even if we confine ourselves to thinking about the distribution of economic resources, we cannot simply think in terms of the spread across individuals. We must also consider the distribution of people across households. How adults form, and sustain, families have significant implications for their – and their children's – exposure to economic inequality. We see this in the interrelated measures of income, wealth, employment and poverty.

Income Inequality

On most measures, and in most rich countries, income inequality increased since the mid-1980s. The predistribution of market incomes is the most important proximate factor.[22] Inequality in individual market incomes is, however, compounded at the household level. Over a fifth of the rise in income inequality in the OECD as a whole between the mid-1980s and mid-2000s can, in a simple decomposition, be accounted for by changing family formation. About half of this effect is rising assortative mating; two-fifths of couples where both partners work now belong to the same or neighbouring earnings deciles, whereas only a third did 20 years ago.[23] The other half reflects the rising share of people who, either because they are unmarried or separated, are not living with partners at all. A study of 16 Western countries finds that an increased prevalence of single-mother families is associated with heightened income inequality – net of differing labour market institutions, social welfare systems and other key demographic and economic indicators.[24]

Family form affects in particular the economic inequality to which children are exposed. Amongst families with children in the US, it is estimated that changes in family composition account for 40 per cent of the overall rise in income inequality from the mid-1970s to the beginning of the twenty-first century.[25] But even in countries with generous redistributive family policies, family form is relevant to economic inequality. The average in OECD countries is for lone parent families to have incomes less than

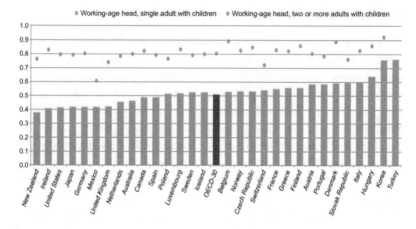

FIGURE 12.1 Household disposable income, relative to a working-age head couple household without children, mid-2000s.
Source: OECD Income distribution questionnaire, 2011. Chart CO2.1.B Relative income by household type, mid-2000s.

half those of coupled families without children (Figure 12.1). Even in Sweden and France for example, while couples with children have incomes about 80 per cent of those of childless couples, the incomes of lone parent families are about half of those of childless couples. In addition, it is the Nordic countries where single parents have seen the biggest relative drop in incomes since the mid-1980s.

Wealth Inequality

Inequalities in wealth greater than those by income, and the effects of family wealth on well-being and children's life chances, are seen over and above those of income.[26] Net of income, education and ethnicity, family structure is highly correlated with wealth.[27] Marriage is associated with increased wealth ownership, relative to cohabitation. The more assortative marriage is by wealth, the more it serves to concentrate wealth. However, one analysis shows that even if marriage were perfectly assortative by wealth, it would still reduce wealth inequality compared to a distribution based on inheritance and chance in returns alone.[28]

Illustrating the connection between family structure and wealth inequality, one analysis calculated that if the US had similar household structures to Spain, median wealth would rise, and the wealth gap between the median and lower quintile would narrow by 63 per cent.[29] The number of people with no assets (mainly women) would substantively decrease. The lower incidence of coupled households with children aged 35 to 55 in the US (16 per cent versus 20.9 per cent) appeared particularly important.[30] Although, as the next section discusses, those who do not form married families often have very little wealth at the time, family instability can prevent this position changing. Marriage's historical role as an institution of wealth consolidation remains important, as marriage is becoming, once again, an institution which the working classes are less likely to access.

Employment

We do not normally talk in terms of the distribution of work, but the welfare effect of an individual being out of work is clearly different for single and couple households. While employment has generally been rising in Western countries, so too has the number of households in which no adult works. Reconciling these two trends, Paul Gregg and colleagues find that much of the polarisation between households that have work and those that do not occurs in single adult households.[31] Male employment insecurity is, as I consider in the next section, a leading explanation for rising family instability. But this is a reminder that key economic trends, such as the employment rate, will have different welfare impacts depending on demographic trends. The ambition to return to 'full employment' – revived amongst social democrats – looks different depending on whether we think about it at the individual or household level.

For those in couples, women's employment income has played an important role in helping attenuate the impact of employment insecurity men experienced in the 'great recession' following the global financial crisis.[32] Female employment, both for single and partnered women, reduces household income inequality across rich countries.[33] But over recent decades, the rise in female employment has not been sufficient to counter the effect of the rise in single mother households on income inequality.[34] Men and women with neither secure careers nor stable partnerships are, in a sense, doubly exposed to the risks of unemployment and poverty.

Poverty

Despite large increases in their employment rate, single parent households remain concentrated in the bottom of the income distribution. In the US in

2000, half of families headed by divorced or separated mothers were in the bottom income quintile, as were three-quarters of families with a mother who had never married.[35] Across the OECD, even against the US federal poverty line (an absolute measure), on average lone parent households have four times the risk of poverty than coupled parent households.[36] Redistribution through tax and benefits naturally reduces the relative risk of child poverty in lone parent households. But it remains about four times as high in countries as varied in social and economic policy as the UK, Canada, Finland, and Norway. In Germany, lone parent families have nine times the risk of poverty as coupled parent families – after tax and transfers.[37]

As the next section emphasises, increased poverty risk definitely does not reflect family form alone. At the point of having children, unmarried men and women are more likely to be lower skilled, already in insecure employment and on low wages. Still, one research team found that women who had a child outside marriage remained between two and three times more likely to be poor than other women – net of the effect of ethnicity, family background, age, education and employment.[38] In the most recent study, of American families with children born in 2000, it is estimated that if the incomes of single parents were combined, it would pull just under half (47 per cent) of poor single parents over the poverty line.[39]

The Limits of Redistributive and Employment Strategies

The heightened economic insecurity experienced by lone parent families would certainly support an argument for redistributive policies towards them. One approach is to see single parenting as an ordinary social risk, and increase employment among single parents or target benefits and tax credits, and childcare services, further toward them.[40] Yet, the scale of the inequalities associated with demography is such that even highly ambitious redistributive, and employment-based predistributive policies would struggle to offset them.

Across the West, lone parents are increasingly employed outside the home, often as a result of welfare reform having made income supports conditional on work.[41] A large part of the reduction in child poverty achieved by the New Labour governments in the UK came from increased employment amongst lone parents, combined with tax credits that subsidised their part-time hours.[42] But, lone parent households still contain the majority of poor women and children. In fact, one analysis found that increased employment amongst lone parents in the US has, as welfare payments receded, done little to actually increase their family income.[43] Also in the US, where lone mother's employment rates are high, more likely to be full time, and where there is no paid maternity leave, one recent estimate finds the conditional wage penalty for unmarried mothers remains, while it has virtually disappeared for married women.[44]

In most rich countries, having two earners in a household is now important not only to access high incomes, but also in protection from poverty.[45] For two-parent households, economists suggest the rise in median incomes since 1975 largely reflects the increased hours worked by women.[46] We cannot assume that resources are pooled or shared equally within couples living together.[47] But as more couples become dual-earning (and egalitarian), single parents are left behind. Even if they work full-time while caring for children, they cannot keep up. And, it seems, neither can government welfare spending.

Family formation's role in the predistribution of resources looks small compared to the principal role of changing labour and capital markets. But changes in families and such markets are related. Not only does demography affect inequality, inequality affects demography. The question of whether the issue is 'demography or disadvantage' is in many ways, as British demographer Kathleen Kiernan has put it, one of 'chicken or egg'.[48]

Inequality's Part in Family Demography

Behind increasingly unequal patterns of family formation lie increasingly unequal young adulthoods, qualitative and quantitative research suggests. For those young adults on a higher income, marriage has again become a symbol of status, with weddings celebrations of the achievement of adult economic independence.[49] Many lower-income couples, meanwhile, say they want to get married but are waiting until they obtain a standard of living they associate with being married; they feel that they do not reach a 'marriage bar'.[50]

Many, however, never reach such a 'marriage bar'. Certainly those groups who have seen their marriage rates decline most are those which have also seen their income drop. In 1970, 91 per cent of median male workers in the US aged 30 to 50 were married. In 2011, over a period where their median real earnings declined around 28 per cent, this had dropped to 64 per cent.[51] Moreover, at the twenty-fifth percentile of earnings, where real earnings fell 60 per cent, half of middle-aged men are now married, compared with 86 per cent 40 years ago. To the extent that marriages are heterosexual, this also reduced working-class women's chances of marrying – despite women's employment and earnings improving at all points of the distribution.[52]

Recent analysis finds that men's labour union membership is associated with higher first marriage rates, with increased income, regularity and stability of employment explaining the link.[53] And beyond work and wages, wealth is independently important: at every age under 40, savings, ownership of a vehicle, or a home each increase the chances of first marriage, net of income.[54]

While economic circumstances matter, the issue is not simply about what men can offer economically. It is about what men and women can offer emotionally, too. For both genders, increased job and income insecurity is reflected in intimate struggles to make relationships and commitments.[55] The core concerns of low-income unmarried mothers are that men do not spend enough time on their relationships, they cannot be trusted to be faithful, and that they would not be good fathers.[56] This is not an issue of committed couples in high-quality relationships actively choosing cohabitation as an alternative to 'traditional' marriages, but individuals not accessing the long-term, quality or equal partnerships they want at all.

Finally, it is not only lower social classes' behaviour that is influencing inequality in family formation. Economists Lundberg and Pollak argue that couples in high social classes use marriage as commitment to a parenting project that emphasises high levels of economic investment in children.[57] In a similar tone, others have interpreted low fertility amongst higher income couples as a response to the greater opportunity costs of children, in terms of parents' own career advancement, wealth accumulation and what they can invest in their children.[58] If true, maintaining inequality in socio-economic status is not only a byproduct of differential family formation: it is a driver of it.

What (If Anything) Can We Do About It?

Even when we recognise the part of family formation in the 'predistribution' of economic inequality, the genuine challenge is: what can we do about it? The trends in family formation are widespread and fairly long-standing, and the number of discrete policies shown to be effective is extremely limited. Yet, significant declines in divorce and teenage parenthood show that demographic trends are not inexorable. Moreover, some rich countries have far more stable, and more equal, family forms than do others. Demography is not immovable destiny.

Of course, a return to a postwar model of family formation – itself historically exceptional – is not achievable. Nor (a point obvious to liberals) is it desirable. Being able to avoid and exit bad and oppressive relationships, and to make mistakes, is an important freedom, especially for women. But so is the freedom to form families in the way you want to, and have these recognised and supported by society. This is the point made in campaigns around the world for gay and lesbian 'marriage equality'. And many, regardless of their sexuality, are not forming families as they would like.

Listening to what People Want for their Families

Contrary to many popular assumptions, ethnographic research with low-income men and women has found that most of them value marriage and family highly. Many single mothers say they want to get married, and they think the best way to raise children is within marriage.[59] In parallel, many non-resident fathers find meaning in their relationship with their children, and want to be more involved in their children's lives, emotionally as well as economically.[60]

Moreover, many of those who have children outside of marriage did not intend to have them. Women who are cohabiting have an unintended pregnancy and birth rate that is over four times that of married or non-cohabiting women.[61] Those women with low education and incomes have a particularly high unintended pregnancy rate – and the latest research concludes it is this, rather than their desire for children or lower opportunity costs, that explains their higher fertility rates.[62] Lower social classes tend to have more children than they want, while higher social classes generally have fewer.[63] Family aspirations are similar across social classes and genders (and sexualities), implying that what differs is the ability to realise them.

There is no necessary tension between a liberal stance toward family, and family stability. Nor is there a necessary trade-off between fertility and family stability. There is no significant association between changes in fertility and changes in family formation across the OECD.[64] Ireland, for example, saw a large rise in non-marital childbearing and decline in fertility, while Norway's fertility declined despite large increases in non-marital childbearing. Addressing the family formation trends that contribute to both demography and inequality, does not require imposing particular 'family values', but rather enabling people to fulfil their own.

The number of single-parent households is projected to rise over the next 25 years in countries across the OECD, by between 22 and 29 per cent.[65]

Even if countries slowed that growth, and those with particularly large disparities in family formation – including the UK and the USA – brought their levels closer to OECD averages it would contribute to a more equal predistribution of economic goods – particularly for women and children. More importantly, it would likely also mean more people forming families in ways they want to, and enjoying greater well-being. How could a government support such a goal?

Learning from what has not Worked

It must be said that neither of the most prominent policy proposals and practice – tax incentives and marriage or relationship education – have strong empirical support.

One recent analysis exploiting variation in the US tax system finds that a $1,000 change in the incentive for marriage has a small (1.9 per cent) effect on the probability of marriage, with those with low education and couples with children most responsive.[66] In general, however, tax and benefits incentives have small or insignificant effects on marriage.[67] Moreover, if marriage incentives lead to early or poorly-matched marriages, without improving relationship quality, it could adversely affect family stability. This finding should not be surprising given the nature of the problem as set out here. Marriage tax incentives assume that people do not get married because they are not sufficiently better-off married. But unmarried parents themselves put forward a different explanation: they are not sufficiently well-off enough to get married.[68]

Although many commentators perceive welfare as a disincentive to marriage and family stability, it is (the few) welfare projects that increased family income supports that have seen improvements in family formation and stability. In the Minnesota Family Investment Project (MFIP), for example, single-parent recipients of higher welfare payments and increased tax credit disregards[69] had increased marriage rates by 4.2 percentage points over three years compared to the control group, who received a smaller welfare payment without disregards.[70] While modest in absolute terms, this is a 50 per cent higher marriage rate.[71] Notably, domestic violence also decreased. Furthermore, by relaxing welfare restrictions for two-parent families, MFIP increased marriage or cohabitation stability amongst two-parent families by nearly 40 per cent compared to the control group. The improvement in family stability remained at a seven-year follow-up.

Further, contrary to the concern with 'marriage penalties' in welfare systems, it is when benefits are tightly targeted and restricted that we see perverse effects on family formation. We can see this comparing the effects in the US of Aid for Dependent Children (AFDC), a needs-based entitlement that went to married couples with families far more than did the much more restrictive, time-limited and work-conditional Temporary Assistance for Needy Families (TANF) that succeeded it. It is estimated that TANF reduced marriages amongst couples with a low education, while AFDC increased it.[72] The effect was small, and we do not know if it led to greater stability. But at a minimum, it confutes the belief that reducing and/ or restricting welfare payments to single parents will increase marriage. It is notable also that in a review of US welfare policy experiments, not one programme that increased economic resources to unmarried women lowered their marriage rates.[73]

Similarly, it seems most marriage and relationship education or counselling programmes come too late, and fail to address how inequality shapes family formation. Amongst middle class couples, a range of couple counselling and marriage education programmes have shown modest improvements in mental health and relationship satisfaction.[74] However, the benefits of such programmes for low-income couples with children are small and short-lived, if statistically significant at all. In fact, in one area testing the programme, enhanced relationship awareness and skills precipitated more break-ups.[75]

Even against the stated aims of 'promoting marriage' then, neither the marriage incentive nor education approach is effective. And yet, the US is currently spending $100 million a year, funds diverted from federal welfare, on marriage education programmes. This works out as $11,000 per couple receiving the service.[76] The UK Conservative Party proposes to spend £700 million a year on a transferrable tax allowance for married couples – one which will be available only to a third of married couples and less than 18 per cent of families with children.[77] My reading of the literature suggests this resource directed to the employment, assets and skills – including relational skills – available to men and women before they have children is more likely to be effective.

Bringing Social Investment Forward

I would recommend a strategy that brings forward a social investment model, typically focused on early childhood, to include the period before families form. It would address the economic, but also the relational and gender aspects, of inequalities in young adulthood that influence demographic behaviour.

There is potential for policy synergy where policies that support economic stability for young adults also promote greater family stability. Some American policy experiments that improved the economic standing of lower skilled men and women also recorded increases in marriage. For example, the Career Academies initiative, a schools programme aimed at improving the transition from school to work, raised men's earnings substantially, and also men's marriage rates (although it had no such effects on women). [78] New Hope, a three-year project in the early 1990s to support poor working adults through earnings supplements, temporary community job guarantees and subsidised child care, produced substantial income gains, and twice the first marriage rates of the control group.[79] Expanded access to higher education, training and apprenticeships may also help young people progress in relationships as well as in the workplace. Addressing youth unemployment, which remains very high across the OECD after the global financial crisis, should be a high priority. Access to assets, including home ownership, may also be relevant to family formation.

Policy can also address relational and gender, as well as economic, aspects of inequality in family formation. Relationship education, for example, could be effective if it came before children.[80] Reproductive rights and access to effective contraception can reduce unintended pregnancy.[81] Encouraging men as fathers and caregivers, such as through more generous paternity leaves, could also feed back into improved relationship quality.[82] Although family policies have often focused on women's employment and fertility behaviour, research suggests that fertility decisions are often tied to men's working hours and contribution to caregiving.[83]

Demographic approaches to predistribution are not short-term or low-cost fixes. But neither are most traditional economic, employment-focused, approaches. The most progress on inequality will be made when economic and demographic strategies, and indeed redistributive and predistributive strategies, work together. Policy, however, must engage with the distributive dynamics that operate not only in labour markets, but also through families.

None of this is to deny the inherent politics in demography and family policy. I have argued, through a review of the academic literature, that demographic trends in family form and stability influence the experience of economic inequality, but also, crucially, that the experience of economic inequality prevents men and women from fulfilling their family aspirations, and undermines family stability. This challenges conservatives to acknowledge poverty and inequality as a primary driver of family instability, and admit, therefore, that policies that fail to address, or worsen, such inequality will disappoint. But it also challenges social democrats to acknowledge that the inequalities associated with family form cannot be redressed solely through current redistributive, or through employment-based predistributive strategies alone.

Central to social democratic thinking is the idea that mutual, just institutions with inclusive membership are indispensible in moderating market-generated inequalities. The family can be one such institution.

Notes

1. OECD, *Divided We Stand: Why Inequality Keeps Rising* (Paris: OCED, 2011).
2. IMF, 'The IMF on the fiscal impact of population aging', *Population and Development Review* 35/2 (2009), pp. 437–42.
3. Ronald Lee and Yi Zhou, 'Does fertility or mortality drive contemporary population aging? The revisionist view revisited', Working Paper (2013). Available at http://paa2013.princeton.edu/papers/132147 (accessed 19 March 2015).
4. S. P. Morgan and M. G. Taylor, 'Low fertility at the turn of the twenty-first century', *Annual Review of Sociology* 32 (2006), pp. 375–99.
5. Fred R. Harris (ed.), *The Baby Bust: Who Will Do the Work? Who Will Pay the Taxes?* (New York: Rowman and Littlefield, 2006), p. 238; Ronald Lee and Ryan Edwards, 'The fiscal impact of population change', in Jane Sneddon Little and Robert K. Triest (eds), *Seismic Shifts: The Economic Impact of Demographic Change* (Boston: Federal Reserve Bank of Boston, 2001), pp. 189–219.
6. Pieter Vanhuysse, 'Intergenerational justice and public policy in Europe', European Social Observatory (OSE) Paper Series, Opinion Paper No. 16 (2014). Available at http://papers.ssrn.com/sol3/papers.cfm?abstract_id=2416916 (accessed 19 March 2014).
7. Adriaan Kalwij, 'The impact of family policy expenditure on fertility in western Europe', *Demography* 47/2 (2010), pp. 503–19.
8. Sara McLanahan and Christine Percheski, 'Family structure and the reproduction of inequalities', *Annual Review of Sociology* 34/1 (2001), pp. 257–76.
9. Sara McLanahan and Wad Jacobson, 'Diverging destinities revisited', Paper presented at the Penn State Symposium on 'Diverging destinies: Families in an era of increasing inequality', 7–8 October 2013; Sara McLanahan, 'Diverging destinies: how families are faring under the second demographic transition', *Demography Association of America* 41/4 (2012), pp. 607–27.
10. The education gap in single motherhood between the most and least educated mothers ranged from 3:1 to 4:1 in other countries. Of eight European countries

with comparable data, only in Italy did women with the highest and lowest levels of education have the same risk of having a birth in a cohabiting union (McLanahan and Jacobson, 'Diverging destinities revisited'; Brienna Perelli-Harris, Michaela Kreyenfeld, Wendy Sigle-Rushton, Renske Keizer, Trude Lappegård, Aiva Jasilioniene, and Paola Di Giulio, 'Changes in union status during the transition to parenthood in eleven European countries, 1970s to early 2000s', *Population Studies* 66/2 (2012), pp. 167–82).

11. McLanahan and Jacobson, 'Diverging Destinities Revisited'.

12. Genevieve Heard, 'Socioeconomic marriage differentials in Australia and New Zealand', *Population and Development Review* 37/1 (2011), pp. 125–60.

13. Neil O'Brien, 'Is Britain "coming apart" as cultural inequality increases?', *The Telegraph* (2012), Retrieved 28 August, 2014.

14. McLanahan, 'Diverging destinies'; Perelli-Harris et al., 'Changes in union status'.

15. Elizabeth Thomson and Sheela Kennedy, 'Children's experience of family disruption in Sweden', *Demographic Research* 23/17 (2010), pp. 479–508.

16. Christine R. Schwartz and Hongyun Han, 'The reversal of the gender gap in education and trends in marital dissolution', *American Sociological Review* 79/4 (2014), pp. 605–29.

17. Juho Harkonen and Jaap Dronkers, 'Stability and change in the educational gradient of divorce. A comparison of seventeen countries', *European Sociological Review* 22/5 (2006), pp. 501–17.

18. Kathleen Kiernan, 'Disadvantage and demography — chicken and egg?', in John Hill, Julian LeGrand, and David Piachaud (eds), *Understanding Social Exclusion* (Oxford: Oxford University Press, 2006), pp. 84–96; McLanahan and Jacobson, 'Diverging Destinities Revisited'.

19. George Akerlof, 'Men without children', *The Economic Journal* 108 (1996), pp. 287–309; Robin Simon, 'Revisiting the relationships among gender, marital status, and mental health', *AJS; American Journal of Sociology* 107/4 (2002), pp. 1065–96.

20. Paul R. Amato, 'The impact of family formation change on the cognitive, social, and emotional well-being of the next generation', *The Future of Children/Center for the Future of Children, the David and Lucile Packard Foundation* 15/2 (2005), pp. 75–96; Kathleen Kiernan and Fiona K. Mensah, 'Unmarried parenthood, family trajectories, parent and child well being', in K. Hansen, H. Joshi, and S. Dex (eds), *Children of the 21st Century: From Birth to Age 5* (London: Policy Press, 2010), pp. 77–94; Sara McLanahan, Laura Tach, and Daniel Schneider, 'The causal effects of father absence', *Annual Review of Sociology* 39/1 (2013), pp. 399–427; Wendy Sigle-Rushton, John Hobcraft, and Renske Kiernan, 'Parental divorce and subsequent disadvantage: a cross-cohort comparison', *Demography* 42/3 (2005), pp. 427–46; John F. Ermisch, Peter H. Frauke, and Katharina Spiess, 'Early childhood outcomes and family structure', in John F. Ermisch, Markus Jäntti, and Timothy M. Smeeding (eds), *From Parents to Children: The Intergenerational Transmission of Advantage* (Russell Sage Foundation, 2012), pp. 120–40.

21. Sophie Moullin, 'Why progressives should be pro-family', *The Political Quarterly* 83/3 (2012).

22. Market income includes income from capital, savings and self-employment, as well as gross (that is, before tax and transfer) wages. Half of OECD countries saw reductions in the redistributive effect of tax and cash benefits since the mid 1980s, but almost all saw increases in inequality in the predistribution of market incomes (Paris: OECD, 2011).

23. OECD, *Divided We Stand: Why Inequality Keeps Rising*.

24. Christoper Kollmeyer, 'Family structure, female employment, and national income inequality: a cross-national study of 16 Western countries', *European Sociological Review* 29/4 (2012), pp. 816–27.

25. Molly A. Martin, 'Family structure and income inequality in families with children, 1976 to 2000', *Demography* 43/4 (2006), pp. 421–45.

26. Seymour Spilerman, Wealth and stratification processes, *Annual Review of Sociology* 26 (2006), pp. 497–524.

27. Lisa A. Keister and Stephanie Moller, 'Wealth Inequality in the United States', *Annual Review of Sociology* 26 (2006), pp. 63–81; Jay L. Zagorsky, 'Wealth inequality in the United States', *Journal of Sociology* 41/4 (2005), pp. 406–24.

28. Alan G. Isaac, 'Inheriting inequality: Institutional influences on the distribution of wealth', *Journal of Post Keynesian Economics* 30/2 (2008), pp. 187–203.

29. Olympia Bover, 'Wealth inequality and household structure: US vs. Spain', Bank of Spain Working Paper Number 804 (2008). Available at http://www.bde.es/f/webbde/SES/Secciones/Publicaciones/PublicacionesSeriadas/DocumentosTrabajo/08/Fic/dt0804e.pdf (accessed 21 March 2015).

30. *Ibid.*

31. Paul Gregg, Rosanna Scutella, and Jonathan Wadsworth, 'Reconciling workless measures at the individual and household level. Theory and evidence from the United States, Britain, Germany, Spain and Australia', *Journal of Population Economics* 23/1 (2010), pp. 139–67.

32. Susan E. Harkness, 'Women, families and the 'Great Recession' in the UK', in G. Ramia, K. Farnsworth, and Z. Irving (eds), *Social Policy Review* 25 (Bristol: Policy Press, 2013).

33. Susan E. Harkness, 'The contribution of women's employment and earnings to household income inequality: a cross-country analysis', Working Paper, Luxembourg, Luxembourg Income Survey Working Paper Series (2010). Available at http://www.lisdatacenter.org/conference/papers/harkness.pdf (accessed 21 March 2015).

34. Kollmeyer, 'Family structure, female employment, and national income inequality'.

35. Martin, 'Family structure and income inequality in families with children, 1976 to 2000'.

36. Janet C. Gornick and Markus Jäntti, *Child Poverty in High- and Middle-Income Countries: Selected Findings from LIS*, UNICEF (2012).

37. *Ibid.*
38. Daniel T. Lichter, Deborah R. Graefe, and J. Brian Brow, 'Is marriage a panacea? Union formation among economically disadvantaged unwed mothers', *Social Problems* 50/1 (2003), pp. 60–85.
39. Wendy Sigle-Rushton and Sara McLanahan, 'For richer or poorer?: Marriage as an anti-poverty strategy in the United States', *Population* (Paris: Institut National d'Etudes Demographiques, 2002); Adam Thomas and Isabel Sawhill, 'For love and money? The impact of family structure on family income', *The Future of Children* 15/2 (2005), pp. 57–74.
40. Gøsta Esping-Andersen, *Incomplete Revolution: Adapting Welfare States to Women's New Roles* (Oxford: Polity, 2009), p. 214.
41. Karen Rowlingson and Jane Millar (eds), *Lone Parents, Employment and Social Policy: Cross-National Comparisons* (Bristol: Policy Press, 2011).
42. Vidhya Alakeson, 'Ending child poverty by 2020. Progress made and lessons learned', *Child Poverty Action Group* (2012), pp. 36–40.
43. Liana Fox, Wen-Jui Han, Christopher Ruhm, and Jane Waldfogel, 'Time for children: trends in the employment patterns of parents, 1967–2009', *Demography* 50/1 (2013), pp. 25–49.
44. Ipshita Pal and Jane Waldfogel, 'Re-visiting the family gap in pay in the United States', CPRC Working Paper No. 14-02, (2014). Available at http://www.childcarecanada.org/documents/research-policy-practice/14/08/re-visiting-family-gap-pay-united-states (accessed 19 March 2015).
45. Harkness, 'The contribution of women's employment and earnings to household income inequality'.
46. Michael Greenstone and Adam Looney, *The Marriage Gap: The Impact of Economic and Technological Change on Marriage Rates* (Washington, D.C.: Brookings Institute, 2012).
47. Jan Pahl, 'Family finances, individualisation, spending patterns and access to credit', *Journal of Socio-Economics* 37/2 (2008), pp. 577–91.
48. Kiernan, 'Disadvantage and demography'.
49. Shelly Lundberg and Robert A. Pollak, 'Cohabitation and the Uneven Retreat from Marriage 1950-2010', *National Bureau of Economic Research* (2013), retrieved from http://www.nber.org/papers/w19413.
50. Christina M. Gibson-Davis, Kathryn Edin, and Sara McLanahan, 'High hopes but even higher expectations: the retreat from marriage among low-income couples', *Journal of Marriage and Family* 67/5 (2005), pp. 1301–12.
51. Greenstone and Looney, *The Marriage Gap*.
52. Those women in the bottom half of the wage distribution, including those women with no earnings, saw there marriage rates decline by 25 percentage points from 1970 to 2011. At the top 10 per cent of earnings, the proportion of women who were married increased ten percentage points (*Ibid.*).
53. Daniel Schneider and Adam Reich, 'Marrying ain't hard when you got a union card? Labor union membership and first marriage', *Social Problems* 61/4 (2014), pp. 625–43.

54. Daniel Schneider, 'Economic standing, marriage, and cohabitation: Evidence from policy experiments', Prepared for the Family Task Force Meeting, 10–11 February 2011, pp. 1–19.

55. Sarah Corse and Jennifer Silva, 'Intimate Inequalities: Love and Work in a Post-Industrial Landscape', American Sociology Association Annual Meeting, Hilton New York, NY, 9 August 2013; Kathryn Edin and Timothy J. Nelson, *Doing the Best I Can: Fatherhood in the Inner City* (Oakland: University of California Press, 2013).

56. Kathryn Edin and Maria Kefalas, *Promises I Can Keep: Why Poor Women Put Motherhood Before Marriage* (University of California Press, 2005).

57. Shelly Lundberg and Robert A. Pollak, 'Cohabitation and the uneven retreat from marriage in the U.S., 1950–2010', National Bureau of Economic Research Working Paper 19413 (2013).

58. Gianpiero Dalla-Zuanna, 'Social mobility and fertility', *Demographic Research* 17 (2007), pp. 441–64.

59. Gibson-Davis et al., 'High hopes but even higher expectations'.

60. Edin and Nelson, *Doing the Best I Can*.

61. Lawrence Finer and Mia R. Zolna, 'Shifts in intended and unintended pregnancies in the United States, 2001–2008', *American Journal of Public Health*, 104 Supplement (2014), pp. S43–S48.

62. Kelly Musick, Paula England, Sarah Edgington, and Nicole Kangas, 'Education differences in intended and unintended fertility', *Social Forces; a Scientific Medium of Social Study and Interpretation* 88/2 (2009), pp. 543–72.

63. S. Philip Morgan and Heather Rackin, 'The correspondence between fertility intentions and behavior in the United States', *Population and Development Review* 36/1 (2010), pp. 91–118.

64. Cristina d'Addio and Mira d'Ercole, 'Trends and determinants of fertility rates in OECD Countries: The role of policies', OECD Working Paper No. 27 (2005). Available at http://www.oecd.org/social/family/35304751.pdf (accessed 19 March 2015).

65. Projections are from mid-2000s to 2025–31. The only exception is Germany, where falling fertility is predicted to offset increased parental separations (Paris: OECD, 2011).

66. Hayley Fisher, 'The effect of marriage tax penalties and subsidies on marital status', *Fiscal Studies* 34/4 (2013), pp. 437–65.

67. Bruce Stafford and Simon Roberts, 'The impact of financial incentives in welfare systems on family structure', Department of Work and Pensions, Research Report No 569, (2009). Available at http://eprints.nottingham.ac.uk/1850/1/rrep569.pdf (accessed 19 March 2015).

68. Edin and Kefalas, *Promises I Can Keep*.

69. Recipients received both a higher basic award and could retain 38 per cent of their earnings, and the 100-hour per month working limit was removed.

70. Lisa A. Gennetian and Cynthia Miller, 'How welfare reform can affect marriage: evidence from an experimental study in Minnesota', *Review of Economics of the Household* 2/3 (2004), pp. 275–301.

71. Stafford and Roberts, 'The impact of financial incentives in welfare systems on family structure'.

72. Robert Schoeni and Rebecca Blank, 'What has welfare reform accomplished? Impacts on welfare participation, employment, income, poverty, and family structure', National Bureau of Economic Research Working Paper 7627 (2013). Available at http://www.nber.org/papers/w7627 (accessed 19 March 2015).

73. Schneider, 'Economic standing, marriage and cohabitation'.

74. Carolyn P. Cowan, Philip Cowan, and Virginia Knox, 'Marriage and fatherhood programs', *The Future of Children* 20/2 (2010), pp. 205–30.

75. Matthew D. Johnson, 'Healthy marriage initiatives: on the need for empiricism in policy implementation', *The American Psychologist* 67/4 (2012), pp. 296–308.

76. Matthew D. Johnson, 'Optimistic or quixotic? More data on marriage and relationship education programs for lower income couples', *The American Psychologist* 68/2 (2013), pp. 111–12.

77. Robert Joyce, 'The new tax break for some married couples', *Institute for Fiscal Studies* (2013).

78. Schneider, 'Economic standing, marriage and cohabitation'.

79. *Ibid.*

80. Thomas N. Bradbury and Justin A. Lavner, 'How can we improve preventive and educational interventions for intimate relationships?', *Behavior Therapy* 43/1 (2012), pp. 113–22.

81. Isabel V. Sawhill and Joanna Venator, '5 Policies that Help Children by Helping Their Parents', Brookings Institute, November 13, 2014. Available at http://www.brookings.edu/blogs/social-mobility-memos/posts/2014/11/13-help-children-by-helping-parents-sawhill (accessed 19 March 2015).

82. Pia S. Schober, 'Paternal child care and relationship quality: a longitudinal analysis of reciprocal associations', *Journal of Marriage and Family* 74/2 (2012), pp. 281–96.

83. Stefanie Brodmann, 'When fertility is bargained: Second births in Denmark and Spain', *European Sociological Review* 23/5 (2007), pp. 599–613.

CHAPTER 13

A 'Family Friendly' Welfare State
Addressing the Gender Equality Paradox

Anke Hassel

Progressive family policies are driven by the fundamental transformation of the role of women in the labour market and society. For young women today, it is hardly conceivable that only half a century ago (until 1957) married women in Germany needed the consent of their husbands to open a bank account, and until 1977, the civil code determined in paragraph 1356 that women were allowed to have a job 'to the extent that it was reconcilable with their duties in marriage and family'. Husbands had to agree to their wives taking a job.

Today, women in the Western world are generally brought up to feel free to take any job at any time. Angela Merkel, Hillary Clinton, Sheryl Sandberg and Helle Thorning-Schmidt are proof of a growing number of women who go for top jobs in business and politics. The norm of gender equality has made it necessary for women quotas on company boards to be on the political agenda in most European countries in the EU. Almost all labour market positions, from head of state to army general, with the sole exceptions of the Catholic and Islamic Church, are open for women. Schools and families put great value on emphasising the norm that boys and girls are not only raised equally, but that girls should be encouraged to be interested in male professions. Girls' days are organised in offices and male-dominated workplaces. Scholarships and special funds are available for women in sciences; anti-discrimination legislation has led to a wave of litigation against employers who are seen to prefer male candidates. In a historical perspective, this is a huge change. Until the twentieth century, gender roles were strictly assigned. For centuries, women were confined to the domestic, caring and child-rearing tasks, while men went out to fight wars, governed the country or made money.

Gender equality in business, the workplace and society has, however, been largely one-sided. While women go out to work in the city or become heads of states, it has remained unclear who, in their absence, is responsible for child-rearing, care and housework, how these tasks should be divided and what the state's role is in service provision. There is evidence that, despite the big increase in paid work for women, they remain the main person responsible for housework and childcare in private households. Mothers' duties are still distinct from fathers' duties, as Ann-Marie Slaughter confessed when she gave up her position in the State Department to be closer to her teenage sons.

The norm of gender equality with which both boys and girls are raised in the developed world usually hits reality when the first child is born in a family and the young parents have to decide who will stay at home, and for how long, to take on the role of carer. The problem will stay with the family for as long as the children are in school and will return when they have ailing and frail parents who might also need to be looked after. Who will take on the task of caring in the family, for how long and under what conditions are the prime questions that a family friendly welfare state must answer.

Progressive family policy must, therefore, first and foremost assess existing family arrangements in the context of the incomplete gender revolution. This includes an assessment of the position of women and men in the labour market, the services needed to make work–life balances manageable and must also find a solution to the ageing populations and falling fertility rates in most OECD countries.

Family policy and gender equality are hotly contested terrains and it is important to be clear about the underlying assumptions. In political and policy debates, the question as to what extent (or even whether at all) female roles should be modelled on male role models has not been solved. The overarching dominant political orientation is based on an understanding that gender equality is, in effect, a process in which women will increasingly behave like men, not only in their professional but also in their private lives. This is contested not only by more traditional political groups and the church, but also by a sizeable minority on the left. The argument is that the move towards gender equality has pushed women into the labour market only to become as commodified as their male counterparts and to spend their working lives in low paid, lousy jobs while neglecting their families. Further integration of women in the labour market is, therefore, not to be aspired to. Proponents of this view are, for instance, in favour of a basic income which would allow women to live the life they choose without the pressure of finding paid employment. While this is not the perspective taken in this brief, it is important to be clear that the view that male employment patterns and work habits are not the ultimate ratio for women is an important argument to be taken into account when discussing policy choices and the politics of family friendly policies.

Five Types of Family Regimes

In the OECD, policies towards families and women vary substantially. This chapter will, therefore, start with an overview of different types of family regimes to identify different constellations of family and employment regimes. In order to illustrate the dilemmas in family policy, the following indicators were chosen: firstly, the difference in working hours between men and women with a family, the female employment rate and the gender pay gap, to illustrate gender equality; secondly, the fertility rate measures the extent to which families are confident and able to have children and thirdly, the use and financing of public childcare for very young children as the key policy that facilitates working mothers.

The correlations in Table 13.1 show two things: firstly, as is well known by now, fertility rates are quite closely related to the employment rate and childcare facilities for the very young. Countries with higher levels of service provisions, higher enrolment in childcare and higher female employment rates are also countries where women have more children. Secondly, gender equality, measured in terms of the gender pay gap and working hour differences, is not related to fertility and only weakly to childcare enrolment and spending on childcare.

The picture becomes clearer when looking at key indicators on gender equality, family policy and the labour market through the lenses of different economic regimes. Various types of capitalism have different ways of dealing with the dilemma of gender equality and family care. Table 13.2 compares differences in working hours between men and women within a family, the gender pay gap, female employment, fertility rates and childcare provisions for a range of OECD countries. It divides them up into five different groups of political economies: liberal market economies (LME), which are mainly co-ordinated by market mechanisms; coordinated market economies (CME), which are co-ordinated by other organisational features, primarily by strong employers' confederations and unions; the Nordic CMEs, in which the public sector plays a distinct role in the economy; mixed market economies (MME) of southern Europe, where the state sponsors co-ordination by direct intervention and the new transition countries of central eastern Europe (CEE).

TABLE 13.1 Correlations of key family and gender equality indicators.

	Female employment rate	Fertility rate	Absolute working hours difference	Gender pay gap	Childcare enrolment (under 3)	Public spending on childcare and preschool
Correlation coefficient	1	0.466*	0.267	0.341	0.607**	0.424*
N	25	25	19	19	23	25
Correlation coefficient	0.466*	1	0.134	0.023	0.591**	0.633**
N	25	25	19	19	23	25
Correlation coefficient	0.267	0.134	1	-0.034	0.073	0.376
N	19	19	19	19	19	19
Correlation coefficient	0.341	0.023	-0.034	1	-0.166	-0.003
N	19	19	19	19	19	19
Correlation coefficient	0.607**	0.591**	0.073	-0.166	1	0.646**
N	23	23	19	19	23	23
Correlation coefficient	0.424*	0.633**	0.376	-0.003	0.646**	1
N	25	25	19	19	23	25

Sources: Female employment rate, fertility rate, childcare enrolment and spending, OECD database (year 2010). On gender pay gap and working hours difference, Hipp and Leuze (2013).

TABLE 13.2 Gender equality and family policy in different types of capitalism.

Type of capitalism		Absolute working hours difference	Female employment rate	Fertility rate	Childcare enrolment (under 3)	Gender pay gap	Public spending on childcare and preschool
LME (Australia, USA, UK, Canada, New Zealand)	Average	-13.43	64.68	1.92	36.80	17.60	0.62
	N	3	5	5	4	3	5
	Standard deviation	1.64	5.22	0.15	6.95	3.27	0.35
CEE (Czech Republic, Hungary, Poland, Slovak Republic)	Average	-9.49	53.30	1.40	6.20	16.00	0.45
	N	4	4	4	4	4	4
	Standard deviation	1.56	2.78	0.06	3.54	7.78	0.17
MME (Spain, Italy, Portugal, Greece)	Average	-14.31	51.38	1.41	30.18	14.15	0.45
	N	4	4	4	4	4	4
	Standard deviation	4.47	6.84	0.08	15.52	6.80	0.26
CME (Austria, Belgium, Germany, Netherlands, France, Luxembourg, Switzerland)	Average	-15.09	63.97	1.64	38.43	16.54	0.60
	N	5	7	7	6	5	7
	Standard deviation	1.23	6.02	0.24	17.17	6.83	0.32

(Continued)

TABLE 13.2 (Continued)

Type of capitalism		Absolute working hours difference	Female employment rate	Fertility rate	Childcare enrolment (under 3)	Gender pay gap	Public spending on childcare and preschool
CME-Nordic (Finland, Denmark, Sweden, Norway)	Average	−6.40	70.78	1.90	48.53	16.80	1.28
	N	3	4	4	4	3	4
	Standard deviation	0.47	2.50	0.07	15.94	1.25	0.150
Total	Average	−12.11	61.38	1.66	32.61	16.13	0.67
	N	19	24	24	22	19	24
	Standard deviation	3.89	8.41	0.26	18.57	5.56	0.38

Sources: Female employment rate, fertility rate, childcare enrolment and spending OECD database (year 2010). On gender pay gap and working hours difference, Hipp and Leuze (2013).

Different constellations of gender equality, fertility and childcare arrangements emerge: the Nordic countries and the liberal countries have the highest fertility rates, employment rates of women and high childcare enrolment. Southern and eastern Europe have the lowest rate of fertility and very low female employment rates. The continental CMEs are in the middle in all categories: fertility, employment and childcare provisions.

Regarding gender equality, the gender pay gap is almost the same in all different regimes and only marginally lower in southern Europe, where both the female employment rate and fertility is the lowest. Equality in working time is highest in the Nordic countries, followed by eastern Europe, which can be seen as a remnant of socialist working arrangements. In all other regimes, including the liberal countries, there is a sizeable difference in working time arrangements between women and men. In fact, in liberal and non-Nordic coordinated countries, women have substantially shorter working hours than men. In both types of countries, this is driven by a high share of part-time employment among working mothers. While in the Nordic states, tax and social policy encourage full-time employment, this is not the case in continental Europe. In liberal and continental countries, the lower rate of childcare enrolment explains a more gendered division of working hours. In other words, in these countries, women spend more time with children at home than their partners. This would also explain women's lower employment rate compared to the Nordic countries.[1]

The Politics of Childcare

Childcare and other social service provisions are at the centre of solving the paradox of gender politics and the family friendly welfare state. Childcare provisions are closely related to both the fertility rate, employment rate and the gendered working hours outside eastern Europe.

Public spending on early childhood has increased in almost all OECD countries and quite substantially in some other countries. In particular, the UK, Norway, the Netherlands, Iceland, Korea and New Zealand have seen a rapid increase in public spending on early childcare. In other countries, such as the US and Canada, public spending on early childcare has remained low and flat (see Table 13.3). In the US, public spending on childcare provision is compensated by private provisions which are primarily used by affluent dual-earning families.[2]

One way of interpreting the data is to assume that there is a general pull towards higher childcare spending, driven by the integration of women in

TABLE 13.3 Public spending on early childcare and preschool in OECD, 1998–2009 (share of GDP).

	1998	1999	2000	2001	2002	2003	2004	2005	2006	2007	2008	2009
Australia	0.3	0.4	0.4	0.4	0.4	0.4	0.4	0.4	0.3	0.4	0.5	0.6
Austria	0.2	0.2	0.3	0.3	0.3	0.3	0.3	0.3	0.3	0.3	0.3	0.4
Belgium	0.5	0.5	0.5	0.6	0.6	0.6	0.6	0.6	0.6	0.6	0.6	0.7
Canada	0.2	0.2	0.2	0.2	0.2	0.2	0.2	0.2	0.1	0.2	0.2	0.2
Czech Republic	0.3	0.3	0.3	0.3	0.3	0.3	0.3	0.3	0.3	0.3	0.3	0.4
Denmark	1.4	1.5	1.4	1.4	1.4	1.4	1.4	1.4	1.4	1.3	1.4	1.4
Finland	1.1	1.0	1.0	0.9	0.9	0.9	0.9	0.9	0.9	0.9	1.0	1.1
France	1.1	1.0	1.0	1.0	1.0	1.0	1.1	1.0	1.0	1.1	1.0	1.1
Germany	0.4	0.4	0.3	0.3	0.4	0.4	0.4	0.4	0.4	0.4	0.4	0.5
Greece	0.1	0.1	0.1	0.2	0.2	0.1	0.1	0.1	0.1	0.1	0.1	0.1
Hungary	0.6	0.6	0.6	0.6	0.6	0.7	0.7	0.7	0.7	0.6	0.6	0.7
Ireland	0.4	0.4	0.4	0.4	0.5	0.5	0.5	0.5	0.5	0.6	0.7	0.8
Italy	0.5	0.5	0.5	0.6	0.5	0.6	0.6	0.6	0.7	0.6	0.7	0.7
Luxembourg	0.5	0.5	0.4	0.4	0.4	0.4	0.4	0.4	0.4	0.4	0.5	0.4
Netherlands	0.0	0.0	0.0	0.0	0.0	0.0	0.0	0.5	0.6	0.7	0.8	0.9
New Zealand	0.6	0.6	0.6	0.6	0.6	0.6	0.6	0.6	0.7	0.8	0.9	1.0
Norway	0.8	0.8	0.7	0.7	0.6	0.7	0.8	0.8	0.8	0.9	1.0	1.2

	1998	1999	2000	2001	2002	2003	2004	2005	2006	2007	2008	2009
Poland	0.2	0.2	0.2	0.2	0.2	0.2	0.3	0.3	0.3	0.3	0.3	0.3
Portugal	0.2	0.3	0.3	0.3	0.3	0.4	0.4	0.4	0.4	0.4	0.4	0.4
Slovak Republic	0.4	0.4	0.4	0.4	0.4	0.4	0.3	0.3	0.3	0.3	0.3	0.4
Spain	0.4	0.3	0.4	0.4	0.4	0.4	0.4	0.4	0.4	0.5	0.5	0.6
Sweden	1.1	1.1	0.9	0.9	1.0	1.1	1.1	1.1	1.2	1.3	1.3	1.4
Switzerland	0.2	0.2	0.2	0.2	0.2	0.2	0.2	0.2	0.2	0.2	0.2	n/a
United Kingdom	0.6	0.7	0.7	0.8	0.8	0.8	0.8	0.8	0.9	1.0	1.0	1.1
United States	0.4	0.4	0.4	0.4	0.4	0.4	0.4	0.3	0.4	0.4	0.4	0.4

Source: OECD statistics.

the labour market, which has taken place across the world. High female employment rates create a demand for public childcare, which governments seek to address. This is accompanied by an increasing share of women in higher positions in business and politics. For instance, the female employment rate is a significant predictor for public spending on childcare – as are the share of women in parliament and the (negative) effect of religious parties in parliament.[3]

However, there are institutional and fiscal constraints for governments to invest in early childcare, which have to do with both the financing and the delivery of services and the general structure of the welfare state. Bonoli and Reber have shown that there is a crowding out effect by public spending on traditional risks: countries that spend highly on old age tend to spend less on childcare.[4]

The precise mechanisms as to how crowding-out occurs are still underdeveloped. In many countries, the budgets for old age spending and childcare are not related and a decision on one does not necessary have an implication for the other. However, insurance-based welfare states, which tend to focus more on old age spending, might crowd out the ability of governments to tax for other purposes. There is, for instance, a negative correlation between spending on early childcare and the share of social security contributions in overall government revenues (−0.333). Another institutional constraint could be the degree of fiscal federalism. More decentralised fiscal regimes are correlated with lower degrees of public spending on childcare for the very young (0.331). In centralised fiscal regimes, governments can more easily shift social spending between different departments. Fiscal decentralisation creates more problems for governments to commit and implement spending on social services.

Conclusion

There is a clear need for family friendly policies in order to address the gender equality paradox. Women have come far in business and politics, but societies have not solved the problem of care for children and families. While this problem has been recognised in many countries, there are a number of hurdles when it comes to the implementation of childcare policies. Firstly, they are easier to implement where the demand, in terms of female employment, is already strong and women have reached a threshold in political representation (both in parliament and also within trade unions). Secondly, old risk insurance schemes tend to crowd out social investment.

This might be due less to the fact that there is competition for one pot of money, but more related to the financing of the welfare state. High social security contributions inhibit governments from increasing social spending from tax revenues. Finally, fiscal decentralisation might also be related to low spending on childcare. Progressive policy-makers will need to proceed in the quest to find sustainable policy solutions for childcare spending. They will find solutions in individual countries and will need to find ways to work around the restriction of insurance-based welfare states and decentralised fiscal regimes.

Notes

1. Lena Hipp and Kathrin Leuze, 'It's not just whom you are with but also where you live! Determinants of working time differences within couples in Europe and the U.S.', Wissenschaftszentrum Berlin mimeo (2013). Available at http://www.gesis. org/fileadmin/upload/dienstleistung/daten/amtl_mikrodaten/europ_microdata/ Presentations_2013/hipp_3rd_uc.pdf (accessed 21 March 2015).

    This finding is also supported by Hipp and Leuze's paper that identifies factors for gendered working time arrangements. They identify childcare enrolment, individual taxation and gender norms as key factors in explaining the working hour differences between men and women.

2. Kimberly J. Morgan, 'The "production" of childcare: how labor markets shape social policy and vice versa', *Social Politics* 2/2 (2005), pp. 243–63.

3. Giuliano Bonoli and Frank Reber, 'The political economy of childcare in OECD countries: explaining cross-national variation in spending and coverage rates', *European Journal of Political Research* 49/1 (2010), pp. 97–118.

4. *Ibid.*, p. 114.

Part V

The Politics of Predistribution

The Political Economy of the Service Transition[1]

New Political Coalitions for Predistributive Strategies

Anne Wren

Over the past 30 years, the wealthiest OECD economies – in Europe, North America and Australasia – have experienced rapid deindustrialisation. A range of factors have contributed to the deindustrialisation process: some, like technological change and changes in the characteristics of consumer demand, are internal to the development process in the economies themselves; others, like increased competition from developing countries in the market for manufactured goods, are external. Whatever its roots, there is no doubt that the impact of deindustrialisation on labour markets has been profound: more than three-quarters of employment in most OECD countries is now in services, while industrial sectors, on average, account for less than one-fifth. In this chapter, I outline the significant challenges that this sectoral shift in the locus of economic activity poses for existing socio-economic models, and ask whether predistributive strategies can offer economically and politically sustainable responses to these challenges.

The Transition to Services: Economic Challenges

One of the most serious socio-economic challenges posed by the deindustrialisation process is a reduction in job opportunities at medium and lower skill levels. The question for governments: as the core of employment in manufacturing sectors shrinks, how, and where, are new jobs to be created? At stake in the resolution of this problem, also, is the future of the welfare state: reductions in the number of industrial workers in stable jobs who are contributors to the system threaten the affordability of welfare state provision, unless new jobs can be created in services.

Low-skilled Employment, and the Employment–Equality Trade-off

One 'solution' to the problem of declining employment opportunities at medium to low skill levels which has been pursued most aggressively in liberal regimes like the USA and the UK over the past few decades, has been to facilitate the expansion of low-skilled (and low-paid) private sector employment in personal, consumer, and social services. These countries have enjoyed considerable success in terms of employment creation in these sectors in recent decades. However, there are marked downsides to the strategy which they have pursued.

The first is that it has been heavily reliant on keeping relative wages in low-skilled service sectors low. The demand for personal and consumer services is very responsive to changes in prices (this is unsurprising when we consider their capacity for home production – think of catering and gardening services, for example). However, the capacity for productivity increases in the provision of these kinds of services is low (waitressing and childcare are good examples to think through here – it might be possible to increase the number of children supervised by one carer, the number of tables served by one waiter and so on, but in the process the quality of care and service will almost certainly decline). Given a low capacity for productivity growth, it becomes particularly important to keep relative wages in these sectors low, in order to generate a demand expansion based on the high price elasticity of demand for these kinds of services. As a result, it is harder to combine the expansion of lower-skilled service employment with equality than it was during the so-called 'golden age' of manufacturing expansion in the 1950s and 1960s (when the simultaneous occurrence of high demand elasticities for new consumer durables, and high rates of productivity growth in manufacturing sectors engendered by Fordist innovations in production processes, meant that relative prices could be kept low at the same time as real wage rates in these sectors were growing).[2]

In liberal regimes then, the dominant response to the trade-off between wage equality and employment creation in low-skilled, low productivity service sectors has been to emphasise the goal of employment creation, with increases in wage inequality facilitated by the removal or reduction of protections on the wages of low paid workers, attacks on the power of trade unions, and decentralised wage bargaining.

As the experience of recent years has made clear, however, increasing inequality has not been the only downside of the liberal strategy for employment growth over the past quarter of a century. In addition to these supply-side adjustments, there was a strong demand-side component to the expansion of employment in low-skilled service sectors in these regimes during this period. Part of this demand resulted from increases in family working hours (as more women entered paid work and more workers began to work longer hours). Increases in working hours raise the demand for consumer and personal services via a substitution effect (women working in the paid labour force purchasing childcare and catered food, for example) and via an income effect (families that work more hours earn more money, and personal and consumer services are 'luxury' items which occupy proportionately more of individual and household budgets as incomes rise).[3] Both of these effects can be seen as outcomes of structural labour market change, therefore, which are not inherently unsustainable. By the turn of the century, however, the expansion of demand, and of employment, in these sectors was also closely linked to the expansion of cheap consumer credit and the asset (in particular house) price inflation which accompanied it. Just how important this highly unsustainable element of the employment growth model had become in liberal regimes by the early part of this century has yet to be accurately assessed: what is clear, however, is that the shock to employment in these countries in the wake of the crisis (when the supply of credit dried up) was relatively severe.

In contrast to the liberal regimes, in the co-ordinated regimes of central and northern Europe, levels of co-ordination in wage setting (and, as a result, levels of wage equality) remain relatively high, and the extent of reliance on employment creation in low paid, low productivity private service sectors in recent decades has been considerably lower. The social democratic regimes of Scandinavia, for example, have (to varying degrees), managed to continue to simultaneously pursue high rates of employment and wage equality by employing large numbers of workers at all skill levels in public service sectors. Meanwhile some continental European regimes – like Germany – have kept unemployment levels down in part by their continued strong performance in traditional export-oriented manufacturing sectors, but also because large proportions of the working age population (and large numbers of women in particular) remain outside the paid labour force. The lower levels of reliance on debt-financed consumer demand in these regimes before the crisis meant that the shock which they experienced when the crisis hit (and credit dried up) was less severe. Meanwhile, the implications for equality of the pursuit of either of these strategies are also more positive than that pursued in the liberal regimes – although the inegalitarian nature of strategies which rely on discouraging labour force participation amongst certain segments of the population should not be overlooked.

Critically though, none of these strategies is, on its own, a sufficient long-term solution to the problem of deindustrialisation. Without a thriving set of high value added sectors to finance them, the expansive public service sectors of Scandinavia are ultimately unaffordable. Without the existence of a core group of well paid workers in high productivity export sectors, the large numbers of early retirees and women working within the home in Germany and other continental European countries cannot be supported. The strategy of expanding employment in low productivity private services, meanwhile, relies not just on low relative prices, but also on rising incomes. Furthermore, as the liberal experience of the past decade has shown, the strategy also relies excessively on the expansion of credit and 'wealth illusion' rather than productivity and income growth as a basis for the expansion of demand and employment in these sectors. These expansions are both unsustainable and economically costly.

Any *sustainable* strategy for employment growth must depend instead on the expansion of output and employment in high productivity sectors and, in a context of deindustrialisation, this means that expansion in high productivity service sectors is, increasingly key. So what does this mean in terms of policy?

Skills and High-end Service Expansion

The revolution in information and communications technologies (ICT) which has taken place over the past three decades has radically transformed production and trade in certain areas of services. In so-called 'knowledge-intensive' sectors – business, finance, and communications, for example – the capacity for productivity growth and for trade have been hugely enhanced by rapid access to large amounts of information, and the ability to communicate that information – both locally and globally – rapidly and cheaply. The transformation has not occurred in all areas of service production. In some sectors, for example the personal and social services discussed earlier, the impact of new technology is less marked. Primarily this is because the provision of these services is, to varying degrees, reliant on face-to-face human interaction: a computer, for example, cannot increase the number of children that can be effectively supervised by a child care worker, nor can it facilitate her in providing this service to children who are not in her immediate vicinity (that is, in participating in international trade).

In these areas then, the uptake of the new technology has been relatively low, and these remain essentially low-productivity, non-traded sectors. In contrast, in the more knowledge-intensive sectors, where provision is less heavily reliant on face-to-face human interaction, and information and its transmission are at a premium, rates of productivity growth and international trade have increased rapidly.

Given their high capacity for productivity growth and for trade, these 'dynamic' service sectors have a critical role to play in any sustainable strategy for employment creation in a context of deindustrialisation. It is of considerable importance then that the skills required by these sectors differ significantly from those on which manufacturing sectors have typically relied.

It is by now well-established empirically that ICT and college-educated labour are complements in production. As Autor, Levy, and Murnane point out, the new technology is highly effective at performing routine tasks which can be specified by stored instructions – even where the required programs are highly complex (for example, bookkeeping or clerical work).[4] As a result, it acts as a substitute for labour in performing these tasks, which are typically carried out by workers at medium-skill levels (those with secondary, or some, but not complete, college education). It is less effective, however, at performing non-routine cognitive tasks requiring 'flexibility, creativity, generalised problem solving, and complex communications'.[5] Rather it serves to complement the skills of the (typically college educated) workers who perform those tasks: faster access to more complete market information, for example, may improve managerial decision-making, but it cannot substitute for that decision-making. Since technology is a complement to, rather than a substitute for, this type of human capital, investment in new technology increases the demand for college-educated labour.

Successful expansion in ICT-intensive service sectors, therefore, is reliant on the existence of an adequate supply of workers with tertiary-level skills. In this regard, the characteristics of the current era of service expansion differ significantly from those of the era of industrial expansion which preceded it. In the 1950s and 1960s, Fordist industrial expansion was associated with an increased demand for labour at low to medium skill levels – and was particularly notable for the existence of complementarities in production between low- and high-skilled industrial labour.[6] In contrast, successful expansion in high-end service sectors requires up-skilling, and increasing the numbers of workers receiving high-quality tertiary education. This underscores, of course, the importance of ensuring effective investment at the tertiary level, and also in facilitating tertiary enrolment and access. Recent research indicates, however, that it also implies a critical role for investment in schools-based learning that begins as early as the pre-primary level, since education at this level is increasingly regarded as a key determinant of tertiary outcomes – especially for children from lower-skilled households.[7]

So how well equipped are existing welfare production regimes to meet the skills demands of the service economy? Liberal regimes have been relatively successful thus far at producing large numbers of high quality college graduates. Levels of public educational investment are low in these countries in relative terms, however, and the system relies on the existence of high levels of wage inequality which create strong incentives for private educational investment (since the relative rewards for such investment are high), and the extensive use of student loans. One clear downside of the model for those concerned with equity of outcomes, therefore, is that it comes with high levels of wage inequality attached; another is that is has been associated with what look like increasingly unsustainable levels of student debt in recent years.[8] Further, there is some evidence to suggest that in spite of the incentives for private investment existing in these regimes, overall levels of educational investment have been insufficient. Goldin and Katz, for example, cite a failure of the US education system to provide an adequate supply of college-educated workers to keep pace with technological change, as one of the primary causes of the increase in inequality in that country at the end of the last century.[9] Wren, Fodor and Theodoropoulou, meanwhile, find that even in the highly decentralised wage setting environments found in liberal regimes, increases in public investment in school and college based education have significant positive effects on employment in dynamic service sectors.[10]

The countries of central and northern Europe face a different set of challenges as regards educational policy. Here, high levels of co-ordination in wage bargaining ensure much higher levels of wage equality. One effect of this though is to reduce the incentives for private individuals to invest in higher-level skills – since the relative rewards to such investment are substantially smaller. In these regimes, then, there is a risk of a shortage in the skills on which expansion in high-end knowledge-intensive services relies, unless the government steps in to subsidise them.[11] In the past, the combination of high levels of co-ordination in wage setting (and equality) with relatively low levels of public investment in tertiary and schools-based education, found in Germany and elsewhere was unproblematic. Rather, as Hall and Soskice[12] have influentially argued, this policy combination formed part of a highly effective educational strategy in which large proportions of the workforce participated in apprenticeship-based vocational training regimes which equipped workers with strong firm and sector-specific skills and formed the basis for comparative advantage in core areas of industrial production (for example, capital goods). The question, however, is whether this strategy remains sustainable in an era in which employment expansion increasingly relies on exploiting the complementarities between ICT and college-educated labour. Even in Germany, the archetype of the successful apprenticeship-based political economy, the proportion of workers employed in high-skilled industrial jobs has declined sharply in recent decades.

In contrast, the social democratic regimes of Scandinavia have combined high levels of co-ordination in wage setting with high levels of investment in school and college based education all the way from the pre-primary to the tertiary level. This has resulted in high levels of tertiary enrolment, facilitating the expansion of high-skilled employment in high-end service sectors.

This strategy has several advantages for those who are interested in furthering the goal of equality by means of predistributive strategies. First, it does not rely on the existence of wage-premia for highly-skilled workers to induce investment in higher-level skills. As a result, it is compatible with predistributive strategies aimed at reducing inequities in pre-tax and transfer incomes. Second, and more directly in terms of its distributional impact, it facilitates greater equity of access to third level education. In the first place, this is because that education is publicly financed, but also because the public financing of education for school-aged, and, even more critically pre-primary, children has knock-on effects on levels of equity in tertiary outcomes for children from different social backgrounds.[13] Finally, investment in early childhood education and care removes some of the costs of caring from women, increasing levels of equity between men and women in terms of access to labour markets, and facilitating women's labour force participation and employment.

The question, of course, is whether the implied spending is affordable in an era of 'austerity'. In a context in which higher-level skills are increasingly critical to expansion in the dynamic, high-value added sectors of the economy, one might equally ask whether countries can afford *not* to undertake investments of this nature. And to the extent that educational investment forms the basis for growth and expansion in high value-added sectors, and the creation of employment in these sectors, this strategy has the potential to be economically self-sustaining.

The Political Basis for Predistributive Strategies in a Service Economy

I have argued so far that expansion in high productivity, internationally-traded service sectors is critical to any sustainable strategy for economic growth in a context of deindustrialisation; and that expansion in these kinds of sectors in turn relies heavily on the development of a strong college-educated labour force. Equitable strategies for tertiary expansion, however, require high levels of state investment in college and schools-based education all the way down to the pre-primary level. So what scope is there for the formation of political coalitions in support of this type of predistributive strategy?

In the face of pressure for welfare state retrenchment stemming from multiple sources (the European debt crisis, globalisation, demographic change, and shifts in the tone of ideological discourse) over recent decades, securing political support for large-scale public investments in university, schools and early childhood education constitutes a political challenge.

One effect of the expansion in high-end traded service sectors has been to significantly increase the numbers of highly skilled workers who are exposed to the international economy: whereas, previously, workers at the highest skill levels tended to be concentrated in sheltered economic occupations (like medicine, public administration, or the law), they are now increasingly likely (and in several countries more likely) to be employed in globalised service sectors like business services or finance.[14] Research indicates, however, that highly skilled workers employed in these kinds of globally exposed sectors are significantly less supportive of public spending, taxation, redistribution (and left parties) than their sheltered counterparts at similar income levels. Amongst the latter, support for the welfare state is typically quite high (approaching, or even surpassing, that of less-skilled workers). Public sector workers, in particular, have often formed an important part of coalitions that favour more generous social policies.[15] The increasing size of the constituency of highly skilled and internationally exposed workers, therefore, potentially constitutes an obstacle to the formation of a stable cross-class (or cross-skill) coalition in favour of any large scale initiative for taxation-based social spending.

In general, state benefits and services offer less to these workers in terms of income replacement than they do to the less-skilled (although obviously the size of this gap varies considerably across countries). In a context of debates about austerity, therefore, they are more likely to be swayed by arguments about the potentially negative effects of social spending and taxation on competitiveness (and hence on the employment prospects of exposed workers). Obtaining the support of this group for a policy of large scale social investment requires that they be convinced that this strategy is essential to facilitate growth and dynamic expansion in the sectors in which they are employed. There is an important role for political leadership here in articulating this strategy as a viable alternative in the context of post-crisis debates about the reform of socio-economic models.

Whilst less-skilled (and lower paid) workers are generally significantly more supportive of higher levels of social spending and taxation, gaining the support of this constituency for public investment in tertiary education can also be politically problematic.[16] Where significant obstacles exist to the progression of children from working-class backgrounds into tertiary education, its public subsidisation can represent a transfer to the middle class. Public investment in schools and in early childhood education, on the other hand, is likely to find more support amongst this constituency. Again there is a role for political leadership here in presenting a coherent and broad based strategy which can appeal to both of these groups.

Possibly the greatest reservoir of potential support for a predistributive strategy centred on public investment in schools and college based education, however, is amongst women. The transition to services has been closely connected with large increases in the numbers of women participating in the labour market in all countries. Female labour force participation closely tracks the expansion of service sector employment, and the indications are that causality in this relationship runs in both directions. On the one hand, women have a comparative advantage in service sector jobs in which they are not disadvantaged, either by a premium on 'brawn', or by labour market experiences which may be interrupted. Service sector skills profiles are particularly relevant here. Service sectors are less heavily reliant on firm and sector-specific skills acquired through long-term experience within a particular firm or sector, and are reliant instead in more general skills, typically acquired initially through college- and schools-based learning, and more easily transferable across firms and sectors. So, women, whose labour market experiences are more likely to be interrupted by childbirth, have a comparative advantage in the production of services which are more reliant on general skills.[17] Meanwhile, reversing the causal arrow, increases in female labour market participation in themselves clearly increases the demand for services which might otherwise be provided in the home (such as, for example, childcare, cleaning, and catering).

This is highly important in political terms because research has shown that female labour force participants are significantly more supportive of redistribution, social spending and taxation than men, or than non-participating women. The increased participation of women in the labour force, therefore, has coincided with a growing gender gap in political preferences on these issues.[18] There appears, then, to be a natural constituency for a predistributive strategy centred on public investment in early childhood, school, and college-based education amongst women. Women are generally more supportive of social spending and taxation than men. They also stand to benefit more directly from this particular set of policies, however. In the first place, this is because access to school- and college-based education is more valuable to them in relative terms, in terms of their labour market experiences. In addition, the subsidisation of early childhood education can play a secondary role in facilitating female labour force participation: the costs of caring are still overwhelmingly borne by women, forming a substantial obstacle to participation in paid employment.

A note of caution is warranted here, however. While women in general display significantly higher levels of support for social spending, taxation, and redistribution, and in general tend to lean to the left of their male counterparts, the evidence does not suggest that this translates automatically into support for the mainstream centre-left political parties: in many countries it is at least partially represented in support for competitor parties on the political left, such as the greens and new left parties. This is possibly representative of the failure, thus far, of the centre-left to coherently articulate a plausible and inclusive new model for post-industrial development – especially in the wake of the global financial crisis. There is an opportunity here to form a politically stable coalition (which is inclusive of women, as well as bridging gaps between low- and high-skilled workers) around an economically sustainable predistributive strategy for the services-based economy – one which prioritises income equality, but also, critically, centres on large-scale public investments in universities, schools, and pre-schools. The task is to clearly articulate the feasibility of that strategy as a basis for sustained growth.

Notes

1. An earlier version of this chapter appeared in *Renewal: A Journal of Social Democracy* 21/1 (2013). The arguments presented here are developed in more detail in Anne Wren, *The Political Economy of the Service Transition* (Oxford: Oxford University Press, 2013).

2. Rudolf Meidner, *Coordination and Solidarity: An Approach to Wages Policy* (Stockholm: Bokforlaget Prisma, 1974); Gosta Rehn, 'Swedish active labour market policy: retrospect and prospect', *Industrial Relations* 25 (1985); Torben Iversen and Anne Wren, 'Equality, employment, and budgetary restraint: the trilemma of the service economy', *World Politics* 50/4 (1998), pp. 507–74.

3. Mary Gregory, Wiemer Salverda, and Ronald Schettkat, *Services and Employment: Explaining the U.S. European Gap* (Princeton and Oxford: Princeton University Press, 2007).

4. David H. Autor, Frank Levy, and Richard J. Murnane, 'The skill content of recent technological change: an empirical exploration', *Quarterly Journal of Economics* 118/4 (2003).

5. *Ibid.*, p. 5.

6. See, for example, Michael Wallerstein, 'Centralized bargaining and wage restraint', *American Journal of Political Science* 33/4 (1990), pp. 982–1004.

7. See, for example, Flavio Cuhne and James J. Heckman, 'The technology of skill formation', *American Economic Review* 97/2 (2007), pp. 31–47; James J. Heckman and Bas Jacobs, 'Policies to create and destroy human capital in Europe', NBER Working Paper, 15742 (2010). Available at http://www.nber.org/papers/w15742.pdf (accessed 20 March 2015).

8. Josh Mitchell, 'Student debt rises by 8% as college tuitions climb', *Wall Street Journal*, 3 May 2012; Joseph Stiglitz, 'Debt buries graduates' American dream', *USA Today Weekly International Edition*, 13–15 July 2012.

9. Claudia D. Goldin and Lawrence F. Katz, *The Race between Education and Technology* (Boston: The Bellknap Press of Harvard University Press, 2008).

10. Anne Wren, Mate Fodor, and Sotiria Theodoropoulou, 'The trilemma revisited: institutions, inequality, and employment creation in an era of ICT-intensive service expansion', in Anne Wren (ed.), *The Political Economy of the Service Transition* (Oxford: Oxford University Press, 2013).

11. See Ben Ansell and Jane Gingrich, 'A tale of two trilemmas: varieties of higher education and the service economy', and Torben Iversen and David Soskice, 'A political-institutional model of real exchange rates, competitiveness, and the division of labor', in Anne Wren (ed.), *The Political Economy of the Service Transition* (Oxford: Oxford University Press, 2013), and Wren, Fodor and Theodoropoulou, 'The trilemma revisited'.

12. Peter A. Hall and David Soskice (eds), *Varieties of Capitalism: The Institutional Foundations of Comparative Advantage* (Oxford University Press), Chapter 4.

13. See James J. Heckman, and Bas Jacobs, 'Policies to create and destroy human capital in Europe', NBER Working Paper 15742 (2010). Available at http://www.nber.org/papers/w15742.pdf (accessed 20 March 2015).

14. Philipp Rehm and Anne Wren, 'Service expansion, international exposure, and political preferences', in Anne Wren (ed.), *The Political Economy of the Service Transition* (Oxford: Oxford University Press, 2013).

15. Anne Wren and Philipp Rehm, 'The end of the consensus? Labour market developments and the politics of retrenchment', *Socioeconomic Review* 12 (2014), pp. 409–35.

16. Ben Ansell, 'University challenges: explaining institutional change in higher education', *World Politics* 60/2 (2008), pp. 189–230.

17. Margarita Estevez-Abe, Torben Iversen, and David Soskice. 'Social protection and the formation of skills: a reinterpretation of the welfare state', in Peter A. Hall and David Soskice (eds), *Varieties of Capitalism: The Institutional Foundations of Comparative Advantage* (Oxford: Oxford University Press, 2001), Chapter 4.

18. Torben Iversen and Frances Rosenbluth, *Women, Work, and Politics: The Political Economy of Gender Inequality* (New Haven: Yale University Press, 2010).

CHAPTER 15

Welfare Futures: Changing Needs, Risks and Tools

Innovation and the New Welfare State[1]

Geoff Mulgan

The long fiscal crisis that followed the 2007/8 crash has put immense pressure on welfare systems to reinvent themselves. Europe is particularly troubled. Angela Merkel regularly repeats a stylised fact that summarises the problem: Europe accounts for 10 per cent of the world's population; 25 per cent of GDP, and 50 per cent of welfare spending. The well-rehearsed challenges of ageing populations, disappearing jobs, welfare dependency and declining willingness to pay in more diverse societies, now combine with shorter-term pressures to cut deficits. As a result, the most prominent accounts of the future of welfare emphasise only retrenchment, salami-slicing cuts and a shift of responsibility from the state to citizens.

Here I suggest a different perspective. There is no doubt that many countries will need to radically overhaul their systems. It is dubious for moral, economic, and political reasons to let present generations benefit at the expense of future ones, and to pass on large debts. But it would be wrong to see only the problems and the limits. Seen at a global level, this is not an age of retrenchment and austerity. In many countries, welfare is expanding. Every developing country has had to build up new welfare rights – to healthcare, pensions, and unemployment insurance. Some have done so very fast, like Korea or Thailand. Others are doing so from a much lower base, including India and China. Meanwhile, the neoliberal arguments for replacing welfare with insurance markets, which became very prominent in the 1990s, and popular with the IMF, World Bank and big consultancies, have largely disappeared, rejected as too costly, ineffective and politically divisive.

New technologies make it possible to organise welfare in very different ways to the administrative systems of the twentieth century, which may make it easier to align welfare systems with the values they aim to represent. The perspective of the richest 10 per cent of the world, experiencing a time of crisis, can distort the bigger picture in which risk is being socialised and managed at larger scales than ever before. For the rich countries, however, the pressures make it all the more imperative to rethink what welfare is for, what tools it uses, how success is to be judged, and how good policies can be legitimated. The changing contexts – of continued deindustrialisation, fragmented family structures, and much greater ethnic diversity in open societies – all demand a level of creativity, both technical and political, that has been lacking in recent years.

In what follows, I briefly address all of these questions. I suggest some of the building blocks that can be assembled in different ways according to context and culture, to revive and reform welfare. I show where the state needs to be more active in direct ways, deliberately providing new infrastructures for payment and support, and where it needs to play an enabling role.

What is Welfare For?

Welfare states are not such new inventions. I have written elsewhere about the very long history of welfare in government, which stretches back to Sumeria (the first ever organised state was primarily a welfare state, organised around the distribution of grain to its citizens).[2] Rome too provided bread. Ancient India provided alms as well as healthcare; and pre-industrial England was one of many countries with a comprehensive, albeit very imperfect, system for alleviating poverty.

Modern welfare states emerged in successive bursts of invention, in response to the new needs of dense, newly industrialised societies in the late nineteenth century. They were borne out of a combination of factors: first, politics and public demand, as recently empowered citizens called for a share of rising wealth to address the risks they could not address on their own; second, the importance of productivity, and the impact of strong evidence that poor health, as well as poor education, undermined the economy; and, third, the arrival of new technologies of provision, in particular large-scale national bureaucracies able to manage complex assessment and payments systems.

These welfare states grew up to socialise a small number of key risks which had previously been seen as the responsibility of the individual, the family or the church. They included poverty in old age, unemployment, and ill-health. At the same time, states were investing heavily in social productive capacity through education systems and infrastructures. What is now called social investment was a major theme of early welfare design – the provision of universal education, maternity and other services to reduce inequalities (and prepare a productive population); and, in many countries, a social contract that involved substantial obligations on employers.

It was fairly obvious that individuals, families, and communities could not address many risks alone. Yet it was also generally assumed that they would be better placed than the state to deal with many other risks and needs, including emotional needs, mental health, most child-rearing, and eldercare.

The New Landscape of Risks and Needs

If we stand back and look at today's needs, we see a landscape that is somewhat different:

- Much longer periods of old age, and infirmity in old age, requiring both means for shifting income across the life cycle but also organising care on a much larger scale;
- Continued challenges of unemployment requiring not only help for short periods out of work but also action to address deeper problems of structural unemployment, obsolete skills, and hollowing out;
- Rising incidence of mental illness, with atomised societies often less able to provide informal support, friendship, and care;
- Related to this, apparently rising incidence of loneliness and isolation;[3]
- Rising incidence of long-term health conditions and disability, partly the result of medical advances;
- And risks that are the result of genetic bad luck as well as risks that are the result of behaviour and lifestyle choices.

The New Landscape of Tools

We can also see a landscape in which there are very different tools available for the daily delivery of welfare, and what we could call new 'operating systems' for welfare, including:

- Predictive algorithms of the kind already used in health services and criminal justice to predict who will be at greatest risk of such events as emergency hospital admission or re-offending;
- Technology platforms allowing not just direct payments into bank accounts but also virtual monies and internet-based payments, secure identities and personal accounts;

- Digital tools allowing states to orchestrate marketplaces for provision, for example of care supports, or learning, using credits provided by the state;
- Multiple feedback channels, and much easier tools to enable peer support;
- Social network analysis, and informal 'collaboratives' to help partnerships and co-operation across professional and organisational boundaries;
- New contracts, conditions and 'commitment' devices;
- And new financing tools, such as social impact bonds to incentivise outcomes and make the notion of social investment more concrete.

Any plausible account of the future of welfare needs to address both the content and the forms. In what follows, I suggest twelve ways in which welfare could evolve, addressing both form and content. The central purpose of welfare, remains as in the past, to protect people from risks they cannot easily manage on their own. Some of those risks are long-lasting (like the facts of old age), and some relate to periods of transition. Which risks matter changes over time, and the means used to address these risks inevitably evolve too; the biggest challenge for reform is how to shift resources from the problems of the past to the problems of the present and future. The arguments around predistribution and social investment are undoubtedly important parts of this story. But they risk missing much of what is happening in daily life, which is perhaps more complex and messier. Here then are twelve prompts, or building blocks, for reformers to draw on:

1. A reassertion of pooled protection against risks beyond the control of the individual

For more than a century, states have attempted to fund welfare through insurance. There are some risks for which insurance makes sense. But insurance markets have well-analysed weaknesses. They work best for the providers when purchasers are ignorant; when the majority of payers do not make claims, and when insurers can avoid the highest risk and highest-cost payers. Bismarck's welfare state was a prime example, designed to pay pensions only for the small minority who lived several years more than the then average life expectancy. Today a wide range of critical risks are essentially about luck and fate: diseases whose main causes are genetic; chronic problems of old age such as dementia that are the result of bad luck, and for which there are few credible cures. For these it makes far more sense to pool risk; insurance systems simply create unnecessary cost and bureaucracy. I expect that we will see a reassertion of some very basic ideas about welfare for some types of issues, with fully pooled risk, provision according to need, and funding through taxation.

2. **A reassertion of personal responsibility for risks over which individuals and families have some control, and incentivising pro-social actions**

The corollary of greater pooled risk for problems that are the result of bad luck, is a greater stress on personal and family responsibility for risks which can be influenced: risks associated with poor diet, smoking, laziness, risky living. In all of these cases support can be made partly conditional; and adjusted according to desert. Much welfare has always been conditional on various statuses (unemployment, disability) or on certain actions (willingness to be available for work). Sometimes, conditionality overshoots – and, like life, punishes children for the errors of their parents. In recent decades, some of the most influential waves of change in welfare have used conditionality more creatively – the better welfare-to-work policies of the rich north; the Bolsa Familial and related programmes in the developing south, that reward parents if their children attend school. All aim to make more explicit the implicit social contracts that underpin welfare and the deep human commitment to reciprocity. How far these go is bound to be controversial: should missed doctor's appointments carry a cost? Should health provision be conditional on signing up for smoking cessation? But some conditionality is essential to avoid perverse incentives and moral hazard.

3. **Cultivating resilience: predictive algorithms and new supports**

The most cutting critiques of late twentieth century welfare focused on its tendency to promote dependency and to address symptoms rather than causes, leaving recipients less, rather than more, able to thrive. This critique was often overdone – since much welfare necessarily has to be tied to needs, and many people are unavoidably dependent. But it contained important truths. So welfare has to be reshaped to help people become more resilient, rather than just supporting needs. That involves an orientation towards assets to fall back on; it requires welfare to include more learning, including both formal skills and the skills needed to be resilient in life, from financial literacy to non-cognitive skills; and it is partly about promoting social networks.

More powerful predictive tools are likely to become more popular. Already, algorithms can predict the risk of an older person entering hospital in the next year, or the risk of a former prisoner re-offending. Companies providing labour market support routinely use their own algorithms to help with triage. The more that large datasets are made open, the more sophisticated these are likely to become, providing guidance to individuals on how they can reduce their own risk factors, as well as guidance to the state and professionals about what interventions can be most effective in preventing future problems.

These can be controversial. The UK's attempt to create a comprehensive database of children at risk to guide preventive action was closed down by the Conservative government in the 2010s. 'Minority Report'-style forecasting of who is likely to be a future criminal raises a host of ethical and practical issues. But the promise of more effective, targeted, and timely welfare interventions is likely to be attractive to many.

If resilience is the goal, new types of intervention are likely to follow. Some will be about early childhood, and helping children to grow up confident, rounded, and smart. Others will focus on older age groups. For example, studio schools emphasise non-cognitive skills such as teamwork, motivation, and grit alongside more familiar skills in maths or science. They are not formally part of the welfare state, but any welfare system that aims to reduce youth unemployment needs something similar. Another example is health programmes that deliberately mobilise support networks for mental health, or 'social prescribing', for patients with long-term conditions to offer companionship, peer support or activity rather than drugs prescriptions.[4] These are much talked about, and there is strong evidence that they can be highly effective in enhancing resilience. But they are rarely made central – perhaps because they require very different ways of organising support, different skills for frontline staff and different metrics of success.

4. **Co-production as well as provision, and the integration of formal and informal support**

Welfare systems that promote resilience are also more likely to complement provision of money and services with more deliberate co-creation of welfare. This is most obvious in healthcare, where long-term conditions now make up the majority of health needs and require self-management and peer support as well as good doctors and hospitals. Turning the home and workplace into places for healthcare requires services with a very different method of delivery, including a much bigger role for coaches and mentors, and orchestrators of support networks. This is part of what I have called the 'relational state': a government that organises its roles, its staff, and its success metrics in terms of relationships as well as entitlements and outputs.[5]

The classic welfare state was conceived primarily in terms of monetary distribution, and service provision by paid professionals. In reality, it was always much more of a partnership with the public – volunteering as drivers, carers, or tutors. Recent fiscal pressures have restored interest in the combination of formal and informal support. Again, healthcare is a good example, where care models try to link together the formal support of the hospital with the engagement of family and friends, or in the case of dementia, with trained volunteers in the community. Nesta's £14m Centre for Social Action Innovation Fund has backed dozens of projects doing this effectively – with tutors for school students, volunteers in hospitals, and business coaches for unemployed young people.[6] Social media technology make it much easier to orchestrate these – and Barcelona's ambitious plans for circles of support for isolated older people could become a model for others to follow. These approaches point to a very different way of thinking about the state. Instead of conceiving its resources as limited to paid staff, and the buildings it owns, the state can think of a much wider pool of community resources to draw on. The Nesta supported Bookshare project captures the difference. Instead of a library consisting solely of the resources within the library building, the Bookshare allows citizens to put their book and DVD collections onto the library database, simultaneously expanding its resources and building social capital. In business, the many ventures of the collaborative economy are showing how the internet can mobilise distributed resources through firms like AirBnB, Buzzcar and many others. In Seoul, the city is using the same principle to reorganise how its assets are managed.

5. **Personal and family budgets and welfare market places**

In some fields the most efficient way to organise welfare is to give credits to claimants and let them decide how to spend money, within constraints. This is how personal budgets already work in many fields, such as care for disability. A similar principle has been explored with individual learning accounts.[7] Getting the detail right is all-important – with the right balance of openness and accreditation/regulation. Some of these budgets are similar to parallel currencies, and smart card technologies have long made it possible for a welfare agency to distribute money with limits on what could be bought (for example, to preclude spending on drink or drugs). The other side of this development is the deliberate organisation of marketplaces of support, for example, of training agencies providing skills, personal care services, and alternative healthcare provision.

6. New parallel currencies to mobilise underused resources

The world is full of parallel currencies sitting alongside traditional fiat money. At times welfare states have provided some of these, through credits that are substitutes for money – food vouchers, for example. Non-state monies include big currencies like the Swiss Economic Circle, an independent complementary currency system in Swizterland (WIR) and there are many thousands of Timebanks, Local Exchange Trading Systems (LETs) and others. Often when the mainstream economy has broken down, new currencies of this kind have grown up to fill the space – from Argentina in the early 2000s to Greece in the early 2010s. One weakness of these is the lack of involvement of the state as guarantor or manager of value, which limits their scale and usefulness. That is why attention has turned to the potential for the state to sponsor parallel currencies as part of reformed welfare systems: very local currencies to encourage circulation of value in towns, rural areas or poor neighbourhoods; currencies linking marginal public resources, and specialised currencies for care or education. There is radical potential for cities or small nations to offer pay and tax in a mix of formal money and parallel currency, creating a parallel market for firms to support the civil economy. Such parallel currencies could, in time, become a fundamental pillar of welfare systems. Technologies make it possible to manage money in very different ways – from mobile payment platforms like MPesa, to digital currencies like Bitcoin and Venn. Nesta's D-CENT programme, a Europe-wide project creating tools and applications for direct democracy and economic empowerment, will be testing out new currencies in various parts of Europe.[8] The full potential of such currencies is unclear – but this should be a period of experimentation, and could enable much more efficient ways of keeping people active, and remunerated.

7. Identities and integrated accounts that make new welfare products possible

Another building block of the future welfare system will be guaranteed identity management. India's Universal Identifier Programme is an interesting pointer to the future – a state-sponsored, biometric identifier which can be used to underpin provision of bank accounts and other commercial services. States may be better placed to provide trusted and authenticated identification services than private companies – and if they do so, can support mixed economies of welfare. A good example is the scope for governments to offer mortgages that are secured over lifetime earnings, with the power of tax agencies to ensure repayment. In principle, it should be possible for states to offer these at significantly lower cost and risk, than private firms because of their superior capacity to avoid default, and because they already have a working infrastructure to manage payments in the tax system. Other types of welfare product would include loans to pay for higher education, apprenticeships or training. In all of these cases, a twenty-first-century state should have major advantages in terms of economies of scale and scope, and should be able to move some parts of welfare from grants to loans, thus allowing money to go further.

8. **Transparency, simplicity, and visible welfare**

A general, if difficult, principle for reform may be to make welfare as transparent as possible, with every recipient clear on their entitlements, with easy access to self-assessment and planning tools. This will mean a drive for legibility and simplicity rather than technical perfection. It is arguably vital that welfare needs to be comprehensible to be legitimate, yet for now welfare remains extraordinarily opaque. A telling moment for me was working with programmers to design online platforms for claimants to assess their own entitlements – which in the UK context turned out to be almost impossible. Single accounts of the kind developed by Denmark may be pointers to the future – allowing citizens to see more clearly all of their payments and receipts from the state, as well as some of their lifetime entitlements. Australia has long adopted a principle of simplicity in its policy design, a principle enforced by its Treasury, which among other things led to one of the simplest systems for paying taxes in the world. At the very least, cognitive overload for citizens should be avoided.

9. **Navigation support – helping citizens make sense of welfare, and sometimes nudging them to change their behaviour**

A more open and complex welfare provision system will require correspondingly better support to help people navigate their way through. Some of this can be done online; some has to be face-to-face or phone-based. Simple self-assessment tools exist already. But coming over the horizon are much more sophisticated supports – for example to help plan curriculum or training choices using big data sets showing pay-offs, or career options. There are also possible new nudges and prompts. Most people are already bombarded with data-shaped communications from business, and the scope for far more targeted communications of all kinds is immense. But how would we feel if the government sent

SMS or equivalent messages to warn that we were not saving enough for our pensions; that our failure to maintain our skills threatened unemployment; that our children were too obese, or that we really should be volunteering more in our community?

10. **Commitment devices**

    Much has been learned in recent decades about how to encourage choices and behaviours that support the interests of the individual, their family and the community. Many of the points described above are essentially about better aligning how welfare works to these. Commitment devices of various kinds have been widely used: in welfare to work, encouraging or requiring claimants to set out a personal plan; home/school contracts to encourage parents to help with their children's education; personal plans in health, agreed with a doctor. Social media technologies make it possible to extend these, and many already encourage people to set goals for themselves that are visible to a circle of friends and family. Any welfare that is aimed at supporting a transition is likely to benefit from some public commitment devices.

11. **Budgets for impact – prevention, outcomes and contracts**

    Public finance is not well suited to the needs of twenty-first century welfare. It tends to be driven largely by demand, to be managed in terms of inputs not outputs or outcomes, and it tends to be time-neutral. Very different ways of organising finance include outcome-based funding like Payment by Results (PBR) or social impact bonds, that only release certain categories of money where outcomes are achieved. These are most appropriate for transitional welfare rather than ongoing support, for example for unemployment, transitions to adulthood or programmes aiming to improve health behaviour. Another example is preventive funding with life cycle budgeting – governments already use life cycle budgeting for some categories such as buildings, but these are hardly used at all for people. The alternative is to look at cohorts, and groups of interventions, in terms of both current cost and the mix of costs and benefits over many decades. This is particularly relevant for preventive health, education and labour market policies. Linking both outcome and preventive funding, some countries have experimented with contracts between different tiers of government, providing funding for investments (that is, into early years provision) but with the lower tier taking some of the risk of failing to achieve outcomes (Council of Australian Governments (COAG) is probably the most developed example). There are undoubtedly many other examples of creative ways of using money to better achieve welfare goals – in conditions of austerity we should expect these to be more widely used.

12. Experimentalism and evidence
Welfare states have tended to be set up by decree – with policies designed in ministries in capital cities, and enshrined in laws and entitlements. There are good reasons why welfare should be stable, predictable and law-based. But there are risks as well: that welfare will not be sufficiently evidence-based or sufficiently flexible to adapt to new needs and new tools. That is why around the core welfare state there is a strong argument for experimentalism: systematic trials of new ways of organising such things as public health, eldercare or skills. This is also why more systematic use of evidence is needed – along the lines of the 'what works' centres in the UK that provide easily used guidance on the state of global knowledge. Great care needs to be taken in how risks are handled – no one wants to be a guinea pig for ill-conceived welfare ideas. But in the long run, a more experimental approach to welfare, combined with more systematic synthesis of evidence, can lead to much higher performance.

Bricolage

These are building blocks not prescriptions. It would be very surprising if the same answers made sense in every environment. Welfare systems reflect history, culture, battles of the past as well as the present. What evolutionary biology calls 'fitness' landscapes may explain why what works in one country is bound to fail in another. Or to put it another way, not everyone could become Denmark even if they wanted to.

But one lesson of history is that there has often been convergence – whether of new tools like income tax, national insurance or welfare-to-work programmes – and it is likely to continue in the future too. Welfare systems are by their nature slow to change – and there is a virtue in keeping them reasonably stable. But the fiscal pressures in the north, and the demographic and political pressures in the south, mean that speed of adaptation will be increasingly important. We desperately need thinking about welfare to become more creative and open, and less formulaic and rhetorical. And we need to recognise that this era can be as much one of invention as of retrenchment.

Notes

1. This chapter is based on a talk given to the Nordic Council of Ministers in 2013.
2. Geoff Mulgan, *Good and Bad Power* (London: Penguin, 2006).
3. For a comprehensive analysis of changing patterns of need in one developed society see 'Sinking and swimming: Understanding Britain's unmet needs' (London: Young Foundation, 2009). Available at http://youngfoundation.org/publications/sinking-and-swimming/ (accessed 21 March 2015).
4. Nesta's 'People Powered Health' programme ran experiments in various parts of the NHS to advance these methods and also showed how much they could achieve in terms of savings.
5. See Geoff Mulgan, 'The Relational State' (London: Young Foundation, 2009); Geoff Mulgan, 'The Relational State' (London: IPPR, 2012).
6. See Centre for Social Action and Innovation Fund. Nesta. http://www.nesta.org.uk/project/centre-social-action-innovation-fund (accessed 18 May 2015).
7. In the UK at least this was a fairly good idea, though it was very poorly implemented.
8. Stefano Lucarelli, Marco Sachy, Klara Jaya Brekke, Francesca Bria, Carlo Vercellone, and Laurent Baronian, 'Decentralised Citizens Engagement Technologies' (D-CENT, 2014).

CHAPTER 16

Moving Towards Welfare Societies
An Inclusive Approach to Growth

Alfred Gusenbauer and Ania Skrzypek

O ne of the key problems with social democracy today is the perception that politics has lost its power. This concern limits debate and overshadows any sparkles of hope that things can be done to change the current state of affairs. This phenomenon is not new. Over the last few decades, much intellectual energy has been channelled into proclamations about the *end* of the era, the *end* of history and the *end* of ideologies. This time the *end* scenario asserts that globalisation is uncontrollable and political parties are unable to protect citizens against anxiety, insecurity and economic and social change. This chapter refutes this 'doomsday scenario'. Instead, we suggest that formulating a new vision for a welfare society can help progressive politics navigate the major structural changes impacting on our economies and labour markets.

Politics versus Invisible, Impersonal, Global Forces

It is paradoxical that in an era when it was possible to set a relatively stable global order, put in place mechanisms enabling the development of fairer societies and foster discoveries that vastly improve the quality of everyday life – that in these years politics has become weaker. Considered a vehicle of empowerment since the French Revolution, politics has melted into a poorly-executed management affair. It is being digested by its own limitations and has abandoned its mission. It has become a profession. It is no longer about long-term plans; it is about surviving the next set of elections. It is no longer about the battles; it is about compromises. In this spirit, politics became an internal feature of the established system – static and subjected to the will of five *invincible, impersonal, global forces*.

First, there is the familiar force of globalisation. Since the 1990s and before, it has split parties and social movements between those who see it as an unstoppable force for good and those who want to roll back time to nation-state social democracy. The position in governments of politicians advocating the former gave rise to the concepts of labour market activation and the need to prepare individuals – as opposed to societies – with the tools they need in the highly-competitive knowledge-based economy. These developments had huge implications for the traditional welfare state and the idea of 'social Europe' – a concept which put the values of collectivism, equality, and solidarity firmly at the heart of the EU.

Second, climate change emerged on the world stage as an impending catastrophe with the emphasis overly placed on alarmism and powerlessness as opposed to a clear statement on how progressive politics could change things and combine a low-carbon transition with social justice – and what this would mean for the welfare state and collective action by different societal actors.

Third, the expansion of financial capitalism and the ensuing 2008 global financial crisis had a perverse effect on the role of the state in providing welfare and social security. To begin, the expansion of financial capitalism meant that the set of values and rules underpinning the global order changed. The foundations of the postwar state came under the pressure of the new, neoliberal logic. The new focus was on competition instead of cooperation and the value of the real economy became increasingly trumped by a focus on efficiency and financial reward.

Fourth, demographic changes and ageing societies, specifically in the EU, have been portrayed as 'unstoppable' and unavoidable 'disasters'. Progressives are left questioning the extent to which the welfare state is at all a plausible political offer. In the reality of ageing societies, the proportion of people active on the labour market has shrunk, less children are born, and citizens live longer and consequently require extended services and pensions. These are all key areas for the new mission of social democracy – providing new societal safety nets and social investment – but instead welfare states are no longer widely seen as the guarantors for social justice or equal opportunities, as the vehicle of social mobility and the protective shield for those in need. To the contrary, they are perceived by many as a burden and judged frequently as anachronistic, and paradoxically, even as a contributing factor in the deepening of societal inequalities.

Fifth, there is the onset of the 'new industrial revolution' and the digitalisation of our economies and societies. Once more, these trends have been presented as invincible, impersonal, global forces. The speed at which technology has impacted on various aspects of professional and private lives has grown intensively – and this has translated into numerous challenges varying from the ethical – defining freedom in the context of data protection, intellectual property rights, and defence against organised crime on the internet – to somewhat more traditional socio-economical dilemmas – accessibility, skills, and a new safety net that would enable a smooth transition between the previous and the new phase of industrial development. But more often than not, these debates are darkened by fear and 'techno-pessimism', with little room for debate on how socio-economic choices and a new welfare settlement can prepare people for this age and harness technological breakthroughs to fight the big challenges of our times.

The tacit acceptance of these five looming unstoppable spectres has eroded confidence in the primacy of politics and the efficacy of centre-left government. Traditional political parties became too resigned to characterising these developments as unstoppable leviathans that dictate the terms of change. These forces provided comfort in serving as an explanation, and frequently also as an excuse for, political drift. The emergence of social movements, protest parties and the recent elections across Europe indicate that this drift cannot continue. Hence political parties have to start reasserting themselves as actors who can tame and shape invincible, impersonal, global forces.

Welfare Societies

A first step involves developing a new understanding of what political choice means. There are three basic criteria that can be applied in order to escape the existing TINA ('There Is No Alternative') logic and to move away from the compromise of established politics. Firstly, political choice needs to be underpinned with distinctive values and clear alternatives, so that the decisions have a political and not a merely managerial character. Secondly, it requires taking risks. Political choice must be about selecting one or another, and not about indecisiveness or creating hybrids. Indeed, perhaps it was true once upon a time that 'elections are won in the middle', but these days *the middle* in question seems to have dramatically shrunk. In order to avoid drifting from one extreme to another, it is indispensable to answer the query: who do social democrats aspire to represent? Thirdly, political choices need to be long lasting. They must be about formulating a path forward, not merely responding to current, pressing and media-propagated affairs. Here they must be part of a long-term mission. The philosophy needs to change – from operating as a governmental party to becoming a mission-oriented political party once again.

This may be obvious on the theoretical level. However, the difficulty lies in moving into tangible recommendations and articulating them in relation to a new concept. Here we suggest the framework of moving towards 'welfare societies'. Following the three criteria above, it is essential to begin with setting the defining lines of a new progressive vision. Social democrats need to focus on the realities of class dealignment in contemporary society – and not the society of the past. In that exercise, it has to be accepted that risks are involved in order to gain more significant support in the future – some voters will be lost in the process. That, however, may be more beneficial than the status quo, with social democracy trying to catch all voters but in reality being left with only a few faithful, but equally frustrated supporters.

The 'welfare society' is by default a concept larger than the welfare state. But it is not only a choice of vocabulary; it must be defined within how progressives think about the state's role and, by extension, the expectations towards the 'social Europe' agenda. The starting point is that progressives will never be able to argue convincingly in favour of welfare policies unless they manage to detach themselves from the notion of simple (unaffordable) redistributive 'spending' and connect with the idea of 'social investment', which is aimed at multiplying assets and ensuring their equitable division. To do so, it is necessary to clarify what is public and what is private. The border has been blurred, since it was public funds that were used to bail out private debts, and consequently public budgets were left in jeopardy. Additionally, it must be stressed that 'public' does not equal 'free' – but instead 'paid from common funds' to which all have *rights* and for which all need to assume adequate *responsibility*. The guiding ethos is that the principles of taxation must be explained clearly, ensuring that everyone, especially the financial sector, is requested to contribute a fair share. Social investment also has to be paired with an active state using predistribution policies to correct market inequalities and outcomes at the source. Broadly, this has to cover four dimensions: opportunities, knowledge, access to resources, and power.

In summary, the concepts of social investment and predistribution should be framed within a move towards welfare societies, which empower individuals to reach their full potential and ensure a level playing field.

Ambitious Goals: Reaching Beyond the Horizon of Bare Minimums

The suggested shift from thinking about the 'welfare state' towards a 'welfare society' should carry two essential components – paving a path for society and designing the future of the labour market. The first step towards a new vision would be to start thinking in terms of a 'society' again. In the last few years, this understanding has arguably faded away, replaced by a three-pillar debate of a different sort. Its components were: preoccupation with individualisation and fragmentation; the neoliberal understanding that there would be a trade-off between collective responsibility and opportunities for individual emancipation; and finally that the split between what society wants and what politics can offer is already too big for politics to influence social processes. Each of the three has become a myth in itself. Progressives should therefore seek to reclaim their core competence regarding social and labour policies.

The second step is about the labour market. The starting point is the question, what role does employment play in one's life and for the community one lives in? If that is, as progressives would claim until quite recently, a value in itself to have and be able to execute a job, then there is a need to ensure that employment in itself is about enabling all to make a sensible contribution, about gratification that allows individual choices and about being a part of a community that has bargaining power vis-à-vis any of the invincible, impersonal, global forces. This is why the entire frame must change. Jobs should not be seen as merely a 'payable occupation', but rather a leverage that, through its quality, stimulates individuals' productivity, allows prosperity to multiply and enables a greater share of welfare for all. The new conceptualisation must take into account the continuing processes, such as technological evolution and digitalisation. There is no reason to fear these changes, as long as there is a readiness on the side of progressives to actively shape the course of this new industrial revolution. Cushioning the effects of change is precisely to where safety nets must extend.

We must therefore think about education and skills in a different way. To begin, they must be about empowerment. Hence they must enable all to comprehend the processes, and within them have a capacity to identify and pursue their individual paths. Education and training must once again become a guarantee for all, translating into enhancing individuals' ability to both adjust and advance. These activation and empowerment criteria should be the guiding evaluation standards regarding the efficiency of the schooling system. The emphasis on equal importance of knowledge and skills should be further pursued, ending the current dualisation and the consequent stigmatisation within societies. If progressives indeed wish to put forward a vision for re-industrialisation, they will need to convince all that practical competences are key. Continuous vocational training should be an aspiration not only for some, but for as many as possible.

Conclusion

If the crisis aftermath and the consequent austerity debate teach us anything, it is that believing that there is no alternative is a self-defeating tactic, especially in a Europe awash with populist actors. There should be no more hiding behind the defensive wall of invisible, impersonal, global forces. Should progressives hope to be chosen to shape the future, they must provide citizens with bolder political choices. That is why we need a new vision for a 'welfare society'. A simple U-turn towards a 'good, old' welfare state concept is not possible; there is a need for a broader, modern vision of welfare.

In that sense, this chapter also connects with an eminent dilemma on how to change the terms of the current debate and induce a different way of thinking about the economy. There needs to be an inclusive approach to growth – one that creates the space to move from the current path of growth 'at any cost' to the understanding that growth must be wide-ranging and sustainable instead. This notion is equally important for offering new ways in which Europe can restore itself as a beacon of hope for the current, disenchanted generation. The realisation of a welfare society agenda would be an essential component of a new social ambition for the EU, proving that the European Social Model is not doomed.

The time is now. On one hand, there seems to be a chance to reverse the tide. On the other, voters are still drifting, but have not yet entirely moved to alternatives to the well-established political forces. To capture this opportunity, progressive proposals need to be bold, brave, and fresh. Now is the moment to stop being defensive, and start framing the future.

References

A. Anttonen and M. Zechner, 'Theorising care and care work', in B. Pfau-Effinger and T. Rostgaard (eds), *Work and Welfare in Europe: Care Between Work and Welfare in European Societies* (Basingstoke: Palgrave Macmillan, 2011).

G. Baiocchi and E. Ganuza, 'Politics without banners: the Spanish indignados' experiment in direct democracy', in E. Stetter, K. Duffek, and A. Skrzypek (eds), *FEPS Next Left Book Series, vol. 5: Building New Communities* (Brussels: FEPS/ Renner Institut/IGLP, 2012), pp. 110–19.

Rémi Bazillier, 'Equality must be the core of economic policies: 17 propositions for equality and efficiency', in E. Stetter, K. Duffek, and A. Skrzypek (eds), *FEPS Next*

Left Book Series, vol. 6: *For a New Social Deal* (Brussels: FEPS/Renner Institut, 2013), pp. 102–33.

Mark Blyth, *Austerity: The History of a Dangerous Idea* (Oxford University Press, 2013).

G. Bonoli and D. Natali, *The Politics of the New Welfare State* (Oxford University Press, 2012).

L. Byrne, 'The squeezed middle and the new inequality', in Olaf Cramme and Patrick Diamond (eds), *After the Third Way: The Future of Social Democracy in Europe* (London: I.B.Tauris/Policy Network, 2012), pp. 203–18.

Olaf Cramme and Patrick Diamond, *After the Third Way: The Future of Social Democracy in Europe* (London: I.B.Tauris/Policy Network, 2012).

Olaf Cramme, Patrick Diamond, and Michael McTernan, *Progressive Politics after the Crash: Governing from the Left* (London: I.B.Tauris, 2013).

Colin Crouch, *The Strange Non-Death of Neoliberalism* (Cambridge: Polity Press, 2011).

Colin Crouch and M. Keune, 'The governance of economic uncertainty: beyond the 'new social risks' analyses', in G. Bonoli and D. Natali (eds), *The Politics of the New Welfare State* (Oxford: Oxford University Press, 2012) pp. 45–69.

Patrick Diamond and Guy Lodge, 'European welfare states after the crisis: changing public attitudes' (London: Policy Network, 2013). Available at http://www.policy-network.net/publications/4320/European-Welfare-States-after-the-Crisis (accessed 22 March 2015).

Gøsta Esping-Andersen, *Why We Need a New Welfare State* (Oxford: University Press, 2002).

—— *Social Foundations of Postindustrial Economies* (Oxford: Oxford University Press, 2011).

J. A. Frieden, 'The many faces of distributional conflicts. Recovery and fiscal adjustement', in Olaf Cramme, Patrick Diamond, and Michael McTernan (eds), *Progressive Politics After the Crash. Governing from the Left* (London: I.B.Tauris, 2013), pp. 45–52.

B. Greve, *Choice. Challenges and Perspectives for the European Welfare States* (Oxford: Wiley-Blackwell, 2010).

Jacob S. Hacker, 'How to reinvigorate the centre-left? Predistribution', the *Guardian*, 12 June 2013. Available at http://www.theguardian.com/commentisfree/2013/jun/12/reinvigorate-centre-left-predistribution (accessed 22 March 2015).

Silja Häusermann, 'The politics of old and new social policies', in G. Bonoli and D. Natali (eds), *The Politics of the New Welfare State* (Oxford University Press, 2012), pp. 111–34.

H. Heclo and A. Wildawsky, *The Private Government of Public Money* (Basingstoke: Palgrave Macmillan, 1981).

Anton Hemerijck, *Changing Welfare States* (Oxford: Oxford University Press, 2013).

N. Kildal and S. Kuhnle, *Normative Foundations of the Welfare State: The Nordic Experience* (London: Routledge, 2005).

S. Moschonas, 'One step forward, one step back? Debt crisis, the PES and the limits of social democracy', in E. Stetter, K. Duffek, and A. Skrzypek (eds), *FEPS Next*

Left Book Series, vol. 7: In the Name of Political Union: Europarties on the Rise (Brussels: FEPS/Renner Institut, 2013), pp. 126–41.

Pippa Norris, *Making Democratic Governance Work: How Regimes Shape Prosperity, Welfare, and Peace* (Cambridge: Cambridge University Press, 2012).

D. V. Preece, '(Re)constructing a neoliberal social Europe', *Dismantling Social Europe: The Political Economy and Social Policy in the European Union* (London: First Forum Press, 2009).

U. Schimank, 'The fragile constitution of contemporary welfare societies: A derailed functional antagonism between capitalism and democracy', Welfare Societies Working Paper 01/2011' (Universität Bremen, 2011). Available at http://www. welfare-societies.com/uploads/file/WelfareSocietiesWorkingPaper-No1_ Schimank.pdf (accessed 22 March 2015).

M. Schröder, *Work and Welfare in Europe: Integrating Varieties of Capitalism and Welfare State Research: A Unified Typology of Capitalisms* (Basingstoke: Palgrave Macmillan, 2013).

Ania Skrzypek, 'The next social contract: a new vision for European society', in E. Stetter, K. Duffek, and A. Skrzypek, *FEPS Next Left Book, Series, vol. 6: For a New Social Deal* (Brussels: FEPS/Renner Institut, 2013), pp. 24–59.

Ania Skrzypek, *Winning for Real: The Next Left Taking the Chance to Shape Europe for the 21st Century – 10 Fundamental Challenges* (Brussels: FEPS, 2013). Available at http://www.feps-europe.eu/assets/794dd776-a325-4393-9782-1fe16f8d812a/ winning-for-real-low-resolution.pdf (accessed 18 May 2015).

—— 'Standing tall: reconnecting with the social question of the contemporary times', in E. Stetter, K. Duffek, and A. Skrzypek (eds), *FEPS Next Left Book Series, vol. 9: Framing a New Progressive Narrative* (Brussels: FEPS/Renner Institut, 2014), pp. 48–71.

P. Starke, A. Kaasch, and F. van Hooren, *Transformation of the State Series: The Welfare State as Crisis Manager. Explaining the Diversity of Policy Responses to Economic Crisis* (Basingstoke: Palgrave Macmillan, 2013).

Joseph E. Stiglitz, *The Price of Inequality: How Today's Divided Society Endangers our Future* (New York/London: W. W. Norton and Company, 2012).

Peter Taylor-Gooby, *The Double Crisis of the Welfare State and What We Can Do About It* (Basingstoke: Palgrave Macmillan, 2013).

Postscript
The Future of the Welfare State

Peter A. Hall

O ne of the messages of this book is that we live in a new world. The world is always in flux, of course, but sometimes it changes so profoundly as to render us 'immigrants in our own land' – in the phrase of Margaret Mead – living in a world our parents never knew. The past four decades have seen the diffusion of radically new technologies, processes of economic and cultural globalisation, and a shift toward employment in services transformative of people's lives. In 1975, the personal computer had not yet been invented, developing economies produced less than a third of the world's output, and more than a third of workers in the OECD were employed in manufacturing. Today, the average American spends 23 hours a week on the internet; developing economies account for more than half of global production; and barely a fifth of the OECD labour force works in manufacturing.

Socio-economic change on this scale has been especially consequential for the social programmes of the welfare state. The welfare state was an invention of the postwar years that assumed its current form during the 1960s and 1970s. To its programmes, the citizens of the developed democracies owe much of their security from adversity, but the adequacy of existing welfare states has been called into question by several challenges facing them today.

The Challenges

The capacity of existing social programmes to provide economic security is being strained by shifts in occupational structure that follow from rapid technological change and more intense international competition. In the developed world, well-paid manufacturing jobs are moving overseas, hollowing out the middle class, as people with advanced skills move into higher paying occupations, while others without them are relegated to low-paid jobs in services.[1] As a result, the distribution of market incomes has become more unequal, a phenomenon exacerbated in some economies by the decline of trade unions and the rise of the financial sector. These developments challenge states in two important ways. First, they increase the pressure on governments to redistribute resources at a time when slow rates of growth and high levels of debt limit the resources available to them.[2] Second, to maintain national prosperity in this new knowledge economy, governments have to ensure that firms have access to technological advances and workers are equipped with sufficient skills to exploit those advances.

These are social as well as economic challenges. From an egalitarian perspective, governments face the task, not only of providing sufficient skills, but of ensuring those skills are distributed widely across the population. Otherwise, a large part of the workforce may be consigned to low-paid, precarious jobs. If they lack the skills necessary for finding meaningful employment in such an economy or the advantages of birth conducive to acquiring those skills, many people will be deprived of the fruits of a high-technology economy. Moreover, failure on this front could have long-term consequences for social stratification. As income inequality increases, rates of social mobility decline, closing off the social escalators that provide a veneer of meritocracy in democratic societies.[3]

There is also an intergenerational dimension to these problems. Young people are especially at risk. In many countries, high levels of youth unemployment are impeding the entry of a younger generation into the core workforce.[4] The absence of stable employment delays family formation and depresses the birth rate, which can be debilitating for societies already facing the prospect of lower rates of growth as the average age of their population rises. Thus, governments face the problem of how to avoid the development of a new underclass, permanently excluded from well-paid employment and from the forms of social engagement associated with it.[5] They confront the spectre of intergenerational inequality with which welfare states that currently spend three times as much on the retired than they do on families with children are ill-equipped to cope.[6]

The political challenges facing those who would like to reform contemporary welfare states are equally great. The Keynesian welfare state was constructed, in the three decades after World War II, out of a politics in which the political cleavage between social classes loomed large. In many respects, that welfare state reflected a class compromise, in which parties representing the organised working class accepted a managed capitalism in exchange for social programmes, while parties speaking for the owners and managers of capital agreed to pay for this social safety net in return for industrial peace.[7] But the class cleavage no longer dominates politics in the developed democracies. As postwar prosperity reduced class-based grievances and the shift of employment to services eroded the blue-collar working class, it has become more difficult for centre-left parties to identify and speak for a cohesive class interest.[8] Today, the advocates for new social programmes face the challenge of assembling support for them from a more fragmented electorate, cross-cut by cleavages rooted in social values, new skill sets and fears about globalisation.[9] Moreover, many must often do so in contexts where scepticism about what governments can accomplish has increased, in the wake of slower rates of economic growth and the growing prominence of neoliberal ideas.[10]

The Roles for Predistribution and Social Investment

The traditional instruments of the welfare state remain important to social well-being. Two kinds of programmes have long supplied the bedrock of the welfare state. Based on contributions from employers or employees, supplemented by general tax revenues, *social insurance programmes* protect people against the loss of income and costs associated with unemployment, retirement, illness and other adverse life events. Alongside them, *redistributive programmes* alleviate the worst effects of poverty and reduce inequalities in disposable household income through the provision of social assistance, tax credits and other types of subsidies.

However, these programmes do not fully address the socio-economic challenges of the contemporary era. For that purpose, two other instruments on which this volume focuses have much more potential. One is a set of measures associated with *predistribution*, so-called because they are designed to address social inequality at its roots, by evening out the distribution of incomes set by market forces, reducing discrimination in the workplace or society, and advancing the life chances of the underprivileged in ways that do not entail fiscal redistribution on the part of governments.[11] Falling under this rubric are steps to enhance the influence of trade unions in wage bargaining; regulations requiring companies to provide more generous pensions, health care or other public goods; and mandates for private sector organisations that improve access to education, among other measures.

In an era when public spending is inhibited by the existence of large entitlement programmes and overhanging debt, policies of predistribution can reduce social inequalities at relatively low cost to governments. Although policy-makers have to be attentive to potentially negative side effects, policies such as these can offset the effects of rampant shareholder capitalism on the inclination of firms to provide public goods and restore some of the 'beneficial constraints' that encourage firms to move their production up the value chain, thereby providing better jobs.[12] Requiring companies to offer better pay and benefits encourages them to produce higher quality products based on innovation and investment in the skills of their labour force. Asking them to pay for the environmental costs of their operations encourages them to seek sustainable forms of production. Thus, predistribution is conducive, not only to more egalitarian societies, but to more effective competition in the global economy.

The second set of instruments serving such purposes are those associated with *social investment*.[13] The defining feature of such policies is their emphasis on improving the skills of the workforce, broadly construed to encompass people's capacities to contribute to society as well as the economy. These programmes often do involve the expenditure of public resources and may target the least advantaged; but, unlike traditional redistributive policies, they are designed to enhance the productive capacities of the nation rather than only to relieve poverty. Such programmes include efforts to improve the educational level of the population, steps to facilitate re-entry of the unemployed into jobs, and measures focused on early childhood development to ensure all children realise their inherent potential.

Social investment addresses the central challenges of the new knowledge economy, which are to ensure that people have the skills to secure good jobs in a system of production transformed by technological change and that no one is denied access to such skills or good jobs by virtue of the circumstances of birth. As the term indicates, effective policies of social investment pay social dividends over time in the form of higher rates of economic growth that flow from better use of all the human capacities available in a society.[14] Genuine social investment does not simply force people into work but equips them to be more productive and socially engaged. Thus, it speaks to the problem of ensuring that the younger generations can enjoy a life as good as, if not better than, that of their parents.

Of course, the boundaries between these four types of instruments are porous. Predistributive measures can promote social investment, and effective social investment often entails some redistribution, as Huber and Stephens observe in this volume. However, policies oriented to predistribution and social investment speak more directly to the socio-economic dilemmas of the contemporary era than traditional programmes of social insurance and redistribution do. As such, they deserve a prominent place on the platforms of progressive political parties.

The Politics of Social Investment

For progressive political parties, however, the issue is not simply whether to espouse policies of predistribution and social investment but how to assemble electoral coalitions around such a platform. As I have noted, many face electorates more sceptical than they once were about the value of state intervention and fragmented into constituencies that are sometimes resistant to the broad egalitarian appeals of the past.

However, it may well be possible for social democrats and their progressive counterparts to assemble a viable coalition around these policies, not least because their principal rivals on the centre-right are also in trouble. Centre-right parties now operate under at least three handicaps. First, in Europe, the traditional appeal of Christian Democracy is waning because organised religion no longer occupies the central role it once had in many households. Women who could once be counted on to support Christian Democratic parties now vote in larger numbers for their Social Democratic counterparts, and a corresponding gender gap favours the Democrats in the USA. Second, the breakdown of longstanding electoral cleavages has also had consequences for mainstream parties on the centre-right. They too face an electoral constituency that is fragmenting, as parties on the radical right draw votes away from them with appeals that combine an attachment to traditional values with calls for social protection, while classically-liberal parties attract members with more progressive social values and a commitment to free markets.[15]

Perhaps most important, the mainstream centre-right lacks an effective policy response of its own to the socio-economic problems of the contemporary era. The suggestion that more intensive use of market competition can resolve those problems, which has been a staple of centre-right platforms for three decades, has lost much of its credibility in the wake of the 2008–9 global financial crisis. As rising levels of income inequality dampen the prospects for social mobility, the traditional promise that centre-right governments would provide equality of opportunity in lieu of more equal incomes has become less convincing. Moreover, because they are generally hostile to further regulation and public spending, these parties are largely unprepared to make the investments in public goods required for prosperity in the context of the new knowledge economy. Thus, the centre-left faces an important political opportunity.

What must social democratic parties do in order to take advantage of this opportunity? There are two sides to their task. From within a fragmented electorate, they must construct coalitions of interest that bring together groups who might not otherwise be natural allies but who benefit from policies of predistribution or social investment. Comparative political economy suggests that political coalitions are always built on shared interests, and many of these policies speak to the concerns of groups that might not normally be seen as political bedfellows. Programmes of early childhood development, for instance, can serve the interests of working women and of the firms that employ them. Measures designed to stabilise or enhance employee pensions can speak to the interests of workers and of segments of the financial sector.[16]

In order to appeal to wide swathes of the electorate, these parties also have to build a new vision of what social democracy offers in the contemporary era. Successful political visions have at least two dimensions. However, they have to make a credible case that the policies being advanced are economically efficient, in the sense that they will address the socio-economic problems of the day. As the chapters in this book indicate, such a case can be made for policies of predistribution and social investment. On the other hand, powerful political visions also have a moral dimension, which is to say they speak to overarching issues about what the people of a nation owe one another and can legitimately ask in turn of their government. Social democrats can find the basis for such a vision in longstanding conceptions of fairness underpinning each nation's understanding of social justice, and refashion it to speak to the circumstances of a changing world. This is not an easy task: it entails capturing and reframing aspects of the zeitgeist that are often elusive. But that is ultimately the craft of politics.

The core of such a vision lies in recognising that income inequality is a social problem but not the only problem confronting developed democracies. The most pressing issue is how to cope with the contemporary transformation in the economic conditions underlying national success. In large measure, that transformation lies behind rising levels of inequality and makes the task of addressing it more challenging. As the chapters in this book note, the rise of a knowledge economy means that national success today depends especially heavily on a nation's capacity to generate and exploit technological advancement. Compounding that problem is the transition to services, marked by the growth of employment in occupations dedicated to the production of services and a corresponding decline in manufacturing employment.

In short, at the centre of a progressive platform for the twenty-first century must be the claim that social democratic parties are best-equipped to manage the socio-economic transformation of the contemporary era. The core challenge is not to rectify the wrongs of the past but to construct the conditions for national success in the future. Everyone's prosperity is at stake, and among the keys to success are policies of social investment and predistribution. Of course, appeals of this sort are not entirely new. They resonate with Harold Wilson's call in 1964 to reforge Britain in the white heat of the scientific revolution. But the terms of the economic challenge have changed and it requires new kinds of policies.

Moreover, rising to this challenge also entails giving some attention to issues of equality. Amidst rapid technological change, national success depends on mobilising the full capacities of a nation's people. Without a well-educated workforce, a country's firms cannot engage in the high value-added production that delivers rising living standards. And securing an educated labour force is not simply a matter of providing access to better schools. Educational achievement is conditioned by the social circumstances of the family. Thus, effective skill formation entails enough redistribution to promote a genuine equality of opportunity.

Progressive parties should note, however, that socio-economic change has not simply created economic challenges. It has also disrupted the set of shared understandings and institutional practices that govern people's relationships with others and with the organisations central to their lives. In this respect, socio-economic change has disorganised what we might think of as the contemporary social contract.[17]

There are many dimensions to these understandings, but some of the most consequential bear on what people can expect from their employers and what a nation expects of the firms at the centre of its economy. On these dimensions, in particular, the contemporary social contract has come unstuck. Under the impetus of more intense competition from open global markets and the influence of neoliberal ideas, many firms have cut costs by eliminating employee benefits, such as defined-benefit pension plans, and sub-contracting tasks to enterprises that offer their workers little job security and few benefits. In the wake of new compensation schemes for senior managers tied to the value of a company's shares, firms have begun to prioritise the value of those shares over returns to other stakeholders such as employees or local communities.[18] Financial manoeuvres to increase share prices, based on buy-back schemes and higher dividends have also drained funds away from investment in research and development, thereby reducing the capacity of many firms to contribute to national innovation and economic growth over the long term. Corporate opposition to environmental policies, such as carbon taxes, have pushed the costs of their operations onto society at large, threatening the sustainability of the economy.

In many instances, these practices have called into question longstanding understandings about what companies owe their employees and communities and generated widespread unease, reflected in contemporary debates about corporate social responsibility.[19] Thus, socio-economic change does not simply pose challenges for the state. By unsettling many kinds of social relationships, it has given rise to a diffuse social discontent rooted in uncertainty about the terms of the prevailing social contract.

In this context, policies of predistribution can be seen as integral components of an effort to establish a new social contract. Social well-being cannot depend entirely on the actions of states. It also turns on what other social organisations, including firms, medical providers and universities, contribute to society, and predistributive measures are meant to ensure that they live up to their responsibilities to the common good. Thus, the times call for a new debate about how to define the terms of the social contract, with a view to shaping the predistributive measures that emerge from it.

Conventional understandings about social relationships at the macro-level, among different segments of society, have also been called into question by contemporary developments and should figure in this debate. Especially important here are questions about what the affluent strata in society owe people who are less advantaged than themselves. This has been a central issue since the dawn of civilisation, and it has been deeply affected by the nostrums of the neoliberal era, which present markets as the most efficient means of allocating resources, thereby privileging mechanisms that render access to many kinds of goods and services dependent on income. In this context, the notion that everyone is entitled to a certain level of public services has waned, and the right to income has been tied more directly to work, much as it was amidst another technological revolution at the turn of the nineteenth century.[20]

Debates about such matters involve issues of social justice, and the contemporary conjuncture supplies social democrats with new arguments to bring to them. They can rely on the fact that most people want to live in a just society. But they can also observe that, in the contemporary context, securing a just society is integral to securing a prosperous society. Social investment in people at the bottom of the social ladder unleashes productive capacities that enhance everyone's prosperity. If working women receive little help, they will not have children, and in the face of a dwindling population societies will decline. If skill formation at the bottom of the income ladder is unsuccessful, countries will be locked into economic regimes oriented to low-wage labour and the kind of low value-added production on which a developed country cannot build a successful economic base.

In short, efforts to advance social justice need not be seen as steps taken in spite of their economic inefficiency, but as measures that increase the efficiency of the nation as a whole, delivering widespread economic fruits. Once again, this is not an entirely novel idea: Victorian social reformers operated under similar premises. But that viewpoint has languished during the neoliberal age and deserves to be revived in light of contemporary socio-economic challenges.

Conclusion

In recent years, disillusionment with what states can accomplish has led thoughtful analysts across the political spectrum to turn away from public action and look for solutions to contemporary social problems in a revived civil society, more socially-conscious enterprises, and new forms of co-operation at the local level.[21] They are not wrong to do so. As I have noted, social well-being cannot depend entirely on the state. Bottom-up concerted action can address many kinds of social problems.

However, states and societies stand in a symbiotic relationship with each other. In some cases, effective social co-operation is easier to secure if public regulations guarantee the commitments social actors make to each other; and addressing some kinds of socio-economic problems requires resources on a scale that can only be assembled by the state. Before giving up on the welfare state as an outmoded structure of ossified social programmes administered by purely opportunistic politicians, then, we should think seriously about how those programmes can be reshaped to meet the distinctive challenges of our age. And, as the chapters in this book suggest, inventive schemes of social investment and predistribution have the potential to speak directly to those challenges.

Of course, they are not a magic bullet capable of curing all the ills of our era, and there are many open questions about how they should be designed and funded. We know more about the desirability of improving the skills of the workforce, for instance, than about just how to do so. Programmes oriented toward early childhood development vary in quality and need to be carefully designed if they are to be effective. Regulations designed to encourage high value-added production can have adverse side effects that must be addressed if they are to accomplish their objectives. In many instances, such programmes must be tailored to the distinctive needs of a particular nation.

Nevertheless, there is real promise in the kind of creative rethinking of the welfare state that the chapters in this volume represent. After several decades in which many countries have seen median incomes stagnate and employment become more precarious, neoliberalism has lost much of its lustre, and programmes of social investment and predistribution look like viable alternatives that can work. In tandem with other social innovations, they surely have a role to play in the future of the welfare state.

Notes

1. David Autor and David Dorn, 'The growth of low-skill service jobs and the polarization of the U.S. labor market', *American Economic Review* 103 (2013), pp. 1553–97; Daniel Oesch, *Occupational Change in Europe* (Oxford: Oxford University Press, 2013).

2. Armin Schäfer and Wolfgang Streeck (eds), *Politics in the Age of Austerity* (Oxford: Polity Press, 2013).

3. Miles Corak, 'Income inequality, equality of opportunity and intergenerational mobility', *Journal of Economic Perspectives* 27 (2013), pp. 70–102.

4. More than 15 per cent of youth between the ages of 17 and 29 in Europe are not in education, employment or training; see also Joachim Vogel, 'European welfare regimes and the transition to adulthood: a comparative and longitudinal perspective', *Social Indicators Research* 59 (2002), pp. 275–99.

5. Robert D. Putnam, Robert B. Frederick, and Kaisa Snellman, 'Growing class gaps in social connectedness among American youth', White Paper of the Saguaro Seminar, Harvard University (2012).

6. Jonathan Bradshaw and John Holmes, 'An analysis of equity in redistribution to the retired and children in recent decades in the OECD and UK', *Journal of Social Policy* 42 (2013), pp. 39–56.

7. Claus Offe, 'Competitive party democracy and the Keynesian welfare state: factors of stability and disorganization', *Policy Sciences* 15 (1983), pp. 225–46; Evelyne Huber and John Stephens, *Development and Crisis of the Welfare State* (Chicago: University of Chicago Press, 2001).

8. Peter A. Hall, 'The political origins of our economic discontents: contemporary adjustment problems in historical perspective', in Miles Kahler and David Lake (eds), *Politics in the New Hard Times* (Ithaca: Cornell University Press, 2013), pp. 129–49.

9. Hanspeter Kriesi et al., *Political Conflict in Western Europe* (Cambridge: Cambridge University Press, 2012); Anne Wren (ed.), *The Political Economy of the Service Transition* (Oxford: Oxford University Press, 2013).

10. Peter A. Hall and Michèle Lamont (eds), *Social Resilience in the Neoliberal Era* (New York: Cambridge University Press, 2013).

11. Jacob S. Hacker, 'The foundations of middle class democracy', in *Priorities for a New Political Economy: Memos to the Left* (London: Policy Network, 2011), pp. 33–8; Peter A. Hall and Rosemary C. R. Taylor, 'Health, social relations and public policy', in Peter A. Hall and Michèle Lamont (eds), *Successful Societies* (New York: Cambridge University Press, 2009), pp. 82–103.

12. Ralph Gomory and Richard Sylla, 'The American corporation', *Daedalus* 142 (2013), pp. 102–48; Wolfgang Streeck, *Social Institutions and Economic Performance* (Beverly Hills: Sage, 1992).

13. Anton Hemerijck, *Changing Welfare States* (Oxford: Oxford University Press, 2013); Natalie Morel, Bruno Palier, and Joakim Palme (eds), *Towards a Social Investment Welfare State?* (Bristol: Policy Press, 2012).

14. James Heckman, *Giving Kids a Fair Chance* (Cambridge, MA: MIT Press, 2012).

15. Tim Bale, 'Turning round the telescope: centre-right parties and immigration and integration policy in Europe', *European Journal of Public Policy* 15 (2008), pp. 16–45; Noam Gidron, 'The center-right in times of crisis: Evidence from the Netherlands'. Paper presented to the American Political Science Association, Washington D.C., August 2014.

16. Jane Gingrich and Ben Ansell, 'The dynamics of social investment: human capital, activation and care', in Pablo Beramendi, Silja Häusermann, Herbert Kitschelt, and Hanspeter Kriesi (eds), *The Politics of Advanced Capitalism* (New York: Cambridge University Press, 2015).

17. See also Albena Azmanova, 'Social justice and varieties of capitalism: an immanent critique', *New Political Economy* 17 (2012), pp. 445–63.

18. Gorman and Sylla; Jiwook Jung and Frank Dobbin, 'Finance and institutional investors', in Karin Knorr Cetina and Alex Prada (eds), *The Oxford Handbook of the Sociology of Finance* (New York: Oxford University Press, 2014), pp. 52–74.

19. Wolfgang Streeck, *Re-Forming Capitalism* (Oxford: Oxford University Press, 2009); Herman Aguinas and Ante Glavas, 'What we know and don't know about corporate social responsibility: a review and research agenda', *Journal of Management* 38 (2012), pp. 932–68.

20. Karl Polanyi, *The Great Transformation* (Boston: Beacon Press, 1944); Peter A. Hall, 'Social policy-making for the long term', *PS: Political Science and Politics* 48 (April 2015).

21. Cf. Kayte Lawton, Graeme Cooke, and Nick Pearce, *The Condition of Britain: Strategies for Renewal* (London: Institute for Public Policy Research, 2014); Rebecca Henderson, 'Business Beyond the Public Sphere'. Presentation, Harvard Business School, 30 January 2014. Available at http://www.hbs.edu/faculty/conferences/2014-business-beyond-the-private-sphere/Documents/Business%20Beyond%20the%20Public%20Sphere%20Introduction%20Slides.pdf (accessed 23 March 2015).

Index